Psalms for Troubled Times:

Prayers of Hope and Challenge

PSALMS
FOR
Troubled
Times

PRAYERS OF HOPE AND CHALLENGE

BARBARA GIBSON

OLYMPIA, WASHINGTON

Copyright © 2003 by Barbara Gibson
Second Printing, 2006

Published by Crestline Press
2438 Crestline Drive NW
Olympia WA 98502

Library of Congress 2003097778

Psalms for Troubled Times:
Prayers of Hope and Challenge by Barbara Gibson
Includes index

ISBN 0-9746566-0-7

Religion and Spirituality

With gratitude to Sophia

For the sake of the whole world

CONTENTS

ACKNOWLEDGMENTS

Many people over several years helped me with their interest, suggestions, and support. I particularly thank Jeanne Lohmann, Katie Cameron, Bob Jones, and my partner Carol McKinley, who read carefully, and inspired me with their theological critiques, literary assessments, and unfailing encouragement.

INTRODUCTION

These are *Psalms for Troubled Times.*

Aren't all times troubled? Perhaps, but in the 21st century we face uniquely challenging crises. We have the power to destroy our planet and ourselves, and we often seem to be doing just that. We are uncertain, angry, grieving, afraid.

In times like these, people seek spiritual help from old traditions and new revelations. *Psalms for Troubled Times* is based on ancient wisdom, and embodies new poetic creations, fresh and relevant for our times. These poems are prayers of comfort, reminding us of our connection to Spirit and to the sacredness of life itself. At the same time, they challenge us to radical new awareness, responsibility, honesty, and courage.

My intention is to make the psalms accessible to those who do not have a personal connection with this source of wisdom, or who might not see the relevance of psalms to their lives. For those who already love and use them, I want to enliven and freshen the familiar texts, to recreate them as a new source of inspiration for individuals and faith communities.

The biblical Book of Psalms is one of the oldest pieces of poetic religious literature that we know, with dates ranging from the tenth century BCE to the third century BCE. The 150 psalms in the Jewish scriptures are outpourings of human feeling and experience: sorrow, despair, triumph, fear, thanksgiving, joy. They were written as statements of faith and of doubt, expressions of a profound relationship between the people of Israel and their God.

As people of the 21st century, we can find in the psalms encouragement to deepen our relationship with God, whatever our religious affiliation.

These are new versions of seventy of the psalms. Many poets have written their adaptations, and I follow in that tradition. I want to bring together the wisdom embedded in these ancient prayers with what I know of poetry, social justice and peace movements, Christianity and Buddhism, and what I know of life after all my years on earth.

I bring current images and contemporary language to these psalms. I have radically revised some of them while remaining true to their spirit. I retain language that is familiar where in my judgment it makes the psalm most effective. In other places I freely substitute words that reflect 21st century realities.

Many of the psalms are prayers, in which the psalmist is speaking to someone. A relationship is implied. To whom is praise expressed, to whom are despair and doubt spoken, to whom is the appeal for wisdom, justice, and peace delivered? Who or what or where is this God with whom the psalmist seems so familiar?

I find God not in the image of an all-powerful and judgmental patriarch, but as an energy that pervades the universe. I see God as cosmic existence, evolving over 15 billion years, as the pattern that connects, as source, deepest reality, ground of being.

At the same time, I want to give a name to that divine other to whom we pray. I want to make that ground of being more accessible and immediate, and to emphasize its relevance to our contemporary personal and communal spirituality. Therefore, instead of the traditional "Lord," I have used names and images such as beloved, earth, and mother.

I also invoke the name of my personal object of devotion: Sophia (the Greek word for wisdom). She appears in the Jewish scriptures as *Hokmah*, a female divinity who is co-equal with Jahweh—his partner in creation, a teacher, bringer of justice, and lover. In the Christian scriptures, Jesus and Sophia are one.[1]

I have created five categories for these songs and prayers: Praise, Earth, Doubt and Despair, Justice and Peace, Wisdom.[2]

---

[1] See the work of Elizabeth Schussler Fiorenza, Elizabeth Johnson, and Hal Taussig's readable *Wisdom's Feast*.
[2] The Books of Psalms is traditionally divided into these groups: Hymns, Laments, Songs of Trust, Thanksgivings, Sacred History, Royal Psalms, Wisdom Psalms, and Liturgies.

Psalms of praise, thanksgiving, and gratitude can be a powerful part of religious and spiritual life in our times, even when we wonder what we have to celebrate in our terrible human tragedies and planetary crises. The psalms remind us that creation itself is always with us as a source of inspiration, hope, comfort and joy. These are the praise psalms.

Another category is Earth, celebrated and addressed in many of my psalms. Earth has the power to bring us to our knees with awe, even to destroy us, whether by earthquake or storm, or in the inevitable end that death brings. But in the mystery of existence, we sense that all aspects of earth are sacred, somehow right and perfect, even in the middle of suffering. We also know that our planet and its inhabitants are in jeopardy due to human ignorance and greed.

Psalms of doubt and despair present our poignant human vulnerabilities. The psalmists speak from the pit of human despair, dread, and anguish. Often they cry out to a seemingly absent God, begging for relief from their doubts. At times the psalmist demands that God punish the enemies, the wicked ones who try to destroy us. Yet the most intimate enemies are the demons within: fears, jealousy, self-hatred, cynicism, impulses to violence, selfishness, arrogance, egotism, and rage.

Individuals are not the only or the most important enemies in our world. The systems of domination, systems of oppression, kept alive by human greed and ignorance, are powerful enemies, and they are named here. Acting to overcome injustice is an integral part of an authentic spirituality, as most religions acknowledge. These psalms belong to the category I call justice and peace.

The wisdom psalms warn us against selfishness and cynicism. They remind us to pay attention to creation itself, in its abundance and generosity, for guidance on how life works best. When we express gratitude and act with compassion, our lives become blessed. These psalms offer the "rules" for a good life.

The theology I find in the psalms is panentheism[3] (not pantheism). The philosophy of panentheism reminds us that God is within us and also, equally importantly, that we are in God. This is the ancient, compassionate, justice-seeking wisdom taught and practiced by sages such as Meister Eckhart, Hildegard of Bingen, and Jesus himself.

The psalms present difficult contradictions: between God or Spirit who dwells within, and the God of whom we are a part, but who lives beyond us. Here are the ever-present God and the distant God. You will read psalms that describe earth as angry and punishing, and earth as healing. At times, justice and peace, the fulfillment of promises, seem just ahead. At other times they seem unattainable, not meant to be. Wisdom is within our grasp, or it is part of the ultimate mystery that we will never know. These tensions are powerful and real. The contradictions are part of our reality, no matter how sophisticated our theology or how devotedly we pray. We live with them.

---

[3] See the writings of Matthew Fox or Marcus Borg for further exploration of Panentheism.

I hope these versions will help you know this glorious poetry and profound wisdom in a fresh way. I hope too that you will be inspired to use the *Psalms for Troubled Times* in your own prayers, and become ever more spontaneous and real in the ways you speak to Spirit.

May these passionately human psalms enrich your life and the life of your communities. May you be moved to re-dedicate yourself to justice for the earth and for all creatures and people. May you find your own peace in these troubled times.

PSALMS

FOR

Troubled Times

True happiness

Who is happy? The people
who have not become cynical
or succumbed to their addictions,
who have not become hard of heart.

They are happy because they follow the path:
they practice wisdom and compassion day and night.

They are like trees planted by the river
which produce bushels of fruit and never wither.
Everything they do works out in the end.

The selfish and the greedy
are like dust the wind blows away.
They doubt and dislike themselves
though they pretend to be on top.

May those who are dedicated to compassion prevail.
May the enemies of wisdom fail.

PSALM 3

Help from Sophia

O Wisdom, how many are my doubts!
My cynical thoughts disturb me,
saying "There is no hope for the world."

But you, Sophia, are a shield against despair.
With you beside me I can lift up my head.
I cry aloud and you answer me
from the deepest place within.

I am defeated by a thousand doubts
that crowd my busy mind.
I lie down and sleep, and then
I wake, for Wisdom calls to me.

Come to us, Sophia;
strike the jaw of our stubbornness
and rattle the teeth of our pride.

Sophia, you are the one
who orders all things for good.
May your blessings be for all beings.

PSALM 6

Prayer for recovery from illness

Source of life, be gracious to me for I am sick.
Heal me, for my bones ache,
and my heart is heavy with fear.
How long will I suffer?

I am tired of being depressed;
I lie awake all night long.
My eyes are dark with worry
and I am dull with hopelessness.

May my sickness come to an end
and my fears go away.
May my body and soul be healed.
May the source of life restore me.

The wonder of the universe and the failings of the people

O universe, how glorious you are!
We see a bright glimpse of you in the night sky.
We look at the moon and stars;
how ancient and mysterious they seem.

How can the universe care for us?
We are tiny in the vastness of time and space,
and yet on earth we are too powerful.

We dominate and exploit the land,
the waters and the air.
We breed and slaughter cattle.
We poison the California condor
and block the sparkling salmon runs.
We have destroyed the passenger pigeon.

O universe, how can you care for us
when we have not cared for you?

For the restoration of justice

With arrogance the powerful exploit the poor.
Let them be caught in their own dire schemes.

The wealthy boast, and the greedy ignore goodness
because they think they are invulnerable.

They prosper, without fear of punishment.
They believe their power will last forever.

The powerful oppress and torture the weak.
They imprison and kill those who oppose them.

They lie about how they have ruined the earth
and threatened the rights of the people.

They lie about the importance of idols, like wealth.
They practice genocide and war.

Rise up, people, and with truth and justice,
lift your strong hands against oppression.

Tell the rulers "We see the evil you have done.
We see the suffering of the children and the poor."

We will listen to the voices of the forgotten,
and strengthen the hearts of the distressed.

Let us commit ourselves to the defense of the suffering.
We will break the grip of arrogance and power.

Taking refuge

In the One I take refuge,
even when I want to flee
like a bird to the mountains.

The wicked are bending the bow.
They fit their arrow to the string
and shoot at the very heart of the world.

Still I put my trust in the One
who lives in the holy temple of my soul
whose throne is in heaven and on earth.

The One examines the good and the bad,
and hates those who make war.

The One causes the fires of regret
to burn up the oppressors;
their guilt is a scorching wind.

The One loves those who bring justice.
Those who do good
will look upon that holy face.

In the One I take refuge.
I put my trust in the One.

Prayer for help from someone

There is no longer anyone who is wholly good.
The faithful have disappeared from the earth.
People lie to one another; they flatter and seduce.

I hope the flattering tongues get silenced,
those boastful tongues that say:
"We will prevail—we own everything—
no one can master us."

Where is help for this?
Where is the someone who sees
how the poor are ruined
and the needy are in pain?

Who will rise up to give them
the comfort for which they yearn?
Where is the helper whose promises are pure,
like silver refined in a crucible?

Help and protect us, someone.
Guard us from the evils we have ignored.
On every side the powerful tell lies,
and many believe them.
Where is the one who knows?

Appeal to the hidden One

How long will I be forgotten, hidden One?
How long will your face be a shadow?
How long must I bear this pain in my soul,
the sorrow that breaks my heart?

Listen to me and give me an answer!
Bring relief to me or I will die.
My demons will say "We won!"
They will be glad I am ruined.

I want to trust that someone will help me
in spite of everything, and that I will be happy.
Someday I want to sing again.
I want to see the hidden One return.

Against cynicism

The cynical people say there is no truth.
They are lost in their own confusion.
They can think of no reason to feel hope.

Meanwhile, creator Spirit looks to see
if there are any among us who are wise,
any who daily seek the truth.

Too many people find no meaning in life.
They have closed their hearts to the mystery.

Don't they know that the bread of life is baked
for them too, not just the earthly bread?
All they have to do is ask.

Creator Spirit, you are present to us always,
in spite of our cynicism and fear.
You are as near to us as our hands.

PSALM 15

To be compassionate

Who may abide in the tent of compassion
and who may dwell on the holy hill of love?

Those who see without blaming,
who do what is difficult but right,
and speak the truth from their hearts,

who do not gossip about their friends,
or hurt people around them on purpose,
who do not hate those who are different.

Those who despise violence and war,
who honor the truths of others,
and who keep their promises even when it's hard,

who give freely to the homeless
and who defend the falsely accused.

Those who do these things
shall be the blessed among us,
though the world trembles and shakes.

The principles of creation

The skies tell the glory of creation
and the galaxies proclaim its power.
Day after day they pour forth speech
and night after night they offer knowledge.

The voice of creation sounds throughout the earth
and travels to the end of the world.

The sky is the sun's tent.
It comes out like a bride
from the wedding canopy.
Like a strong racer
it runs its course with joy.
It rises at one end of the sky
and crosses to the other.
Nothing escapes its heat.

The workings of creation are wonderful,
refreshing the soul.

The teachings of creation are sure,
making the simple ones wise.

The patterns of creation are right,
rejoicing the heart.

The demands of creation are clear,
opening our eyes to what is.

The principles of creation are true;
they are deep and full of mystery.

The gifts of creation are worth more than gold,
even the finest gold,
and sweeter than honey
from the dripping honeycomb.

The workings of creation are a lesson:
fitting ourselves to the whole brings harmony,
though it is easy to think only of ourselves.

May we not be unconscious and ignorant.
May we be saved from arrogance and lust for power
so that we may preserve our home the earth.

Let the words of our mouths
and the meditations of our hearts
be in harmony with you, creation,
our water and our rock.

Blessings for a friend

May you find answers in the day of your troubles!
May the names you call on protect you!

May help come to you from a sacred place,
a place which you can call home.

May your friends remember your goodness
and honor the gifts you have given.

May your heart's desire be granted
and all your hopes fulfilled.

Some people are proud of possessions
but you value the truth inside.

Some fall into despair;
may you stand up and be happy.

Help comes to the seekers.
An answer comes from somewhere
to those who pray with heart.

PSALM 23

Trust in the goodness of creation

Creation takes care of me
and gives me what I need.
I lie down on the green grass,
I swim in the clear river.
My heart is whole.
I do what is right for the earth.

Even when I walk in a dark valley,
the shadow of death behind me,
I am not afraid
because creation is with me:
the trees and the mountains comfort me.

Earth's table is set for us
even when we doubt.
Earth's plenty flows over us like balm,
more than enough for everyone.

Surely goodness and mercy
are here for us every day of our lives.
We dwell in the house of earth forever.

PSALM 24

The blessings of earth

The earth is one and all that is in it:
the world and those who live in it are one.

For the earth rests on the great oceans
and the water of life flows in every river and stream.

Who shall ascend the holy hills?
And who shall stand in the sacred forest?

All who have clean hands and pure hearts,
who do not worship the marketplace or the bank,

who do not give their souls to profit and war,
and who refuse to believe the social lies.

All will receive the blessings of earth
as long as they seek the truth with every breath.

Such is the company of those who honor the earth,
who honor the sacred face of creation.

The earth speaks in the storm

The voice of earth is heard on the waters.
In her glory she thunders over the mighty seas;
the voice of earth makes a powerful roar.

The strength of earth breaks the tall cedars.
Lightning cracks hemlocks in the deep forests;
the power of earth flashes forth in a storm.

Earth shakes the houses and towns.
Storms make the strong oaks whirl
and strips the redwood forests bare.
Earth flows and rages in great floods.

Let all in the temple of earth cry "Mother!"

May earth give her strength to the people!

Prayer for renewal of faith

As a deer longs for fresh water
so my soul longs for you, beloved.

My soul thirsts for the One.
When will I see the face of the beloved?

Salt tears flow into my mouth.
People tease me, saying: "Where is your God now?"

I remember how I used to pray
and how I went to the house of the One.

We sang hymns and danced; we gave thanks
and we celebrated the high holy days.

Now all that is a memory
and my soul is utterly cast down.

I remember when I was a child:
my faith was sweet and innocent.

I loved God with my whole heart, and
love poured over me like the ocean.

At night I felt safe when I prayed
"Now I lay me down to sleep."

Now my friends say: "Where is your God?"
And I ask: why is the beloved no longer with me?

Why have I been forgotten?
Why do I walk around with a broken heart?

The presence of Spirit

Spirit is our refuge and our strength,
always present, even in times of trouble.
Therefore we are not afraid,
even when the earth rumbles
and volcanoes erupt beneath the sea
when ocean waters foam and roar
and mountains tremble and shake.

There is a calm river which flows in our hearts,
the place where Spirit lives.

Spirit lives in the cities, moving
among the people, comforting us.
Spirit is present to give help when the changes come,
when the nations are in uproar and governments totter.

Spirit inspires us to break the grip of war,
to shatter the power of missiles and bombs,
to ban all nuclear arms forever.

Come, let us see what Spirit can do
when people find their strength,
when Spirit brings hope.

Be still and know the One!
Among the people and on earth,
nothing is higher or deeper.

Spirit is with us, our refuge and our strength.

Praise the mother

Clap hands, all you people!
Shout your songs of joy.
The earth inspires our awe;
She is the mother of all creation,
greater than any of us,
greater than any of our thoughts.
We have inherited her
and we give love back to her.

Praise earth with a great shout,
and with the sound of a trumpet.
Sing praise to earth, sing joy,
sing praise to all creatures of earth,
for earth is mother to all.
Praise her with prayer and with action.

The earth is greater than any nation.
She includes us all.
The people of earth
come together as her children.
She holds us forever, and
when we die we return to her.

The folly of money and power

Hear this, everybody!
Pay attention, world!

Whether you're rich or poor,
powerful or forgotten,
Wisdom speaks to us
in the meditations of our hearts
and the understanding of our minds.
Wisdom speaks in parables,
in riddles, and in songs.

She tells us: in times of trouble
when you are persecuted and oppressed,
remember those who think they are safe
because they are wealthy,
those who rely on their power;
they will suffer and die like everyone.

Everyone perishes: the wise,
the foolish and the ignorant.

Money? You can't take it with you.
Power? It can't insure you against dying.
The man who has a city named for him
still ends up in the grave forever.
Some poor fools don't know this.
They are lost in their pride and arrogance.

Wisdom speaks to us
in the meditations of our hearts.

The earth demands respect and selflessness

The mighty one, the earth, speaks to us
from the rising of the sun to its setting,
and she shines forth at night.
The earth speaks in her beauty.

She calls out with a powerful voice:
"Come, my people.
We are bound together, you and I,
and the time has come to wake up!

"In your churches you pray
and in your councils you legislate.
But your prayers and your laws are flimsy
compared to the needs of the people, the animals,
the birds of the air, and all that moves on me.
I am suffering in my water, air, and soil.

"You must discover how to thank and honor me.
You must promise to put me first, before your selfish needs.
You must stop giving lip service to my laws,
pretending to love me while you submit
to the advertisers and greedy corporations.
You are addicted to prosperity and success.
You lie to each other and you exploit the poor.
You slander other races, people of your own family.

"These things you have done, and I have been silent.
You thought you could ignore me and exploit me.

I rebuke you now and remind you of your mistakes.
Remember these warnings, you who have forgotten me,
or you will be struck by poisons, plagues and wars.

"Get on the path! You know what is right!
Honor me and yourselves; show respect
for the planet you live on, and the creatures
who share it with you, even the water and the air.
Act without selfishness! Wake up!"

Regret and repentance

Have mercy on me, O Spirit,
according to your steadfast love.
With your abundant compassion
blot out the errors I have made.

Forgive the mistakes I've made in the past;
I know what I've done and I'm sorry.
I have sinned against you, Spirit,
and against myself, my friends, and the earth.

I just want to be truthful and sincere!
Wash me inside out and I'll be clean,
ready to start over and make a new self.
Teach me everything I need to know.

I'm ready for happiness, Spirit;
my sore and aching body will rejoice.
Wipe away the stain of my self-hatred,
and teach me how to accept who I am.

I need to remember your presence,
I need to remember your beauty each day.
May I be given the joy of wholeness and
may I find my willing heart.

Spirit, open my mouth, and I will sing to you.
I know you don't want more guilt from me;
you don't want me to beat my breast in shame.
All you want from me is my joy.

The search for meaning

The cynics say "There is no truth, no justice."
They think they can do anything, no matter how wrong.

That's not the way the world works best.
We have to search for meaning and wisdom.

The cynics are lost in their ignorance;
they think humankind is all there is,
and that human logic explains everything.

Too bad they're so misguided, because they do a lot of
        harm,
misleading people, lying about what's important,
thinking we can control the world and have whatever
        we want.

They live in constant fear, with their false belief
that we're alone here. They ignore the vast mysteries
of the cosmos, the mysteries of microscopic life.

Who will defeat greed and arrogance?
Where is the defense against hatred and war?
How can people learn wisdom and compassion?

Prayer for help from Sophia

My soul longs to hide in you,
to find safety beneath your soft wings
until these bad times pass.
Come and be with me, Sophia.

Tell me what you want from me.
I'm asking for your help.
Save me from myself
with your never-ending love.

I lie down among the hungry beasts
of my imagination. They try to eat me.
My doubts stab me like spears and arrows,
my hateful thoughts are like sharp swords.

I call out: only you can help me, Sophia!
You understand everything in the universe!
I want to know you and sing your praises.
I want to serve you and do your work.

My selfishness and fears had trapped me,
and I was ready to give in to despair.
But now my anguish has been stilled,
thanks to your presence, Sophia.

I'm back on my feet again and
my heart is full and satisfied.
I'm ready to sing a song!
I'm awake! I'm grateful!

I want to play music in the morning
and greet the new day with joy!
My praises are for you, Sophia.
Devotion to you makes me happy.

You rule in my soul and in the universe.
Your love is as high as the heavens
and your faithfulness stretches past the sky.
May you dwell in my heart forever.

PSALM 58

Prayer that evil systems may be defeated

Does justice prevail in America?
Do our people get a fair chance?
No, because the politicians are corrupt;
they owe their power to the wealthy.
They cater to the gun lobby and
the oil companies—the rich and the selfish
who don't care about people or the land.

They never stop lying and their lies
are like the venom of a snake.
They are deaf to the call of conscience.
They are seduced by the voice
of their addictions and their greed.

Somebody's got to break the teeth
of the systems that oppress!
Tear out the fangs with which they bite the poor.
Let oppression vanish like water that dries up;
let it wither away like dead grass.
May the powerful be helpless as the slug
that dissolves in its own slime,
and may all their plots come to nothing.

The downtrodden will be glad
when they see oppression disappear.
They will rejoice when tyranny bleeds and dies.

The people will say: "At last justice has been done.
At last truth has prevailed, and we are free."

Earth's suffering and promise

The earth is angry,
she rejects us, she breaks us down.
The land is torn with earthquakes,
it is cracked and shaken.
The people are suffering
and they turn to the idols—
money and fame—
that make them crazy.

Give us something to believe in!
Give us a sign that things will improve.
The people still love you, mother earth,
but we need help. Come and inspire us.

Earth promises her bounty in the fruit and grain,
in the beauty of the Mississippi river,
and the glory of Mt. Everest.
Earth shows us the way in the mighty Columbia,
and in the gentle Shenandoah valley.
Earth encompasses all these wonders.
The message is clear, but somehow we miss it.

Help us understand and when we do, to act.
Help us read the messages in the sun and water.

Waiting for help

My soul waits in silence for the One,
for a message that can save me.
The One will be my rock and my salvation,
the place from which I cannot be removed.

How long will my doubts and fears attack me?
I'm like a crooked wall, a rickety fence.
"You're your own worst enemy," people tell me.
I can't stop lying, even to myself.
I seem like a nice person,
but inside I'm full of envy and anger.

My soul waits in silence for the One;
my hope is in the presence of the sacred.
The One will be my home and my rock,
the place from which I cannot be removed.

I will be saved from fear
when I learn to be peaceful and not hate.
The power of the sacred is my only hope,
the one place I will find safety.

Misery is a fleeting breath,
and pride is a delusion.
The truth is that I'm ordinary,
just a fleeting presence on this earth.
I can't cheat and lie and steal my way to happiness.

Even if my luck improves, it won't help.
The whole thing is not just about me.
It's about everybody, everything, the whole.
It's about trusting in the best of who we are,
and putting aside our pretensions and our fears.

How can I learn to trust?
Where will I find refuge?
When will my heart be whole?

Praise to the beloved

You are my beloved
and I seek you,
my soul thirsts for you,
my flesh faints for you.

I am an arid, weary desert;
the water of life has dried up in me,
though I have looked for it
in all the sacred places.

I know your power and your love;
your passionate love is better than life.
My mouth will praise you, and
I will adore you as long as I live.

When I reach out my hands
and call your name, beloved,
you satisfy me with a rich feast.
My mouth praises you with loving lips.

When I think of you on my bed
and call to you in the night,
then you come to me;
you hold me in the shadow of your wings.

When the enemies within
assault me with doubt and fear,
your arms encircle me.

I embrace you and sing for joy.

Only you can ease
my loneliness, beloved.
Come to me now.

Praise to abundant earth

Gratitude to you, O earth!
You answer all our needs
while we live, and after death,
we return to your loving arms.

You are our faith and our hope;
from the far-off snowy mountains
to the depths of the distant seas
you surround and comfort us.

You calm the roaring of the oceans,
then stir up the crashing waves.
We watch with wonder as the tides
rush in and out on every shining shore.

Rain visits the soil and soaks it;
the rivers are full of running water.
The fields are nourished with sun
and softened with sweet showers.

You bless our crops in country and city.
You crown the year with your bounty.
Paths overflow with richness
and pastures are drenched with green.

Bountiful lilies color the hills

and meadows clothe themselves with sheep.
Grain adorns the pleasant valleys.
All nature sparkles and glows.

Because of you, we shout for joy
at the gateways of the morning
and the windows of the night.
Gratitude to you, O earth.

PSALM 66

A prayer for the task ahead

Make a joyful noise,
all you people,
sing the glory of the earth,
give praise to all creation.

How awesome is the universe!
We study distant stars
with amazement, and tremble
at their mysterious power.

Come see the wonder of the galaxies
and marvel at the tiny seed.
Bless earth and walk softly on it.
This is how we give thanks.

Our faithfulness and wisdom are tested now.
Earth is bringing us into her net of being;
we bear the burden of past sins and errors.
Our task is to make things right.

Earth can still be Eden for us
and we can come into a fertile place.
We must repent for how we have abused her,
and promise to change our ways.

We must forget our selfish needs,

and offer our wisdom and energy
as if they were burnt offerings,
as our ancestors did in the old days.

People who love our earth, come and hear
what she has done: given us life!
Earth waits for us to return to her ways.
She will cherish us if we respond to her.

A desperate prayer

Save me, someone,
for the waters are up to my neck,
I'm sinking in the mud
and there is no place to stand.

The water is deep here
and the flood sweeps over me.
My throat is raw from crying.
I can barely see or hear.

My miseries are more
than the hairs on my head.
I'm ruining myself and
I don't understand why.

I thought I was on the right path
by staying with the old rules.
I humbled myself by fasting
and I wore secondhand clothes.

What did I do to deserve this?
Now everyone thinks I'm pathetic;
people gossip behind my back.
My family has disowned me.

Answer me, someone!

Why are you hiding your face?
Can't you see how I'm suffering?
Can't you see how ashamed I feel?

I am lowly and desperate and in pain
and I'm asking for salvation.
If someone comes to help me,
I'll give praise and gratitude.

I'm still willing to pray,
if only someone would answer me.
I want to believe God hears the needy.
I want to live in the city of God.

Help in old age from the Mother

In you, Great Mother, I take refuge;
may I always know your love.

Be my refuge and my rock
where I may dwell in peace.

You are my hope, Great Mother,
and have been since I was young.

I know you were with me
even in my mother's womb.

Keep me from the cruelties of age,
keep me from loneliness.

I'm afraid I'll be ignored,
sent away from the home I love.

I'm afraid I'll be neglected,
sent to live with strangers.

Please don't forsake me in old age,
when my strength is almost gone.

You have taught me from childhood,
and still I learn from you every day.

Even in old age, wrinkled and gray-haired,
I am your loving disciple.

Do you know how long I've worshipped you?
Do you know you are my rock?

Do you hear me sing your praise?
I haven't lost my love for you,

I tell everyone about your power.
I tell everyone about your beauty;

I tell the world about your love.
Each moment I thank you for my life.

PSALM 72

*Prayer for a righteous world
and an enduring earth*

May all the people in the world find justice,
and all other creatures as well.

May the mountains convey justice to the people,
and the valleys send a message of peace.

May the earth last as long as the sun shines
and as long as the moon sheds her light.

Let knowledge of the sacred fall like rain on the grass,
like fresh showers that water the earth.

May peace and justice reign from sea to sea,
from high mountain tops to the lowest desert.

May those who have exploited the earth
wake up and learn to respect life.

May the exploiters and the polluters pay back
what they have stolen from the earth.

May all people work to restore balance and harmony
to the earth, the water and the air.

Only when we recognize the earth as our sacred mother,
when we recognize how precious she is,

will we save ourselves from poverty of spirit,
from oppression and war, from every kind of violence.

May there be abundance of food in every land,
may the old growth forests sway in the wind.

May the orchards give sweet fruit, the cow good milk,
and may the people flourish in the cities.

Long life to the earth! May we honor her forever,
when we work and pray, and when we love.

May all beings be well; may all beings be happy.
Blessed be the sacred earth, our mother.

Envying the rich

I used to envy the rich and the famous,
the arrogant, successful ones.
Their bodies are sleek and healthy.
If they get in trouble, they buy their way out.

The rich wear their pride like a necklace;
they wear the threat of violence like armor.
Their eyes shine with greed,
and they act out terrible fantasies.

They do what they want to people like us.
They get together to plan our oppression;
they look down their noses at us and mock us.
Worst of all, they have no respect for the sacred.

I'd been trying to keep my hands clean.
But it got me nowhere. How come people say:
"Virtue is its own reward"? I didn't notice:
in fact, I was still poor and miserable.

Nothing made any sense until I began to pray.
Then I saw the emptiness of lives
where people have to keep running,
trying to stay ahead of each other.

I began to see how fearful
the arrogant people are, worrying
about holding on to what they have.
Their lives must be nightmares.

Spiritually, though, I was just like them.
So I'm giving up my envy and bitterness.
I'm trying to be generous to all,
and to act with compassion to everyone.

Now I stay in the presence of Spirit,
praying and meditating every day,
listening to the wisdom of nature.
I feel a rush of comforting, consistent love.

The Mother stands against war

The name of the Mother is known everywhere.
Her name is great among the nations.
Her house has been built on earth,
and she dwells among the people.

She tells us: "Break the flashing rockets, the tanks,
the bombers, and all the weapons of war."
She tells us: "Destroy all nuclear arms!"

Through her, we are filled with power
like the mighty mountains.
We will strip the warriors of their loot, and
the warmongers will fall into a trance.
Their missiles and their cluster-bombs will fail.

Indeed you are sublime, great Mother!
When you speak in judgment against violence,
we cannot help but listen.
You demand that we work to stop the wars.
Your anger becomes our energy.

We promise to praise you and
to serve you among the people.
This is our gift to you: to work against war.
We bring you our promises and our gifts.

Absence of the One

I cry aloud to the One, I raise my voice.
I cry aloud, hoping the absent One will hear me.

All night I stretch my hands out,
but my soul is not comforted.

I think of the One I love and I moan.
I try to pray but I almost faint.

All I can think about is the past,
the old days when I was happy.

I worry that I'll never be at peace.
I'm afraid I'll be alone forever.

Absent One, where are you?
Maybe you've forgotten all about me.

Are you angry with me?
Have you stopped loving me?

You helped me in the past.
Please, dear One, I need you in my life again.

Strength for the restoration of the earth

Hear us, O Mother,
you who send angels to shine
on the ruined earth.
Come back, O Mother,
and renew us.
Let your face light the way
to the restoration of our earth.

O Mother, we deserve your anger.
We have fallen into selfishness and despair.
You see how we fight among ourselves,
how we hate our neighbors.

You planted goodness like a vine;
you cleared the soil around it.
The vine took root and filled the land.
The mountainsides were covered
with the shade of its green leaves.
Its branches reached to the sea
and its shoots to the river bank.

Now the vine is ripped apart,
stolen and used for profit
by those who come like thieves.
They have burned it with chemicals
and ripped it to pieces with machines.
You frown on those who destroy.

Turn to us again, O Mother,
look at us in our need and help us.
Restore the vine which you have planted.
Let your hand be upon the shoulders
of those who work for you.

Because we love you,
we will not give up.
Because you gave us life,
we call your name.

Song of the beloved

Sing aloud to the beloved,
who is our strength.
Speak words of praise to the beloved.

Raise your voices in song
and play the violin and flute.
Play a clarinet at the new moon,
and at every celebration.

I hear the voice of the beloved singing,
"I will lift the burden from your shoulders
and free your hands from their heavy weights.

"Call to me in your trouble.
I will answer you in thunder,
and swim with you in the warm rivers.

"Be true to the power of love
and don't bow down to wealth.
I am the truth and the light;
open your mouth and I will fill it.

"I will feed you with the finest bread,
I will feed you honey from the rock."

For the law of life is love,
and the beloved is with us always.

Abandoned by the hidden One

Hidden One, I cry to you all night.
Let my prayer come before you.
Listen to my pain.

My soul is full of agony
and my life is hell.
I have gone down into the pit,
with the others who have given up,
the helpless ones.

I feel forgotten, like the dead,
cut off from love,
abandoned by you.
You have forgotten me.

I live in darkness and despair,
angry at myself and at you,
overwhelmed by waves of sadness.

No one cares for me anymore;
not my friends, not even myself.
I am trapped and I can't escape.
My eyes grow dim with sorrow.

Every day I call on you, hidden One,
Every day I reach my hands to you.
My only friend is the darkness.

Hidden One, I'm crying out to you.
Why have you abandoned me?
Why do you hide your beautiful face?

The brevity and wonder of life

Creation is our dwelling place
and earth has been our home forever.

Yet in the end life throws us to the dust;
we are a moment in the vastness of time.

We are grass that blooms in the morning
and by night is withered and dry.

Our days are full of suffering
and our years are ended with a sigh.

O life! How long shall we mourn?
We are your lonely servants.

Teach us to honor our passing days
that we may acquire a peaceful heart.

Fill us in the morning with your warmth,
that our hearts may rejoice and be glad.

Make us glad through the painful years
and let us rejoice in spite of the evil around us.

Let the wonder of life shine among us.
Let our time on earth be a blessing.

Steadfast love

We live in the shelter of love
and we dwell in the shadow of the One.
The One is our refuge, in whom we trust.
May love deliver the people
from the snares that would bind us,
from the poisons that would make us sick.

We seek refuge under the wings of love,
we find safety in its faithfulness.
May we not fear the terror of the night
or the arrow that flies by day,
the dangers that stalk in the dark,
or the destruction that ruins the noonday.

We have made the One our refuge, and
the beloved is our dwelling place.
May love send angels to guard us
and hands to bear us up
so that we do not stumble.
May love defeat the lions of fear,
the serpents of doubt that assail us.

Love comes to us in trouble
and stays with us each day.
Loving is the way to a good life;
loving the One brings peace and wisdom.

Love and praise for creation

It is good to give thanks,
to sing praises in the name of creation.
It is good to declare our steadfast love by day
and our loyal faithfulness by night.

Play music on the harp and flute
and sing a song of rejoicing.
For the works of creation make us glad;
the beauty of creation brings us joy.

How great you are, creative One!
Your works are very deep.
We try our best to understand;
but sometimes we cannot grasp your ways.

To love you is to blossom like the apple tree,
to flourish like the ancient cedars.
We are planted in the orchards of creation.
We flourish in the forests of the One.

In old age may we still be fruitful,
full of sap and green.
May our love for creation bring joy;
may the One be our happiness and our rock.

Worship of the beloved

O come, let us sing to the beloved,
let us make a joyful noise to the one who loves us!
Let us come before her with thanksgiving
and praise her with songs and dance.

The beloved holds the depths of the earth,
and the heights of the mountains are hers.
The sea belongs to her, for she made it,
and also the dry land, which her hands have formed.

O come, let us worship and bow down,
let us kneel before the One who made us.
for we are the sheep of her pasture
and the people of her very hands.

O listen to the voice of the beloved!
Do not harden your hearts
with cynicism and doubt.
Come listen to the voice of the beloved!

PSALM 96

The sacred story of the cosmos

O sing to the beloved a new song;
sing to creation, all the earth.
Sing to the beloved, bless his name,
and tell of his wonders day and night.

Declare the glory of creation to the world,
and its marvelous works among the people.
For great is creation and greatly to be praised.
The One is to be honored above all.

Some people worship petty things,
but the universe is vast and glorious.
Energy and mystery dwell in creation,
where beauty and wisdom live as well.

Study the story of the universe,
learn how energy exploded
learn how galaxies were formed
consider how life arose from the sea.

Let everyone be glad, and let the earth rejoice.
Let the sea roar and all the life within it.
Let the fields exult and all that grows come forth.
Let the trees of the forest sing for joy.

The realm of the One

Praise the realm of the One!
Let the many floating islands rejoice.
A cloud of mystery surrounds the One,
and she sits at the heart of the world.

Fire goes before her and
burns up all our doubts.
Her lightning lights the world,
and the One admires creation.

Mountains erupt with fire
when she comes near.
The sky proclaims her beauty
and all the people adore her.

Those who worship wealth
and power are ashamed.
They are small compared
to the vastness of the One.

The One loves those who hate violence.
She guards the souls of the peacemakers.
Light dawns for the unselfish
and joy for the pure of heart.

Rejoice in the One!
Give thanks to the sacred One!

Joy in the beloved

Sing praise and be thankful
to the beloved, all the lands.
Worship the beloved with gladness
and come into his presence with singing.

Know that the beloved is with us.
We were made in mystery
and we belong to the beloved.
We are the people of the One.

Enter the sacred gates with thanksgiving,
and go into the world with praise.
Give thanks to the beloved, bless his name.
For the beloved is always good.

The love of the One endures forever.
We are the people of the One.

A psalm and prayer in the Buddhist manner

I ask for right action and right relationship,
as I take refuge in Buddha, Dharma and Sangha.
I will study the path of wisdom and compassion.

I will walk without idolatry and dogmatism
in my heart and in my actions.

I will not avoid contact with suffering,
and I will stay with those who are in pain.

I will not grow wealthy while others are in need.
Money and fame mean nothing to me.

I will not maintain anger and hatred;
to the best of my ability, I will forgive.

I will not gossip or spread rumors,
or speak in a way that causes discord.

I will not kill, and I will do what I can
to prevent others from killing.

I will try to love my neighbor as myself,
so that we may live together in peace.

Morning by morning I will let go of my attachments
and sit quietly, praying for a compassionate heart.

PSALM 102

Utter despair and doubt

Hear my prayer, O hidden One;
let my cry come out to you.
Don't hide your face from me
in the day of my distress.

My days are passing away like smoke,
and my bones burn like a furnace.
My heart is dry as grass,
and I forget to eat my bread.

I'm like an owl in the wilderness,
living in a gloomy wasteland.
I lie awake all night
alone like a bird on a wire.

I'm so tired of myself.
I curse my very name.
I feel like eating ashes.
Tears fall into my cup.

All day long I'm tormented
by my thoughts.
I'm angry about my life.
I feel abandoned by everyone.

Some people worship you.
They pray to the stones you made.
They say you have compassion.
I'm waiting to feel it.

They tell me you don't despise anyone,
that you hear the groans of the needy,
that you set free the doomed,
that you look at us with pity.

How about me? I'm praying to you:
don't let me die—I'm still young.
Let me live a few years more,
let me age and endure like you.

Why should I believe in you?
Hear my prayer, and answer me.
Save me from my suffering,
O hidden, absent One.

The goodness of creation

Bless creation, O my soul,
with all that is within me.
Bless creation, O my soul,
and never forget its goodness.

Creation satisfies us with goodness
so we fly like eagles, even in old age.
Creation works to bring justice
to those who are oppressed.

Creation is merciful and gracious,
forgiving us when we have done wrong.
Creation does not slander us,
but remembers our errors.

Creation is generous to us,
considering how ignorant we are.
As vast and mysterious as the cosmos,
so is creation's love.

As far as the immeasurable galaxies,
so far does compassion reach.
For we were made from stardust,
marked with the original flaring forth.

It's true that our days are like grass,

blown by the wind and forgotten.
But we are always part of creation;
we never leave the earth.

All creation asks of us is
to walk softly on the earth.
Creation asks that we honor
the universe of which we are a part.

Bless creation, all beings:
angels, people, animals, and trees.
We are part of the intricate web of life.
Let us bless and honor all creation.

Creation's bounty

The sky stretches out like a tent;
the clouds are a great chariot
riding the wings of the wind
riding the fiery lightning.

The earth spins in its orbit,
held fast by the field of gravity.
The moon wanes and waxes in season
and the sun knows the time for setting.

Before the mountains emerged,
oceans covered the earth.
Thunder roared over the seas,
and when the time was right,

the waters receded, forming lakes and valleys,
making the land abundant with plants.
Now springs gush forth
and flow down the mountainsides,

giving water to the wild animals,
quenching the thirst of all.
Rivers flow from the melting glaciers
and the land is abundant with grain.

Grass grows for the cattle and sheep,
and nuts and fruit for the people.
Birds perch along the banks of the streams,
and sing among the leafy trees.

The heron and eagle build nests in the firs,
and robins in the cedars and hemlocks.
The mountain goats leap on the heights
and the prairie dogs whistle in their holes.

People go out to their work
and return to their homes at evening.
They cultivate the fields
and harvest crops from the land.

They press grapes to gladden the heart
and oil to make the lips shine,
bread to strengthen the body:
all these are gifts of the earth.

The earth is rich with life, and the sea
also is crowded with creatures,
huge whales and the swift dolphins,
the intricate octopus and tiny crab.

May the wonders of creation endure forever;
may all creatures rejoice and sing.
May all creatures bless and praise.
Praise all that is! Praise creation!

Prayer of hope in hard times

O give thanks to the One,
for many were redeemed from trouble
when they listened and woke up.
May it be so for us today.

Some wander in desert wastes,
lost and abandoned,
hungry and thirsty for meaning,
fainting from loneliness.

May their cries be heard by the One.
May they find their way
and come into a safe place.

Some sit in darkness and pain,
prisoners of poverty and hate.
Their hearts are broken
because when they fell
no one helped them.

May they break out of darkness,
and shatter their heavy bonds.

Some are sick of body and soul,
failing, close to the gates of death.
They are ill and in pain,
alone, without friends.

May they find deliverance.
May their suffering be healed.

Some have plunged into addiction,
tossed by storms of craving.
Without the strength to resist their bondage,
they stagger in confusion and pain.

May the storm in their souls be stilled
and the waves of guilt be quieted.
May they find a safe haven.

Because of human ignorance and greed,
rivers have become deserts
and springs of water have dried up.
Fruitful land has turned into a salt flat.

But deserts can become pools of water
and springs will return to the parched land.
The hungry will live in fruitful land again,
sowing the fields and planting vineyards.

The harvest can be abundant
when we follow the ways of the earth
rather than our selfish ways.

Bless those who live simply and respect all creatures.
They do not overpopulate the land.
They build their houses and tend their crops
without polluting the earth.

Let those who seek wisdom hear these words.
Let all who have suffered know the love of the One.

Prayer for help with anger

Listen to me, wise and powerful One.
Wicked and lying forces are at large,
doing deeds of hate and violence
even against those who are harmless.

They attack those who are innocent and good:
the children, the animals, and the old.
In the courts, the oppressed are found guilty;
the suffering are made to suffer more;
the poor and the aliens are held and imprisoned.

It makes me furious! I want to punish
the punishers, and oppress the oppressors.
What shall I do with my rage?
I want the corrupt and heartless to suffer the way
they make others suffer!
I want them to go into debt
and to be evicted from their luxurious homes.
I want them to be given no kindness.

I want them to be unforgiven,
for these oppressors are not kind;
they are cold and indifferent.
They do not look at suffering close up;
they do not face what they have done.
They walk away from the poor;
they lie to the people.
They live for profit rather than for love.

Wise One, what can be done about this?
Deliver me from my vengeful thoughts
and my impulses of rage!

I have fled into the shadows of my despair,
and I feel completely worthless.
My knees are weak from fighting myself,
and my poor body reveals my inner war.
I have become my own enemy,
treating myself as the oppressors treat the poor.

Help me, wise One! Bring me your compassion.
Take away my despair, and show me
how to love in spite of everything.
Keep me from hatred and revenge.
If others do evil, let me do only good.

I praise you every day with my prayers.
May I learn to praise you with my life,
with the way I live, not just with words.
May my work be praise.
May my life be a prayer to you.

Devotion to Sophia

Sophia says to me:
"Sit at my right hand
and I will make your troubles
your footstool."

Sophia makes me powerful,
because she makes me wise.
She helps me defeat my inner demons
so I can oppose the wrongs of the world.

I walk in the holy mountains
and inspiration comes to me
like dew in the morning sun.

Sophia has promised me:
"You are my priestess forever,
as long as you keep my ways."

Sophia is always with me,
showing me how to conquer
pride and arrogance,
showing me how to oppose
the deathly injustice I see.
Sophia shows me how to break
the ugly bonds of shame.

She shows me how to drink
from the stream of wisdom
that flows beside my path.

Therefore she lifts me up;
she lifts me to herself.

Happiness comes from gratitude

Happy are those
who praise life
and who understand
the intricate ways of creation.

They are blessed with wisdom
and have the gift of satisfaction
because they are in right relationship
with the planet and the people.

Those who praise life
give light to all around them.
They are gracious and compassionate.
They work for justice and peace.

They are generous to everyone,
even those they dislike.
They are fair to all,
even their enemies.

Those who praise life
stay on the difficult path.
They are remembered
for how they tell the truth.

They are not afraid of the future,
because their hearts are firm,
and they continue to do what is right
no matter what price they pay.

They acknowledge their anger
and are not trapped by it.
They use their anger
to make the necessary changes.

Again and again
they give up their selfishness.
They never blow their own horns,
but defer to the wise and worthy.

Happy are those
who praise creation
and who understand
the intricate ways of life.

Giving thanks to the many names of God

When peoples and nations go out from slavery,
when the persecuted come to a new land,
when the exiles return home,
the people give thanks and praise.

The very oceans give thanks
and the mountains skip like rams,
like lambs on the hilltops,
when the people rejoice in their deliverance.

Rejoice, O people, in your liberation
in the presence of Allah
in the presence of Yahweh, and Christ
in the presence of the Mother
Mary, Kwan-yin, and Gaia
in the presence of Life and Source
in the presence of all the sacred names.

When the people are liberated,
Spirit turns rock into a pool of water,
and flinty stone into a spring of life.

Trusting in Spirit, not idols

Not to ourselves alone, O Spirit,
but to you we give honor,
because of your never-ending
wisdom and compassion.

Why do people say "Where is Spirit?"
Spirit is in us, but we are small
compared to the greatness of life around us.

Some people have forgotten this;
they worship the idols of profit and pleasure;
they worship wealth, domination and fame.
Their idols are the work of human ego.

These have mouths but not do speak;
eyes, but do not see.
They have ears but do not hear;
noses, but cannot smell.
They have hands, but do not feel;
feet, but they do not walk.

Those who worship power are empty
and all who trust in wealth are fools.

O people of the world, trust in Spirit.
Spirit is everywhere: in us and around us.
Spirit is our comfort and our hope.

Creation is the guardian

I lift up my eyes to the hills.
Where does my help come from?
My help comes from creation,
my help comes from sky and earth.

I know my foot will not slip.
Sky and earth do not sleep.
The forces that help me
do not slumber or sleep.

Creation is my guardian,
protecting me from harm.
The sun will not hurt me by day
or the moon by night.

Sky and earth will keep me from harm,
protecting my very life.
Creation will watch my going out
and my coming in, now and forever.

The sacred places

I was glad when they said to me:
"Let us go to the holy places!"
Now our feet are standing
on the sacred realms of earth.

In fields and forests and beaches
we find it easy to give thanks.
Even in the dirty, crowded cities
we discover the sacred sites.

We sit in quiet and give thanks.
We thank creation for all we are given.
We thank the people who have loved us,
and the people who have worked for justice.

When we meditate we pray for peace
among all the cities and nations:
"May happiness live within your walls
and safety and love dwell in your houses."

We pray: "Peace and goodness be with you.
May the trees and air and water and soil
be protected to the seventh generation."
We do this for the sake of the whole world.

Prayer to the loving Spirit

I lift up my eyes to you, Spirit
who lives among us and beyond us.

As the eyes of a child
look to the face of her mother,
so my eyes look up to you,
waiting for love and compassion.

Have mercy on me, Spirit,
have mercy on us all.
My soul has suffered enough contempt.
I've had more than enough failure,
more than enough self-doubt.

I lift up my eyes to you,
Spirit who lives among us.
Come to me.

Devotion to Wisdom

If I did not have Sophia in my life,
if I had never learned about her,
when self-doubts attacked me,
they would have swallowed me alive.

When I was angry at myself,
a flood of self-hatred would have drowned me;
I would have been lost in the raging waters.

Thank you, woman of wisdom.
You have saved me from being prey
to my insecurities and fears.

I have escaped the worst of my doubts
like a bird flying free from its cage.
I have broken the trap of my fears
and abandoned the prison of my own making.

My help came from you, Sophia,
You who are with me always.

The realm of the sacred

When we come into the realm of the sacred,
we can hardly believe our happiness.
Our mouths fill with laughter
and our tongues with words of praise.

We chant out loud to each other:
"Great things have been given to us."
We understand and we are grateful.
We create a celebration.

May these times be forever and always.
May our joy flow like the mountain streams.
May those who have sown tears
now reap with shouts of joy.

May those who go out weeping
bearing the seeds to be sown,
come home with pleasing songs,
carrying their sheaves.

Great things have been given to us
and we are grateful.

How Spirit works in us

Unless Spirit helps raise the house,
those who build it labor in vain,
Unless Spirit pervades the city,
those who care for it watch in vain.

In vain we rise up early
and stay up late at night.
Without Spirit we eat the bread
of our hard labor in vain,
for Spirit alone gives us peace.

Children, art, honest work, love—
all are gifts of Spirit.
Those who receive them carry Spirit within.
Happy are we who honor Spirit
in our selves and in the world.

Love of creation

Happy and blessed are those who love creation
more than wealth, and who walk in its ways.
They shall eat the fruit of their labor with their hands;
they shall be content, and know that all is well.

Their families are like a beautiful vine in garden,
friends and children like green trees in the yard.
Those who love creation and keep its ways
are rich and peaceful in their souls.

May they live a long time in health.
Peace be to all beings.

PSALM 130

Putting trust in the source

Out of the depths we cry to you, source of all!
Beloved, hear our voices!

Let your ears be open
to the sound of our prayers!

We wait for your presence; our souls wait,
and we hope for a comforting word.

Our souls wait for the beloved one
more than those who watch all night for the morning
more than those who wait for the sun to rise.

O people let us put our hope in the source!

For there we will find wisdom and compassion
and the power of renewal and change.

From the source of all, the people will find
the help we need in these terrible times.

Spirit brings abundance

Spirit of life, remember me
and all the hardships I have endured.
I have promised to myself and to you:
I will not enter my house and go to bed,

I will not give sleep to my eyes
or slumber to my body
until I find a place for you in my heart,
until I meditate and pray with you, O Spirit.

I hear of you in many places,
I seek your wisdom in books and hymns.
I want to live with you in my heart,
and give you honor every way I can.

Spirit, come to your home inside me,
come to your place in my soul.
May I be clothed with your compassion
and may your wisdom feed me.

Spirit has promised me and will not turn back:
"I am with you always and I love you.
Pay attention to the truth you hold inside,
and you will never be abandoned.

"Your heart is my resting place.
I live with you and give you peace."

Praise of unity

How good and pleasant it is
when people of the earth
live together in unity!

It is like precious oil on the head,
a scented balm for the face,
a salve for the dry body.

It is like snow on a mountain glacier
which melts and flows
into a great wide river.

When they live together—people,
mountains and rivers—all these
are blessed and will be blessed forever.

Lament for the earth

By the rivers of New Jersey and Oregon
there we sat down and wept
when we remembered the old days.

On the bending willow branches
we hung up our fiddles and guitars.
For there our captors,
greed and illusion,
begged us, "Sing the songs
of the good old days."

How could we sing those sacred songs
in a polluted land?

If we forget how the world
was once beautiful,
let our right hands wither!
Let our tongues cling
to the roof of our mouth
if we do not remember and cherish you,
clear water and running salmon,
if we do not value the sacred wilderness
above our selfish desires.

Remember, people, how ignorance
and greed brought down
the old growth forests,
how the timber barons shouted
"Cut them down! Log them!
Down to the bare earth!"

O America, you Devastator!
Happy be those who will make you pay
for what you have done to the earth!
Happy be those who will take your dirty money
and use it to restore the land!

The presence of Sophia

O Wisdom, you have searched me and known me.
You know when I sit down in sadness
and when I rise up in joy.

You know my hidden thoughts;
you search out my shameful fantasies
and my terrible fears.
You know me through and through.

Even before a word is on my tongue,
Sophia, you know it completely.
You lay your hand upon me,
to discipline and teach.
Such power is frightening to me,
so awful that I run from it.

Where can I go to get away from you?
If I try to think noble thoughts, you laugh.
If I become cynical, you are displeased.
If I fly off into ignorance and illusion
even there your hand holds on to me.
Your presence holds me to the truth.

I say, "Surely hopelessness and grief
cover me and the light is turning to night,"
but even despair is not dark to you.
The night of despair is bright as day,
for Sophia tells me that my pain is not my failure.

You formed my inward parts, Sophia,
you knit me together in my mother's womb.

Who I am is not hidden from you:
all the ways I have held onto secrets
all the ways I have been hurt.
You know all about me and still
you look at me as a precious being.
You write my name in your book.

How beautiful are your ways to me.
How vast and intricate you are.
I try to count your mysteries—
they are more than the sand.
When I wake from sleep in the morning,
we are still together, you and I.

I wish you could quiet the hatred within me,
and make my selfish thoughts go away:
the times I speak of others with contempt,
the times I wish bad luck to those I envy.

At this moment, Sophia,
I renounce whatever is in me
that takes me away from you.
I let go of everything
that keeps us apart.

Search me and know my heart.
Test me and know my thoughts.
Have compassion on all that is hurtful in me.
And lead me in your ways forever.

Gratitude to the universe

Praise the universe!
Praise creation, O my soul!
I will praise creation as long as I live.
I will sing praises to the universe all my life long.

People, don't put your trust
in the rich or in politicians.
They can't possibly save you.
When they breathe their last
they too return to earth,
and on that day their money and their power
are buried with them in the dirt.

Those who praise the universe know better.
Their hope is in the energy
that was there at the beginning,
energy that made the galaxies,
that created and sustains all life,
energy that embraces us right now.

The universe seeks right relation.
Through the energy of our work on earth,
we bring justice to the oppressed,
food to the hungry, solace to the sick,
freedom to the prisoners of deception,
and eyes to those who are blind to the wonder.

Creation itself embraces those who fall down,

lifts up the lonely ones, and watches over
strangers, the homeless, and the very young.
But those who show no compassion to others
will never find peace for themselves.

Creation is eternal.
The energy is here for all of us.
Praise creation!

The gift of life

Praise life!
Sing a new song to creation,
praise goodness wherever the people meet.

Let people be glad they're alive.
Let the children of earth rejoice
in the gift of life.

Let us praise life with dancing,
let us make music with violin and drum,
for we are meant to be happy.

We are meant to see the oppressed
rise up and be satisfied.

Let the people be grateful to life itself.
Let us sing aloud in our houses,
let us praise the sacred with our dance.

Let the people overcome fear and illusion.
Let us take the sharp-edged sword of wisdom
and set things right in our nations!

Let us destroy the systems that oppress,
and rebuke the madness for possessions
that binds us in chains!

Let us see through illusions of money and hate
and rid ourselves of selfishness and greed.

This shall be done
for the well being of all people!
Praise life!

Praise and joy for life

Praise life!
Praise life in our small selves
and praise it in the vast universe.

Praise life for all its riches
and praise it for how it is good.

Praise life with the saxophone
Praise it with guitar and bass!

Praise life by dancing in a circle
Praise it with violins and flutes!

Praise it with clashing cymbals
and praise it with tall conga drums!

Let everything that breathes praise life.
Praise life!

Praise for Robyn Gigl and *By Way of Sorrow*

"An intelligent and resourceful protagonist with an unusual back-story . . . Erin's ability to navigate the intricacies of the law is just as fascinating as the subsequent perils she encounters. Gigl, an attorney, offers some enlightening insights into the workings of the legal world." —*Publishers Weekly*

"This enthralling series debut features a twisty plot full of surprises and a cast of exciting characters—most notably tough, relatable defense attorney Erin McCabe—all while diving into the mud of corrupt local politics. An original legal thriller that is sure to be among the year's best!" —Edwin Hill, author of *Watch Her*

"Does a remarkably effective job of mixing an exciting legal thriller with the personal story of its protagonist. Gigl shows the good and the bad that comes along with Erin's transition. The depictions of bias, discrimination, and feelings of disconnect that come with losing your friends and family are shown to varying degrees and to a range of resolutions. But the message doesn't overwhelm the medium. Readers will find that *By Way of Sorrow* is a compulsively riveting page-turner with a complex heroine, a captivating plot, and no easy answers. It's one of the best thrillers of the year."
—*Mystery Scene*

"A taut, engaging page-turner with a lot of heart. Lawyer Erin McCabe and her law partner Duane Swisher are on the case of a transgender teen accused of murdering the scion of a ruthless politician bent on burying the case, and the accused, at all costs. A good read. McCabe's a protagonist with a lot of depth. Two thumbs-up for Gigl." —Tracy Clark, author of *Runner*

"Robyn Gigl has delivered a compelling, provocative legal thriller like no other. It's addictive as hell, one of those 'just one more chapter' books that keep you reading late into the night. Topical and fast-paced, *By Way of Sorrow* grabs you on the very first page with a brutal murder, and then sends you on a twist-filled thrill ride that doesn't let up until the startling finale. Gigl introduces a new kind of heroine with attorney Erin McCabe—she's brilliant, resourceful, a little vulnerable and completely unique. Bravo! Is it too soon to ask when we can expect the next Erin McCabe thriller?"
—Kevin O'Brien, *New York Times* bestselling author of *The Bad Sister*

Books by Robyn Gigl

BY WAY OF SORROW

SURVIVOR'S GUILT

Published by Kensington Publishing Corp.

BY WAY OF SORROW

Robyn Gigl

KENSINGTON
PUBLISHING CORP.

www.kensingtonbooks.com

For Jan—Since our first dance all those years ago, your star has been fixed in my firmament. Thank you for sharing life's adventures with me. With love.

For Tim, Colin, & Kate—Thank you for being who you are. You are the three greatest joys in my life.

PROLOGUE

April 17, 2006

*H*IS BROWN EYES WERE OPEN, THE SHOCK OF BEING STABBED still reflected in his dilated pupils. Sharise pushed his naked, lifeless body off of her, and he tumbled heavily from the bed to the floor, landing on his back.

Fuck, she thought, breathing heavily, *I got to get out of here. No. Take your time, don't panic. It's two in the morning, no one will miss him for a while.*

She leaned up on one arm so she could look over the side of the bed at his body, the blood pooling beneath him on the cheap mustard-colored motel carpet. *Fucking bastard. You got what you deserved, you piece of shit.* Turning away from him, she looked down at her own blood-soaked body, and the wave of nausea came without warning. She retched over the side of the bed, adding a final indignity to his corpse.

Shaking, she pushed herself to the far side of the bed and swung her feet to the floor, hoping she could stand, hoping the nausea would retreat. She steadied herself by bracing her hand against the wall, and slowly felt her way to the bathroom, where she found the light switch and the toilet just as she vomited again, grabbing her cornrows with her right hand to protect them from the insides of her stomach and the murky waters of the bowl. As she heaved and gagged, her mind drifted back to when she was little and her momma would sit next to her when she was sick, comforting her through the ordeal. God, she could use her momma now, but it had been four years and there was no going back now.

When there was nothing left to come up, Sharise lay on the cold tiled floor, her body trembling, not wanting to budge from where she was. Finally, the reality of what she had done began to settle in, and she knew she had to move.

She dragged herself into the shower, where she watched his blood swirl down the drain, and desperately tried to come up with a plan. Her fingerprints would be all over him and the room, not to mention they'd probably be able to get her DNA from the vomit, which she had no intention of cleaning up. She had been arrested enough to know that Homicide would find a match in the system before their coffee even cooled. So not only would she have to somehow disappear, she had to avoid getting arrested for the rest of her life; not likely in her line of work, and especially since her mug shot would be plastered all over the place.

She found her dress in the far corner of the room and put it on sans underwear, which she'd left in the bathroom, soaked with his blood. She sat on the edge of the bed and zipped up her thigh-high faux suede boots. She looked in the mirror, dug her lipstick out of her purse, and reapplied it. The only other makeup she carried was mascara, but she decided to forego reapplying that for now.

Why the hell had this white boy picked her, anyway? She found his wallet still in his pants pocket. William E. Townsend, Jr., age twenty-eight, according to his license. *Great*, she thought as she rifled through the wallet, *one of those guys who carried no cash.* Besides the fifty dollars he had already given her, he only had another thirty dollars in his wallet, not even enough to pay for what he wanted. She grabbed the money and his Bank of America ATM card. Then she found his phone, flipped it open, and scrolled through his contacts. *Stupid motherfucker.* There, under the name "BOA," was his ATM PIN number. That should be good for three hundred, she figured.

Taking the keys to his BMW out of his front pants pocket, she looked at his phone again. Two forty-five. She wasn't exactly sure where they were, but she knew it wasn't too far from Atlantic City; maybe she could still grab a change of clothes and get to Philly before daylight. She could ditch the car there and hop a train to New York. It was a long shot, but she couldn't think of any better options.

Studying the scene, she tried to figure out if she should take the knife with her or not. It's not like it mattered if they found it. They sure as hell were going to be able to put her in the room if she ever got caught. Might as well take it, she reasoned, just in case.

She walked over to where he was lying. His face was already pale, the blood that had provided the color now in a puddle under him. His hands still clutched the knife protruding from his chest. She unclenched his hands to pull the knife out, then rinsed it off in the sink before stuffing it in her purse.

Time to go. She turned off all the lights and hung the DO NOT DISTURB sign on the door. With a little luck, she'd be in New York before they found his body. Maybe if she was really lucky, it would never make it beyond the local news. She took a deep breath and headed out the door.

CHAPTER 1

*E*RIN HADN'T BEEN IN THIS COURTROOM IN OVER FIVE YEARS. A lot had changed since then. She smiled as she made her way down the aisle thinking of all the time she had spent here ten years ago, right after she graduated law school, as the law clerk for the Honorable Miles Foreman. She had learned a lot that year, watching the lawyers in the courtroom, both the good ones and the bad. And she had learned a lot from Judge Foreman, also some good and some bad. Today she expected she'd experience the bad. She could deal with that. What other choice did she have?

"Erin, are you out of your mind?" said Carl Goldman, who represented her client's codefendant, his eyes wide as she slid into the seat next to him.

She dropped her purse, which doubled as her briefcase, onto the bench and smiled politely. "I'm not sure I follow, Carl."

"Foreman is going to go absolutely insane. Why did you file this motion? Not only is he going to take it out on your client, but he'll crucify my client as well."

"Does your client have a defense?"

He studied her, trying to make the connection. "No. But what does that have to do with your motion for Foreman to recuse himself?"

She laughed. "My client has no defense either. Which means, at some point, I'll be looking to get the best plea deal I can for him. I listened to all the wiretap recordings, and you're in the same boat. Correct?"

"Yeah, so?"

"Who hands out the toughest sentences in the county?"

"Foreman," he answered.

"Exactly. We need a judge who is going to see this case for what it is—a simple gambling case, not an organized crime, money-laundering one. Our clients should be looking at a couple years tops, not the eight or nine years Foreman will want to give them. And as long as Foreman has the case, there's no reason for the prosecutor's office to be reasonable, because he won't be when it comes to sentencing."

"But what are the grounds?"

Her grin was slightly evil. "Foreman's homophobic."

Carl stared at her. "What on earth does that have to do with anything? My client's not gay. Is yours?"

She shook her head. "No, Carl, my client isn't gay. It isn't about him. It's about me."

Carl stared at Erin, a look of confusion spreading across his face as he looked her up and down. She was wearing a navy-blue business suit over a low-cut white silk blouse that accentuated her breasts, with a skirt that came several inches above her knees. She had on four-inch heels and her makeup was done to perfection. With her copper-colored hair and the dusting of freckles that ran across the bridge of her nose, she was usually mistaken for being far younger than her thirty-five years. She thought it more than ironic that she was often told she had the girl-next-door look.

"But you don't look gay," he finally offered.

She cocked her head to one side. "And exactly how does

someone who's gay look? Not butch enough for you? Besides, who said—"

Erin was cut off by the entrance of the courtroom deputy. "All rise."

Judge Miles Foreman charged out of the door leading to his chambers onto the bench and looked out over his packed courtroom. "*State v. Thomas*," he said, not even trying to mask his anger.

Erin and Carl made their way up to counsel table, where the assistant prosecutor, Adam Lombardi, was already stationed. Lombardi's olive complexion, jet-black hair, which he wore slicked back, Roman nose, and taste in expensive suits sometimes led those who didn't know him to believe he was a high-priced defense attorney. But his reputation as a top-notch prosecutor was well earned, and he showed no signs of wanting to switch sides.

"Appearances, please," Foreman said without looking up.

"Assistant Prosecutor Adam Lombardi for the State, Your Honor."

"Erin McCabe for defendant Robert Thomas. Good morning, Your Honor."

"Carl Goldman for defendant Jason Richardson, Judge."

Foreman looked up and lowered his glasses so he could peer over the top of his lenses. To Erin it didn't look like he had aged in the five years since she had last appeared in his courtroom, or for that matter in the ten years since she clerked for him, but that wasn't a compliment. Bald, with a dour expression and a demeanor to match, he had always looked ten years older than he was. Now, at sixty-five, he finally looked his age. "Everyone have a seat, except for Ms. McCabe." He picked up a stack of papers in his hand and waved them about. "Good morning, indeed," he started. "Do you mind telling me what this is, Ms. McCabe?"

Erin smiled politely. "I presume that's the motion I filed, Judge."

"Of course it's the motion you filed. Do you want to tell me the meaning of this motion?"

She knew she had to walk a fine line between provoking him

and being held in contempt. "Absolutely, Judge. It's a motion seeking your recusal from this case."

"I know what it is!" he exploded. "What I want to know is where do you get the temerity to challenge my impartiality?"

An answer quickly ran through her head—*I think it must be genetic, probably from my mother*—but she opted for the safer, "I'm not sure I understand, Judge."

"What don't you understand, Ms. McCabe? You say you want me to remove myself from the case, but you filed no affidavits in support. You simply say you want to present an affidavit for me to review privately, in camera, as you put it in your motion. If you have something to say about me, I suggest that you say it in public, on the record."

She looked at him, trying to gauge how close to the line she was. "Judge, I'm not sure you really want me to do that."

He slammed the motion papers down on the bench. Placing both of his hands flat on his bench, he leaned forward. "Who do you think you are to tell me what I do or don't want? Either you put it on the record, or this motion will be dismissed. Am I clear?" He paused, and then with emphasis added, "*Ms*. McCabe."

Erin slowly inhaled. "Very well, Judge. For the record, I was your law clerk ten years ago. During my tenure as your law clerk, your honor handled a case called *McFarlane v. Robert DelBuno*, Mr. DelBuno, of course, being the Attorney General at the time. Perhaps your honor recalls that case?"

Foreman glared down at her. "I remember the case," he replied, a tinge of concern evident in his voice.

"I thought you would, Judge, because the case involved a constitutional challenge to New Jersey's sodomy laws, laws which your honor upheld but were subsequently reversed on appeal. Now, if Your Honor may recall, Mr. McFarlane was represented by—"

The bang of Foreman's gavel brought her to an abrupt stop. "I want counsel in chambers immediately. Now!" Foreman leapt up from his chair and stormed down the three stairs and through the door leading to his chambers.

Adam Lombardi followed behind her as they headed back to Foreman's chambers. "Erin, this better be good, because if it's not, you'll need to get someone down here with bail money pronto."

She smiled at Adam. He was a decent guy, just doing his job. She knew if it were up to him, he'd put a fair plea offer on the table. "I think I'll be okay. But if things go south, put in a good word for me with the sheriff, okay?"

"Sure. I'll see if they can get you a cell with a good view."

"Appreciated," she said as the three of them headed back to Foreman's chambers.

Foreman was pacing back and forth behind his desk, still in his robes, when they walked in. He stopped pacing long enough to run his eyes up and down his former law clerk. "You . . ." he started. "You have a hell of a lot of nerve attacking me this way. So I got reversed in McFarlane. So what? Judges get reversed every day. This is a gambling case, not a prostitution case. What's McFarlane got to do with this?"

She held out a document. "Judge, this is my affidavit that I wanted you to review in camera," she offered. "I did it that way so you could review my affidavit privately in chambers and then decide if you wanted to make it public."

He reached out and snatched the papers from her hand, then picked up a pair of reading glasses from his desk and began reading. His face began to flush almost immediately. When he finished, he scowled at her.

"These are lies, damnable lies. I never said the things you attribute to me. Never! I should hold you in contempt for writing these scurrilous allegations. Maybe a few days in the county jail will refresh your recollection. What do you say to that, Ms. McCabe?"

She knew she had him by the short and curlies. Sure, it was his word against hers, but she was confident he wouldn't want any of this aired in public.

"Judge, I have tried my best to refrain from having any of my recollections regarding your comments about Barry O'Toole, Mr. McFarlane's attorney, placed on the record. I'll be happy to supply copies to counsel if you want, and of course, if you hold me in contempt, you will have to place my affidavit on the record."

He threw the papers at her, but they fluttered harmlessly to his desk. "Get out of my chambers," he spit out. But as they started to file out, he suddenly called her back.

She stopped and turned to look at him. "Yes, Your Honor?"

"You're worse than O'Toole, you know that. At least O'Toole never lied about who he was."

She studied him, his anger visible and real. "Judge, ten years ago, a man who I consider to be one of my legal mentors told me that doing what was right for a client was a lawyer's highest responsibility. He told me that even if a judge disagreed with my position, a judge should always try to respect that I was doing it for my client. I've tried to live up to that advice, placing my clients' best interests over any reaction I may get from a judge. Like me—and as evidenced by my affidavit—that mentor is imperfect. Given my status, I felt that it was likely my client might suffer as a result of certain biases. Nonetheless, regardless of my mentor's imperfections, I will always respect him for his help and guidance when I worked for him." She let her last words linger, hoping he'd be convinced of her sincerity. "Will there be anything else, Your Honor?"

Foreman reached down and picked up the affidavit from his desk. He slowly ripped it into pieces. "Here's what I think of your affidavit, Ms. McCabe," he said, his contempt evident. "And if your little speech was meant as an apology, it's not accepted. Get out, and don't worry your pretty little head about coming back. I will make sure I recuse myself from any case you're involved in, because I could never treat you fairly after reading your scurrilous lies. And frankly, I hope I never see you again."

She was tempted to respond, but another piece of advice moved front and center: Quit while you're ahead.

"Thank you, Judge," she said, turning and heading back to the courtroom.

CHAPTER 2

"**Y**OU NEED BAIL MONEY?" ERIN'S PARTNER, DUANE SWISHER, asked when she answered her cell phone.

"No, Swish. I'm just leaving the courthouse now," she said with a chuckle, appreciating his warped sense of humor.

"So?"

"He recused himself from this and any other cases I'm involved in."

"Wow. What was in your affidavit?"

"Oh, just some choice quotes from a homophobic judge. Where are you?"

"I'm with Ben. Trying to decide how to play things with the U.S. Attorney's Office."

"Got it," she replied, hoping that Ben Silver, one of the best criminal defense attorneys in the state, could keep her partner out of the crosshairs of the Department of Justice, who once again appeared intent on pursuing him for a leak of classified information to a reporter from the *Times*. Three years earlier, Duane had been forced to resign from the FBI under a cloud of suspicion that he was the leaker. Now, with a new book out based on the leaked information, he was once again the target of the DOJ's investigation.

"Listen, do you think you'd have time to meet a potential new client?" Duane asked.

She ran her calendar through her head. "Yeah, I should be able to. I have to get some stuff out today, but I have time. What time they coming in?"

"Actually, you have to go see him at the Ocean County jail."

"Okay, not exactly dressed for jail, but what kind of case?"

"Murder. Wouldn't be surprised if they go with capital murder."

"Wait. We're not on the public defenders' pool list anymore."

"It's not a pool case. It's a referral from Ben. He doesn't feel he can do it. He knows the victim's father. It's a big case, E."

"Yeah, if you're talking death penalty, I'd say it's a big case. Which case?"

"Do you remember about four months ago a kid by the name of William E. Townsend, Jr., was found stabbed to death in a motel?"

"Sure. His father is a big player down in South Jersey; it was all over the news. Didn't they pick someone up a couple of weeks ago on that?"

"That's the one."

"Why is Ben recommending us? I mean, I appreciate it and all, but Ben knows everyone. Plus, I've never done a death penalty case."

"A number of reasons. He really likes the work you've done helping him out on my case and he thinks you're a good lawyer. Second, almost everyone Ben knows is going to have the same problem he has—they either know or can't afford to cross Mr. Townsend."

She let out a reflexive laugh. "Yeah, guess we're not in that league."

"Last, but not least, Ben thought you might be able to relate better to the defendant than most."

She was about to question him more, when she remembered the news reports and realized what he was talking about. She paused for a moment, internally weighing the pros and cons. "Well, if it's not a pool case, how we getting paid?"

"Seventy-five thousand retainer up front, bill at three hundred an hour, and payment is guaranteed by Paul Tillis."

"And I should know who Paul Tillis is because . . . ?"

"Ah, what has become of you, my friend? Paul Tillis, point guard for the Pacers. Who also happens to be married to Tonya Tillis, née Barnes, the sister of defendant Samuel Barnes. Sister says she hasn't seen her brother since mom and dad threw him out of the house back in Lexington, Kentucky. But they're willing to pay for his lawyer."

Erin let out a low whistle. "Guess I'll drive south. Let me meet Barnes, and then I'll decide if I think we can do it."

"Great. I just spoke to the public defender who has the case now. Said he'd leave you a copy of what he has at the front desk; just ask the receptionist for a package with your name on it. Said the only things he had at this point were a rap sheet for Barnes and the initial arrest report from when they picked him up in New York City. He'll also fax authorization over to the jail for you to see his client for purposes of possible representation. By the way, he's thrilled someone might be taking the case. Apparently, no one in his office wants to piss off Mr. Townsend."

"Wonderful."

"You can say no."

She thought for only a moment. "Let's see what happens."

"Okay. I'll be in the office this afternoon. We'll talk when you get back."

Had Erin known she'd be headed to the county jail, she would have worn something a little more conservative. She wasn't sure which was more demeaning, the catcalls from the inmates or the leering looks from the corrections officers.

She walked up to the bulletproof glass, her identification in hand; she always left her purse locked in the trunk of her car.

"Can I help you?" the lieutenant on the other side said without looking up.

"Here to see an inmate."

"You got to come back later. Visiting hours aren't until two," he said, an air of annoyance circling his words.

"I'm an attorney," she replied.

Rubbing the back of his neck, he slowly leaned back in his chair to look her up and down. "You sure you want to go in there, honey? Those guys can play rough," he said with a smile. "Maybe you want to stay out here and keep me company."

While his eyes were focused on her chest, she picked out the name on his name tag: WILLIAM ROSE. *Jerk*, she thought, smiling back. "You don't have to call me 'honey,' Lieutenant. And Rosie, you may be the one, but unless you'd like to bring my client out to see me, I don't think I have a choice," she said, placing her license, attorney ID card, and car keys into the metal drawer.

He stared at her, his smirk telling her that he was trying to decipher if she was flirting or mocking. "So who you here to see . . . *honey?*" he asked as he opened the drawer and looked at her ID.

"Samuel Barnes."

His grin disappeared. "A freak and a murderer. You're gonna need more than your good looks and charm for that one."

"Never know," she said, holding her tongue, aware that Sam Barnes would reap what she sowed.

The lieutenant turned around and picked up a phone. "Rose here. Get Barnes and bring him down to attorney meeting room two. He's got an attorney here to see him. Her name is Erin McCabe." He walked back to the glass partition, put a visitor's badge in the tray, and slid it out to her. "I hold your license, attorney ID, and keys until you come out and give me the visitor's badge back. Don't want anyone sneaking out disguised as you," he said with a chuckle.

"Thanks, Lieutenant," she said, taking the visitor's badge out, putting it around her neck, and walking toward the metal doors to wait to be buzzed in.

No matter how many times she heard it, the clang of the heavy doors behind her always sent a claustrophobic ripple of fear through her like an electric shock. Being locked in and at someone else's mercy to be let out was not a feeling she enjoyed. Dressed as she was, the fact that she was locked in a men's jail made her more apprehensive.

After she went through the metal detectors, the guards thoroughly searched the paperwork she had to make sure there were no paper clips or staples, finding only the copied police reports from the public defender, her business card, and a legal pad with the name *Samuel Barnes* written in her neat script. After satisfying themselves she wasn't trying to sneak anything in, one of the officers led her to a small room that held a table and two chairs, where she sat in the chair closest to the door as she'd learned early on in her career as a public defender. That way a guard checking through the window on the door could always see her and her facial expression.

Ten minutes later, she heard the key in the door, followed by the clang of the metal door as it was pulled open to reveal Sam Barnes. Just a hair under six feet, he was rail thin. She quickly estimated that he weighed no more than 150 pounds. His brown face had several small cuts, and there was swelling around his lips. Even from the table, she could make out the dark bruises on his cheeks and under his eyes. His hair was in cornrows, hanging down to his shoulders.

He shuffled in, shackled at his ankles and his wrists, a thick chain running between them. In ten years, she had never seen a prisoner shackled inside the jail when visiting their attorney.

"You can unshackle him while he's with me," she said to the guard.

"Look, honey, I don't tell you how to do your job, you don't tell me how to do mine, okay? He's in PC. He stays shackled."

The guard grabbed the chair and pulled it out, then put his

hands on Barnes's shoulders and pushed him into the chair. "Pick up the phone behind you when you want out or if Mr. Barnes here gives you any problems. It rings in the control room." He turned and walked out, closing and locking the door behind him.

Erin slowly sat down, studying Barnes's battered face as she did.

"You not my attorney," he said defiantly and in a distinctly feminine voice.

"My name is Erin McCabe. I'm an attorney. I'm here to see if you'd like me to represent you."

"And why I want you to represent me? Shit, girl, you ain't even old enough to be a lawyer. I already got a public defender. Why I need you?"

She paused, wanting to earn Barnes's trust, but she didn't want to overplay her hand. "What would you like me to call you?" she asked calmly.

"You wanna be my lawyer and you don't even know my name?"

"I know the name on your rap sheet is Samuel Emmanuel Barnes, but I suspect that isn't the name you prefer."

The room fell silent. "Look here, lady, don't worry your white, liberal, bleeding heart over what I prefer to be called. Why you really here?"

"I told you why. To see if you want me to represent you."

"Who send you? I don't have no money for no lawyer."

"Your sister, Tonya, and her husband."

Barnes stiffened and his eyes narrowed. "I haven't seen my sister in four years. She don't know where I am. Besides, where she get the money to pay for some schoolgirl lawyer?"

"Honestly, I don't know where she's getting the money from; I suspect her husband. But my partner spoke to both your sister and her husband a couple of hours ago and they asked if I would meet with you. Your arrest apparently made the news back in Lexington. That's how they knew where you were."

"Yeah, hometown kid makes big." Barnes stopped and looked

across the table. "You keep saying my sister and her husband, they live in Lexington?"

"No, Indianapolis. But your parents are still there and they told your sister."

At the mention of his parents, Barnes seemed to retreat further into himself. "What's her husband name?" he challenged her.

"Paul Tillis."

For the first time, Barnes seemed to let his guard down just a shade. "Good for her. She marry Paul. I use to joke with her when they first meet that if they married, she'd be Tonya Tillis. Don't know why, but I always thought that sounded funny."

"I spoke to her briefly on the way here and she asked me to tell you that she loves you and misses you. She's been looking for you for the last four years. She wished she had been there when your mom and dad threw you out. She might not have been able to prevent them from doing that, but she would have taken you in. She hopes that she might still get to know"—Erin paused—"her sister," she said softly, finishing the sentence.

A tear seemed to hang momentarily in the corner of Barnes's eye, but he leaned forward and quickly wiped it away with the back of his shackled hand.

"You just be trying to take my sister's money?" he demanded, his protective mask quickly slipping back into place. "Is that it? You understand I stabbed some white boy whose daddy is some big shot. Either they execute me or I'm going to spend the rest of my life locked up. And the way things going, it be a very short life at that. So I don't want my sister wasting her money on you."

"Who beat you?"

Barnes threw his head back and laughed. "You really are one crazy bitch. First you come in here saying you wanna represent me; then you start asking stupid shit to get me killed." He glared at Erin. "I tripped and fell. Clumsy me," he said, rolling his head.

"You really should be more careful. Looks like you fell multiple times. Look, based on what your sister told my partner, I suspect you're a transgender woman. Has anyone talked to you about trying to get you moved to the women's jail?"

Barnes closed his eyes. "Please, ain't no one gonna move me to no women's jail."

"You're probably right. But it's one way to try and protect you without ratting anyone out. Even if they don't move you, you've drawn attention to the situation, and maybe some judge will be a little bit more sensitive to the fact that you're getting the shit beat out of you while you're supposedly in protective custody. Sure as hell doesn't look protective to me."

Before Barnes could say anything, Erin continued. "Look, I can't make you talk to me. Your sister asked me to see you. I've seen you. You want me to leave? I'll leave. I suspect what really happened on the night of April 17 is far different from what has been reported in the press. And as best I can tell, only two people know for sure what happened, and one of them is unavailable for the trial. You want to talk about it, fine; you don't, that's fine too. But what do you have to lose?"

Barnes looked at her across the table. "Okay, Ms. Big Shot, my public defender says he's tried fifteen murder cases. You try any?"

"Three."

"How you do?"

"Lost them all."

Barnes laughed. "And you think I should hire you? You don't sound very good to me, honey."

"I never said I was. But if that's the way we're going to mea-sure how good a lawyer is, do you know how many your public defender won?"

"No, didn't ask him."

"Maybe you should. If he's lost all fifteen, I'm five times a better lawyer than he is."

Barnes frowned, unimpressed by Erin's logic. "The public de-fender guy told me they probably want to give me the death penalty, but he said don't worry, nobody gets executed in New

Jersey. He said that his office have a special team that handles death penalty cases, and that they be the best attorneys in the state. You ever handle a death penalty case?"

"No, I haven't. And honestly, I'm not here to argue whether or not there are good lawyers in the public defender's office. I was a public defender for five years. And he's right; on death penalty cases they draw from a pool of outside lawyers to form a team who will defend you really well. The PD's office usually assigns the best lawyers to represent defendants in capital cases. It's also true that no one has been executed in New Jersey since the 1960s. There's no guarantee, but there is an effort to have the death penalty repealed. But right now, it's still there, and if it's still around when you go to trial, chances are the state will be seeking it in your case."

"If there's no death penalty, what I looking at?"

"Either life in prison with no parole or thirty years to life."

"Fuck," Barnes said to himself. "Look, whatever your name is, I don't have a fucking chance in this case. But if somehow I did, it ain't gonna be with some redheaded, freckle-faced lawyer who doesn't know shit about what my life has been like. I have no idea why my sister pick you, but you go back and tell her if she really wants to help, get me some pit bull lawyer who is gonna rip the piss out of the other side."

"Fine. I'll let her know. Here's my card if you ever need it," she said, sliding the card across the table.

"Why you?" Barnes asked as she turned around to reach the phone that would let her call the guard. "I mean, if she got money, why not get me Johnnie Cochran?"

Erin snorted and turned back so she was facing Barnes. "No matter how good or bad I might be, I'm a better choice than Johnnie Cochran." She paused. "Unfortunately for you and for Mr. Cochran, he's dead."

Barnes squinted at her, not sure if he believed her that Cochran was dead. "So what be so special about you? You ain't

Black. You ain't some white guy who's tried a million cases. You the daughter of the judge or something? I don't get it. Why Tonya pick you?"

"Probably because you and I have one thing in common," Erin replied.

"You whoring to make a little extra money?" he said with a laugh.

Erin studied Barnes, knowing where this was going, even if he didn't. "No, nothing like that. Just that I know a little about being rejected."

"What, you didn't get into Harvard?"

"No, I know what it's like to have family and friends struggle to accept who you are." She hesitated and slowly inhaled, suspecting that his reaction would be different from just about everyone else's. "Up until about two years ago, my name was Ian."

Barnes stared at her. "Wait! What you saying? You telling me you're trans?"

Erin nodded. "I transitioned a little over two years ago."

Barnes sat there shaking his head in disbelief. The only noise that punctuated the silence in the locked meeting room came from the prisoners out in the hallway screaming at each other. It remained that way for several minutes as Barnes weighed his options.

He slowly lifted his shackled hands and laid them on the table. "Sharise," the voice barely audible. "My name is Sharise."

Then Sharise gently laid her head on her arms and quietly began to weep.

"He tried to kill me," she said, choking back a sob. "He had the knife, and he tried to kill me . . . when he found out that I was trans."

CHAPTER 3

"*S*o?"

Erin looked up from her computer screen to see the commanding figure of Duane Abraham Swisher, "Swish" to his friends, standing in the doorway to her office. At thirty-five, her partner kept himself in great physical shape. Even in a suit and tie, you could tell by the way his shirt stretched across his chest that he was ripped. His six-foot-two-inch frame, dark brown skin, and well-trimmed goatee always made an immediate impression. A Brown University alum, he had been the starting shooting guard there for three years, first-team All-Ivy two of those years. His shot from three-point range was so sweet that even if his last name hadn't been Swisher, "Swish" would have been a perfect nickname.

"Hey," she said, "where've you been? I thought you'd be here when I got back."

"Stopped and had lunch with Cori."

"Oh, that's nice. You're such a good husband."

He looked at her and wrinkled his brow. "Yeah, not so sure she feels that way. When you marry an FBI agent, you generally think he's going to be the one doing the investigations, not the one being investigated."

"Sorry. Anything I can do to help?"

He paused for a moment. "Thanks, but don't think so. Besides, I'm not sure whose side you'd be on."

Erin chuckled. "That's easy—Corrine's."

"That's what I was afraid of."

She motioned for him to come in, and he took a seat in one of the three beige club chairs that formed a semicircle in front of her desk. "So how did it go this morning with Ben?"

"He has a meeting with Andrew Barone from Justice tomorrow. Martin Perna from the *Times* has a new book out, which is based on the FBI's targeting of Muslim Americans post 9/11. As a result, the FBI's Office of Professional Responsibility has reopened the investigation into the leak. Since I was part of the team that was involved in the surveillance, and complained internally about the fact that it was unconstitutional, they suspect I leaked classified information to Perna. They issued a subpoena to Perna trying to find out who his source was, and apparently the *Times*'s lawyers have already filed a motion to quash on reporter's privilege and First Amendment grounds."

"Why OPR? You've been out for three years."

"Because they ran the investigation when I was still an agent. So they're just picking up where they left off."

"Anything I can do at this point?"

"Pray," Duane said, shrugging his shoulders.

"Not my forte," she replied. "But for you, I'll give it a shot."

"Thanks," he offered with a small grin. "How'd things go with Mr. Barnes?"

"Pretty good. Interesting case, that's for sure. But, Swish, if we get into this case, our client's name is Sharise, and it's 'she,' 'her,' and 'Ms. Barnes.'"

Duane quietly laughed, shaking his head. "Guess Ben made the right recommendation."

"I don't know if he did or not, but if we're going to represent her, I want to make sure she's given the respect she's entitled to. And that starts with recognizing who she is."

"I get it. No problem here. After all, I've always been politically correct with you, right?" he said.

She raised her eyebrows. "Are you for real? How many other women in your life have you asked, 'Is it hard to walk in heels?' 'Do you miss standing to pee?' And my favorite, 'Is it fun having tits?'"

"I think I said breasts," he offered in his own defense.

She shot him a look.

"Okay, maybe I didn't. But come on, you're the only one I know who's changed teams. Who else am I going to ask the questions that have stumped men for eons? I always want to know what it's like for people in different situations. I remember my senior year at Brown, a guy transferred in from Princeton. At that time Princeton had won the Ivies a couple of years in a row and had made it to the NCAAs. We, on the other hand, never even had a winning season. Shit, we all wanted to know what it was like playing for Princeton."

"What did he say?"

"Said Princeton sucked and he hoped to get some decent playing time at Brown."

She laughed. "That about sums it up for me too. Being a man sucked; hoping for some decent playing time as a woman." She paused, tilting her head to one side. "Now, can we please get back to Sharise?"

Duane nodded. "Sure, sorry."

"So where do I start? Yes, she is interested in us representing her. I think the next step is for us to have a conversation with her sister and brother-in-law to go over what will be involved. If they are in agreement, then . . ." She sat there shaking her head. "Then there is a shitload of work to do."

"We have a defense? Like she was in Detroit at the time of the murder?"

"Self-defense."

"Witnesses?"

"Her and Mr. Townsend, Jr."

"Yeah, I was afraid you were going to say that. And they were together why?"

"They had become acquainted on the streets of Atlantic City, where young Mr. Townsend was so enamored with her that he offered her fifty dollars for a blow job."

"Unfortunately, I think I know where this is going."

"Yeah, spoiler alert, Junior gets his hummer, but it's his last. Apparently, when he discovers she was not assigned female at birth, he flips out and tries to kill her. In defending herself, Mr. Townsend is stabbed."

"Any brilliant thoughts on how we defend this?"

She shrugged. "Change of venue, maybe? After all, Townsend senior is such a force in South Jersey that Sharise could never get a fair trial south of the Raritan."

Duane rubbed his chin. "And we're going to ask to have it transferred where?"

Good question. Up until a few hours ago, Erin had known very little about William Townsend. But a quick Internet search showed that his power and influence in the southern part of the state were very real. He had built a commercial real estate empire south of the Raritan River that had made him one of the wealthiest men in the state. Using his wealth, he moved on to politics, and had been elected as a state senator. The combination of his wealth and political clout gave him a hand in just about every political appointment in South Jersey. A lot of very important people were beholden to William Townsend. Some people had friends in high places; Mr. Townsend put his friends in high places.

"How about the Bronx?" she finally offered.

Duane laughed. "Yeah, that'll work. All we have to do is make it part of New Jersey."

"Shit, I don't know. Let's talk to Sharise's sister and brother-in-law, and then, if we're retained, we can start sorting out these minor details."

Duane looked at her, and she could sense he was concerned about something.

"What's the matter?" Erin asked.

Duane ran his hand over his short, neatly trimmed 'fro. "I just want to make sure you've thought this through. To most people you're just an attractive female attorney. This case will change all of that; the defendant is transgender, and you can bet your ass that people will find out that the defense lawyer is also transgender. That could make for some real interesting headlines." His eyes narrowed. "This is going to be a high-profile case, E, and with Townsend lurking in the background, this has the potential to get really ugly for you. Are you sure you're prepared to be outed in a big way?"

She got up from behind her desk and walked over to one of the windows. Her office was perched in one of the second-floor turrets of a former Victorian home that had been converted into an office building twenty years ago.

She watched the Rahway River running gently past their building on its way through Cranford, now nothing more than a gentle stream, and thought of the times that a heavy rain would turn it into a raging torrent. Like the river, life could certainly be unpredictable. Ten years ago, when she was still Ian, both newly married and newly admitted to the Bar, she never thought she would transition, but here she stood. She also knew Duane was right; taking this case probably would turn her life into a raging torrent. Was she really prepared to deal with that?

She turned around to face him. "I know you're right, and no, I'm not sure I'm ready for what's likely to happen." She hesitated, trying to find the words to express something she felt from the moment Sharise had told Erin her name. There was a connection between them, and that connection meant something. "I think I can make a difference in this case," she finally said, the confidence in her voice surprising her. Silent was the self-doubt that had eaten at her for the last two hours.

"You've had enough issues with your family over your transition; they're not going to be happy if your name and picture are all over the place."

"You're right." She took a deep breath. "But it's not about them, Swish," she said, hoping she was being truthful. "I don't know what it's like to be thrown out of your home by your parents and forced to live on the streets, like Sharise was. But maybe what I've been through gives me enough of a window to help us defend her."

"Or maybe it's your attempt to show some people in your life that they're wrong about you?"

Ouch. She hated that there were times when Duane seemed to know exactly what she was thinking. "And your basis for this is your BS in psychology or your years of training as a special agent?"

"None of the above. It's from knowing a little bit about my very talented but sometimes insecure partner."

"I'll be okay," she replied, not even convincing herself. "What about you? How are you going to feel if everybody knows your partner is transgender?"

"Whatever. If everybody's focused on you, maybe I'll just fly under the radar."

She gave the slightest bit of a laugh, and nodded. "We're good to go then?"

"There is one other minor detail."

"What's that?" she asked, walking back to her desk.

"I'm going to have to tell Tonya and Paul I'm under investigation. Agreed?"

She nodded. Duane had lived under the cloud of the investigation for almost four months. Even though he'd never admit it, she could see the strain he was under.

"Speaking of things we need to discuss, do they need to know about me?" she offered reluctantly, knowing how awkward that conversation could be.

Duane grinned sheepishly. "Yeah, it kind of came up when I spoke to them the first time."

"It kind of came up?" she replied, her voice rising into a question.

"Well, they wanted to know about us and why Ben had recommended us, and, well, I mentioned to Tonya the fact that you had transgendered."

She winced. "You'd think that after spending as much time with me as you have, at least you'd learn the correct terminology. *Transgender* is an adjective. I'm a transgender woman. It's not a verb. *Transition* is the verb you want."

"Got it," he said.

She gave him a generous smile. If anyone had suggested to her three years ago that Swish would still be her partner after she transitioned, she would have said they were crazy. But, as her therapist had warned, the way people reacted to her news was totally unpredictable. People she thought would always support her never spoke to her again, while others, like Swish, who she figured would fade from her life, had become a port in the storm.

"No problem. You stuck with me through this," she said, spreading her arms wide, "so you get a pass on terminology."

"Thanks," he replied.

"Why did you stick with me?"

"Never occurred to me not to, I guess."

"Really?"

"Yeah," he said, his look displaying his surprise at her reaction. "Look, when we started the firm, you didn't ask me a lot of questions about why I left the Bureau. I suspect you knew then that there was more to me leaving than I could tell. But you welcomed me with open arms." Duane hesitated and in a gentle voice continued. "I saw what was happening. I know a lot of people who were close to you had trouble with your situation."

She nodded, her thoughts swallowing her. Some losses had

been harder than others, none more so than her former wife, Lauren, her dad, and her brother, Sean. And in Sean's case, it also meant her losing contact with her nephews, Patrick, now twelve, and Brennan, now ten, both of whom she adored. Before she transitioned, Erin had been a fixture at their soccer games, having played in both high school and college. That ended when she came out to her brother. God, she missed seeing them.

"Thanks," she said, a sad smile slowly gracing her face. "I'm glad you didn't bail on me," she offered with more than a hint of appreciation in her voice.

The call with Tonya and Paul went well. It probably didn't hurt that Paul's agent had played for Harvard when Duane played for Brown and he had put in a good word for Duane. Duane's FBI experience had also given him some cred on the investigative work that needed to be done.

Now came the hard part: figuring out how to prove a nineteen-year-old transgender prostitute killed the only son of one of the most powerful men in the state in self-defense.

Erin locked the office door and started walking the four blocks from her office to her apartment, thinking it might be a nice night for a run. She lived so close she always left her car in the office lot, saving the hundred and fifty dollars a month on the municipal parking permit she'd need if she parked by her apartment.

She walked briskly down Union Avenue and crossed Springfield Avenue into the downtown section of Cranford. When she got to North Avenue she turned right, passing Nino's Pizzeria and a gift shop called In Clover, where she bought her greeting cards, before the North Side Bakery came into view. Ah, the North Side Bakery, home of her favorite cheese-crumb Danish. Her one-bedroom apartment sat on the top floor of a former bank building on North Avenue, which ironically ran east-west.

She retrieved her keys from her purse and unlocked the glass door just past the entrance to the bakery. DR. KEITH OLD, D.D.S.

was stenciled in gold lettering on the glass, the *G* in his last name having been mischievously removed, probably by an unhappy root canal recipient. She started up the dingy wooden staircase that led to the dingy corridor off of which was Dr. Gold's office. Up another fifteen stairs was a burnt-red wooden door marked with the letter *A*. Be it ever so humble, she had called it home ever since she and Lauren had separated almost four years ago.

To characterize the building as run-down was being charitable. It may have been grand when it was built during the Depression, but now it was just depressing. Everything in the apartment was old—the pipes, the sinks, the shower, the toilet, the steam heating system. It wasn't hard to figure out why it had been on the market for six months before she rented it. The only things she had insisted on were an apartment-size washer/dryer and two wall air-conditioning units. The landlord, desperate at that point, had readily agreed.

With the other apartment in the building vacant, when Dr. Gold's office finished for the day at six p.m. the only noise she ever had to deal with was the rattling and knocking of the heating pipes. Coming on the heels of her marriage crumbling, she initially found the solitude overwhelming, and the loneliness had almost consumed her. But slowly, as her transition went from possibility to reality, she had come to relish the privacy that the old building offered, especially when she first started to venture out as Erin.

She turned on her computer and changed for her run while it loaded. Slowly she went through her stretching routine. She had run since college, but over time running had morphed from exercise to therapy. She honestly believed that she did her best thinking when she was running. She hoped that would hold true today, because somehow, against the odds, they had to come up with a way to defend Sharise.

She had forgotten to check her e-mails before she left the office, so she clicked on her remote access to see if there was anything important. It wasn't the e-mail address that caught her

eye—soccerman@aol.com—it was the subject line: "Hi Aunt
Erin." She nervously clicked on the e-mail, not knowing what to
expect.

> Hi Aunt Erin
> It's Patrick (and Brennan). We hope you're doing okay. we
> guess dad didn't think we'd be able to find you but since we
> knew where your office was we did a quick search and found
> attorney erin McCabe at your address. we checked out your
> picture and you look really nice.
> We just wanted you to know we miss you. Our soccer
> team (that's right aunt erin I'm now playing up on patrick's
> team) is in the state cup starting on Saturday at 130. We
> really miss seeing you at our games. our first game is against
> westfield at tamaques park and we wondering if you could
> come since it's close to where you live—maybe in disguise or
> something. Dad might not be there so maybe you could
> come. it's ok if you e-mail us here just do it before we go to
> bed around 10—dad sometimes checks our e-mails after we
> go to bed but we'll delete any from you. He doesn't say any-
> thing about you but we know he misses you too. mom keeps
> working on him. we haven't told him yet that we know you're
> our aunt erin now but we wanted you to know we still love
> you. maybe we'll see you saturday.
> love patrick & brennan
>
> ps in case you forgot we play for Princeton united—our team
> is the cobras

Erin stared at the screen, wiping the tears from her eyes. It
took her three tries before she was able to compose what she
hoped was a good response.

> Dear Patrick and Brennan,
> Thank you so much for e-mailing me. It is so wonderful to

hear from both of you. I miss you guys and it was great to
hear that you're both doing well—and Brennan, congratula-
tions on playing "up." I know exactly where Tamaques Park is
and I'll definitely come to the game. So you know who I am,
I'll wear a white Adidas baseball hat, dark sunglasses, and an
Arsenal shirt. I don't want to cause any problems, so I'll avoid
wherever your mom and dad are watching from, and it's
probably best if you pretend like I'm not there even if you see
me. It will be so great to see you guys. Good luck and know
I'll be cheering for the Cobras!

    Love—Aunt Erin

She hit send, hoping that she wouldn't get them into trouble.
She took a deep breath. God, she missed them.

A chime from her computer let her know there was a new
e-mail.

    Yea. we don't want mom or dad to get mad so we won't
say anything. We're deleting these e-mails now and emptying
the deleted e-mails. don't worry, mom and dad are really
smart but we know more about computers than they do. see
you saturday. go cobras.

She smiled. Go Cobras.

CHAPTER 4

"*T*HIS IS JUST TOO GOOD TO BE TRUE. ONE OF MY LAWYERS is trans and her partner is everything I want in a man. Maybe my world is looking up," Sharise said, eyeing Duane and tilting her head seductively.

Duane shifted uncomfortably in the chair. *It's not a guy flirting with me*, he repeated to himself, *Sharise is a woman*. Still, he was having trouble processing the incongruities in the situation. He was in a men's prison, with an inmate dressed in the standard men's orange jumpsuit, yet Sharise clearly had some feminine qualities, including the inflections and pitch of her voice.

"Cat got your tongue, honey?" Sharise asked with a deep-throated laugh. "Mmm-hmm, you the first man I've seen in a while makes me sorry I'm in these chains—unless you're into chains," she added with a wink.

"Sharise, enough. I happen to be a happily married man."

"Most of my customers are, love," she shot back.

"As much as I hate to ruin your fun, I'm here to talk about your case, not flirt."

"Can't blame a girl for trying." No longer playful, she asked, "So why you here at eight thirty in the morning? I told your girl-friend what happened, what else you need to know?"

"Let's get some things straight," Duane began, finding his footing. "Erin is not my girlfriend—she's my law partner and a damn fine lawyer. She's over at the prosecutor's office right now, speaking to the prosecutor handling the case and picking up the discovery. Both of us are going to do our best, not only to keep you from getting the death penalty if the state goes that route, but to try and prove your innocence. Assuming you'd like to help save your own life, I need to know everything about you—every-thing—up to and including the day you got arrested on this mur-der. It's going to be long, tedious, and probably painful at times, but I need it all, the good, the bad, and the ugly. So it's up to you, you going to help us or not?"

"You a former cop?" she asked accusingly.

"FBI."

"So what happen that you no longer a FBI guy?"

"They seem to think I broke the rules."

Sharise laughed. "Why, they didn't realize you were Black when they hire you?"

"Got nothing to do with that."

"Honey, you either the dumbest motherfucker around or lying. It always got something to do with being Black." Her stare betrayed no self-pity, simply her cold reality. "So where do you want to start?" she asked.

"From the beginning. Where were you born?"

Erin paced the waiting area of the prosecutor's office. Because she hadn't had many cases in Ocean County, she had called around to attorneys she knew who practiced down here to find out what her adversary, First Assistant Prosecutor Barbara Taylor, was like. To a person, everyone had said she was an excellent lawyer and had a reputation for being fair.

"Ms. McCabe, I'm Assistant Prosecutor Roger Carmichael,"

said the young man walking toward Erin with his hand extended. "Nice to meet you."

"Nice to meet you as well," Erin replied, shaking his hand.

"So we received your substitution of attorney yesterday indicating you'll be representing Mr. Barnes in this matter."

"That's right."

"So I presume you've met your client then," he said with a wry smile.

"I have," Erin said.

"A little weird, right? I mean, he looks somewhat like a guy, but talks like a woman."

Unfortunately, no witty rebuttal sprung immediately to mind, so she simply answered, "I'm okay with it."

Roger raised an eyebrow and shrugged. "Whatever. Come on back and I'll introduce you to First Assistant Prosecutor Barbara Taylor. Barbara's in charge of the case."

They walked through the maze of cubicles that made up the interior of the Ocean County Prosecutor's Office, eventually coming to the office of First Assistant Ocean County Prosecutor Barbara Taylor. As second in command, Taylor's office sat prominently next to the office of Prosecutor Lee Gehrity. Taylor had joined the prosecutor's office right out of law school, and over the course of the next twenty years had slowly risen through the ranks.

Roger gently knocked on the open door to Barbara's office. "Come on in," she offered when she looked up and saw them standing there.

"Barbara, this is Erin McCabe, new counsel for Mr. Barnes. Erin, Barbara Taylor."

Barbara rose from her chair. "Nice to meet you," Barbara said, flashing a pleasant smile as she reached over her desk and shook Erin's hand. Barbara appeared to Erin to be in her mid-forties, with short sandy hair, which was nicely layered to accent the gentle curls framing her face. She was attractive, and her makeup was subtly done to accentuate her best features. Her eyes, which were robin's-egg blue, were drawn out even more by her royal-blue silk blouse and black skirt. She looked to be several inches taller than Erin, but without knowing if she was wearing heels, Erin couldn't be sure.

"Likewise," Erin replied, sensing Taylor taking her measure.

It had taken Erin a while, but she had come to understand that professional women took the measure of one another far differently than men did. With men, it was always about who had the biggest dick—usually not literally, although she had been in enough locker rooms to know that sometimes it truly was the question du jour. More often than not it was a euphemism for who was the toughest in the room, the alpha male, taking on all comers.

For women, it was much more nuanced. And with time, Erin had come to sense when the gaze of another woman was gauging her looks and her confidence. It was the look Barbara Taylor had just given her, and it was the look she had just given Taylor.

"Have a seat," Taylor offered, pointing to the two chairs in front of her desk. "So you'll be representing Mr. Barnes."

"Yes, my partner, Duane Swisher, and I were retained a few days ago. I came down to pick up the discovery," Erin replied.

"Very good. After you've had time to review the discovery, if you want to talk, just let me know. At this point, we haven't decided whether we're going to seek the death penalty or not, and depending on what happens in Trenton, it may be moot. But, as I'm sure you know, the victim was a stellar young man whose father is very well-known in this part of the state. Needless to say, there has been a public outcry for us to seek the death penalty. But as I said, no final decision has been made. Perhaps if your client was willing to resolve this case quickly with a plea and spare the family the horrors of a trial, we may be persuaded to forego the death penalty," she said with the confidence of someone who felt they held all the cards. "But I can't guarantee that," she added quickly. "I don't know if you've had the chance to see your client's rap sheet yet, but he has quite the criminal history—

assault, aggravated assault, prostitution, drugs. Kind of hard to believe he's racked up that kind of record and he's not even twenty years old."

Play it close to the vest, Erin told herself. No point pissing them off, at least not until she found out if they'd consent to moving Sharise. "Thanks, but at this point I've only talked with my client once and haven't seen the discovery yet, so it's way too soon to know what my client will want to do. My partner is over at the jail now, and I'm heading there once I'm done here. We'll see what happens."

"Of course, I understand," Barbara offered. "Just so you know, though, your client's prints and DNA were all over the motel room where the victim was found. The victim's car was found abandoned in Philadelphia, and if you're taking the category of Fingerprints for $500, the answer is: 'What is your client's prints were in the car too?' So you see, Erin, this is pretty much an open-and-shut case as far as we're concerned. And you should also know that apparently your client was impersonating a woman at the time he killed Mr. Townsend."

Here we go, Erin thought. "Actually, my client wasn't impersonating a woman, my client is a transgender woman. Prior to being incarcerated, my client had been taking female hormones for almost three years. As a result, she has developed breasts and other feminine features. One of the reasons I wanted to speak with you was to see if your office would be willing to consent to her continuing to receive medical care and having her transferred to the women's section of the jail. Despite being in protective custody, she is in constant fear for her safety."

Barbara looked at Erin, puzzled. "You're asking for us to consent to putting your client in the women's section of the jail?" she finally said.

"Yes, as a transgender woman, my client isn't safe in the men's section. She's not a man."

Barbara snorted and looked over at Roger, shaking her head. "Look, Erin, I don't want to be rude, but your client is no more a

woman than Roger is. I've read the police reports on your client—
he's a transvestite hooker. He pretends to be a woman so he can
rob and assault poor shmucks who mistakenly think he's a woman.
How in good conscience could we put him in the women's section? The bottom line is he's got a penis and he's a murderer.
There wouldn't be a woman in the jail who would be safe. That
would be like putting the fox in the henhouse," she said with a
chuckle. Then added, "Honestly, I'd like to think I'm fairly reasonable, but even if I wanted to, which I don't, the sheriff would
have a cow. He's in charge of the safety and security of the
county's prisoners, and I can assure you, he would never agree.
It's just crazy."

"Actually," Erin offered, "it's really not crazy at all. I can appreciate that most people don't understand what it means to be
transgender, but in my client's case, she truly is a woman who
just happened to be born with male genitalia."

Barbara gave an exasperated sigh. "Did you hear what you just
said? 'She,'" Barbara said, drawing air quotes, "is a woman born
with a penis. I'm a woman. You're a woman. I have many friends,
colleagues, and acquaintances that are women; none of them
have penises. There is no such thing as a woman with a penis."
Barbara cupped her hands on either side of her nose and slowly
dragged them down over her mouth and chin. "Let me know if
your client is interested in talking about a plea. Otherwise we'll
move this matter forward." Barbara stood up, indicating their
meeting was over. "Roger will provide you with copies of the discovery. If there are any discovery issues, please deal with him on
those. A pleasure meeting you, Ms. McCabe."

Erin stood and nodded. "A pleasure meeting you as well.
Thank you for your time. We'll talk soon, I'm sure."

After Erin and Roger left, Barbara replayed the last part of her
discussion with McCabe. *Strange*, she thought. It was clear to her
that McCabe was more focused on where her client was being
held than in discussing a quick resolution to the case. She had

been at this for almost twenty years, long enough to learn the hard way not to underestimate an adversary, but this was a potential death penalty case. Why hadn't McCabe jumped at the possibility of avoiding a lengthy trial? She picked up her phone and dialed the extension for Thomas Whitick, the Chief of Detectives for the office. "Hey, Tom. It's Barbara."

"Hey, Barb, what's up?"

"Tom, do me a favor. I need as much information as you can get on an attorney by the name of Erin McCabe. Her office is in Cranford, and according to the Lawyers Diary, she was admitted in '96."

"Anything in particular?"

"No, I just met her. She's been retained to represent Barnes, and my antennae are up. Besides, I'm sure Townsend is going to want to know everything about her."

"Will do. Sounds like you want it ASAP."

"I do, thanks. Oh, and while you're at it," she said, looking down at the cover letter from McCabe & Swisher, LLP, "check out her partner, too, a fellow by the name of Duane Swisher."

Erin sat in a small attorney conference room in the courthouse, looking through the box of discovery she had just received from Carmichael. The twenty-two-page summary investigative report contained no real surprises. Townsend's body had been discovered by a cleaning woman, Maria Tejada, at about 8:45 a.m. at the Bay View Motel. The DO NOT DISTURB sign was on the door, but after knocking several times, Ms. Tejada used her passkey to open the door. After calling out to see if anyone was in the room, she entered and discovered the body on the far side of the bed. She called 911 and then her manager. Tuckerton Police were there within ten minutes. Tuckerton in turn called the Ocean County Prosecutor's Office, who had investigators on the scene by 9:34 a.m. Identity of the victim was preliminarily established through his driver's license, and OCP Lee Gehrity was notified. Forensics was called in, and fingerprints were lifted from the scene. In addition, blood and vomit samples were collected, along with several hairs and a pair of women's underwear, all of which were sent to the state laboratory for DNA testing. Motor vehicle search revealed the victim was the owner of a 2004 BMW 545i, and an APB was put out.

At approximately 2:15 p.m., OCPO received a call from Philadelphia PD, who had an abandoned car matching the description of the victim's vehicle.

Erin flipped the page. OCPO had a preliminary match on the DNA at 16:35 hours on April 18, 2006: Suspect Samuel Emmanuel Barnes, aka Sharise Barnes, aka Tamiqua Emanuel.

She found the coroner's report and skimmed through it. Cause of death, one stab wound measuring 127.8 mm in depth, which punctured the right ventricle, resulting in tamponade. By appearances, the wound appeared to have been made by a knife, possibly a switchblade.

After leafing through the rest of the discovery to see what else was there, she took the box out to Duane's car and headed over to the jail to join the meeting between Duane and Sharise.

"What do you think?" she asked as Duane hit the gas, merging onto the Parkway North on the way back to the office.

"Honest?"

"No, lie to me and make me feel better," she said. "Of course honest."

"Her story sounds plausible."

"Plausible? That's not a ringing endorsement. You believe her?"

"Is that important?"

"Yeah, if she can't convince you, and you're on her side, what chance does she have with a jury of strangers—probably twelve white strangers?"

Duane scratched his head. "E, I'll be honest. None of this makes sense to me. Why is a good-looking twenty-eight-year-old guy—a twenty-eight-year-old *single* guy whose father is very rich—picking up a Black hooker in AC, then taking her to Ocean

County? Christ, I have to think he could have gotten a blow job anytime he wanted, and cops are always looking to pull over white boys from the suburbs in expensive cars that are in high-crime neighborhoods, usually because they're buying drugs. By the way, you get a chance to look at the toxicology report—anything there?"

"Nothing. His blood alcohol was .04, consistent with a couple of beers. No other drugs in his system."

"Shit," Duane mumbled under his breath. "It just doesn't add up. It doesn't seem like it was about sex—it was something else. It's almost as if his plan from the start was to kill her."

She turned quickly to face him. "You're not serious? He picked her up with the idea of murdering her?"

"As crazy as it sounds, yeah, that's exactly what I'm thinking."

"Swish, I know you don't know a whole lot about the trans community, but trans women, and especially trans women of color, are often the victims of violence when the guy they're with discovers their secret. It's called trans panic. Men freak out, thinking the fact that they were attracted to a woman with a penis somehow makes them gay."

He stole a glance at her, his eyes narrowing. "You know, you compute."

"Yeah, so I've discovered." His look conveyed his confusion. "I'll explain later," she offered. "By the way, not sure if or how this plays into anything, but time of death is around two a.m. on April 17."

"Yeah, so?"

"Sunday, April 16 was Easter Sunday." She paused. "Not sure it means anything, and I have no idea how religious the Townsend family is, but strange way to end your Easter. 'I think I'll go out looking for a hooker.'"

She looked out the passenger window, watching the landscape whiz by. When she was a kid, they'd vacation at the Jersey Shore. Back then it always seemed so different from where they lived. She remembered there being sand on the shoulder of the Parkway, endless stretches of pine trees, and of course, the beaches. It was a place people went to vacation or retire, not live there. Now it appeared no different from North Jersey—housing developments, strip malls, and industrial parks. Sure, the beaches still made it different, but it had lost some of its rural charm.

Maybe she really wasn't the right person for this case. Who the hell was she to think that she could take on a capital murder case? This was different from the murder cases she handled as a PD. Sure, there was the whole trans angle, but Erin actually believed Sharise had acted in self-defense. It wasn't like she had never had a client she believed was innocent before, but in her three prior murder trials, the evidence against her clients had been pretty overwhelming. So the pressure of defending someone in a capital murder case, who she truly believed was innocent, was something she had never experienced before. And now, the realization that Sharise's life might literally rest on her skills as a lawyer had begun to sink in.

"You never answered me. Do you believe her?" she asked Duane.

"I don't know. There's also something about her story that bothers me. I just don't know what it is. Maybe once we have someone take a look at the autopsy report, I'll have a better sense of how I feel." He looked in her direction. "You know if she's telling the truth she made one very bad decision, don't you?"

"Yeah, I realized it when you doubled back and asked her to go over how he was stabbed. If what she said is the truth, and all she did was parry his attempt to stab her, her prints wouldn't have been on the knife—just his."

"You got it. But then she took the knife, so we'll never know, will we?"

"No, I guess we won't," she said. Swish couldn't be right, she thought. Townsend going there to kill Sharise made no sense. Why would he do that?

"You coming next Saturday?" Duane asked, breaking her train of thought.

"You know I wouldn't miss Austin's birthday."

"You didn't come last year."

"Yeah, well, it was kind of hard to since I was lying in a hospital bed recovering from surgery."

She smiled as she watched Duane cringe at the reference to her surgery.

"You know Lauren will be there?" he asked.

She laughed. "Yeah, I kind of assumed she would since she's Austin's godmother."

"Her husband will be there too."

"The nerve of her, bringing her husband."

"Just didn't want you to be surprised."

"Thanks." Her eyes stared straight ahead, but her mind was still trying to process seeing Lauren again. "I may be a little late." She paused. "I got an e-mail from Patrick and Brennan," she said, her voice barely above a whisper. "They invited me to their soccer game next Saturday afternoon."

He glanced over at her. "They invited Uncle Ian or . . ."

"Aunt Erin."

"Do Sean and Liz know?"

"From what the boys said in their e-mail, that would be a negative," she said. Before he could say anything, she continued. "Kids know how to do Internet searches. They found the firm website, which has my contact info, and extended an invitation. I used to go to all their games."

"You going to go?"

She smiled warmly. "Wouldn't miss it." Sensing his uneasiness, she quickly added, "Don't worry, I'm going incognito, and the boys aren't going to tell Sean and Liz that I'm there. It's all good."

He laughed. "You're too much."

"Whatever," she said dismissively. "Let's get back to Sharise. What can you tell me about DNA evidence?"

"You mean the index the FBI has—CODIS?" he asked.

"That would be the one."

CHAPTER 5

WILL TOWNSEND STOOD IN THE DOORWAY WATCHING AS LEE
Gehrity, Barbara Taylor, and Tom Whitick came up his walk.
Townsend was tall with close-cropped gray hair, and it looked
like he could still fit into his army dress uniform that he had put
away thirty-five years before. He worked hard on his look, including getting up every morning at five a.m. to do his exercise
regimen.

"I like it when people are punctual," he said, motioning for
them to come in. He shook each of their hands in turn as they entered, closed the door behind them, and led the way toward the
kitchen, which was toward the rear of his summer home, a
10,000-square-foot Tudor on the ocean in Mantoloking. The
kitchen was bright and airy, and sitting on the center island was a
spread of croissants, bagels, Danish, juice, and coffee.

"I figured this early on a Saturday morning, I had to at least
give you something to eat and some coffee," he said, then
pointed to a man seated at the kitchen table. "I'm not sure if all
of you have met my personal counsel, Michael Gardner. Michael

was my XO back when we were in Vietnam and worked for years with the government. After he left the government, I hired him to keep me out of trouble."

Michael stood and walked over to meet them. He was reed thin, with tufts of salt-and-pepper hair on either side of his bald dome. His craggy face, square jaw, and thin lips appeared unfamiliar with the concept of smiling.

"Michael, this is Ocean County Prosecutor Lee Gehrity, First Assistant Barbara Taylor, and Chief of Detectives Thomas Whitick." As Michael shook hands and said hello to each of them, Will urged them again toward the food. "Please help yourselves to some coffee and grab something to eat. We have plenty of room to spread out at the table."

They walked around the island, gathering something to eat and fixing their coffee. Then, one by one, they made their way over to the table.

"Lee, I really appreciate you folks making the trip this morning," Will said. "I'm sure all of you have better things to do on a Saturday morning."

"Will, stop. Don't be silly. We needed to talk and we appreciate your hospitality. How's Sheila doing?"

Townsend took a deep breath, shaking his head. "She's still a basket case. Barely comes out of our room back home. I'm not sure she's ever going to recover from losing her Billy. This house was always her favorite place, but she didn't spend one day here over the summer. Too close to where Bill was murdered. Seems like I not only lost a son, but my wife too."

"I'm sorry, Will. I truly am."

Silence filled the room. Finally, Michael said, "Lee, we need to talk about the case. We appreciate how your office has kept Will advised about what has gone on over the last few weeks, the arrest, etcetera, but where are we now?"

"Sure," Lee began. "The suspect is—"

"Wait," Michael interrupted, "he's more than a suspect. I was told you have his DNA and fingerprints all over the room and in Bill's car. This is the guy, correct?"

"Yes, Michael. We have no doubt the person who has been arrested is the murderer, but to avoid any breaches in what we are permitted to say ethically, it's just force of habit to refer to him as the 'suspect' or the 'alleged assailant.' Be that as it may, the person who murdered Bill is Samuel E. Barnes. What we know of Mr. Barnes is that he apparently disguised himself as a woman and worked as a prostitute in Atlantic City. Not counting his juvie record, he has eight prior arrests, one for assault, one for aggravated assault, three for CDS—drugs—and three for prostitution. On some of these occasions he reached a plea. Almost all of the charges were handled in the Atlantic City Municipal Court. On one of the CDS charges he was given a conditional discharge, and the aggravated assault, which occurred when he assaulted an undercover police officer, was downgraded to a simple assault.

"We know from interviewing some of the other prostitutes who were with him the night of the murder that he was dressed as a woman, and we believe the motive for Bill's murder was robbery."

He paused and looked around the room, then continued. "Will, one of the main reasons we wanted to talk to you is that on Friday the eighth, Barnes will be arraigned on the indictment. At that time, we're obligated to give defense counsel notice if we intend to pursue the death penalty. If we are, we have to provide counsel with notice of which aggravating factors we are going to rely on under the statute. We believe we have two aggravating factors—that the murder was done during the commission of a robbery, and that the murder was done to avoid apprehension."

"Sounds like the second one is weak," Michael offered.

"We agree," Lee replied, "it is certainly the weaker of the two. But on the robbery, we believe we have a slam dunk. Bill's ATM card and car were stolen. After the time of death, three hundred dollars was withdrawn from Bill's bank account with his ATM card. There was also no cash in his wallet, so we believe it is likely that was stolen as well. Given all of this, we believe we have a strong death penalty case. We have all the paperwork prepared, but obviously wanted to talk to you before we made it public."

Will sat at the head of the table, lost in thought. "Polling," he said at last, "shows seventy percent of New Jersey voters are against the death penalty, including fifty-three percent of registered Republicans. Sometime in the near future, probably December, my good friend and soon to be lame-duck governor Neil Rogers is going to issue a moratorium prohibiting implementation of any death sentences until a panel he appoints studies whether New Jersey should ban it altogether. When you couple that with the fact that our Supreme Court reverses about three quarters of the death sentences handed down, no one has been executed in this state since 1962. So what are we doing?" he asked, looking around the table. "Just think how magnanimous I will look when the press learns that I stood against the death penalty even in the case involving the murder of my own son. I'll give cover to a lot of Republicans opposed to the death penalty, not to mention to the governor, who will be indebted to me when he moves to ban capital punishment. We need to use this to our political advantage, and I think taking a principled stand now gets us the biggest political bang for our buck. What do I care if Barnes dies from a lethal injection or in prison? He'll be just as dead."

No one spoke. Finally, Lee asked, "Are you saying you want us to announce that you asked us not to pursue the death penalty?"

"Of course. I'm not going to make you take the heat for my decision. It has to be public knowledge I made the call, or I can't use it politically. Don't worry, I'll have my people come up with a statement for you to issue."

"Oh . . . uh, okay," Lee stuttered.

"Look, I have to do something to divert attention from the

fact that my idiot son picked up a drag queen hooker and took him to a motel. Even if the press treads lightly out of fear of pissing me off, Christ Almighty, it's not like you can hide what he did—it's the reason he's fucking dead. Hopefully, this will help divert some of the attention away from his stupidity."

"I assume it's too early to know if Barnes has any interest in taking a plea?" Michael asked.

Barbara spoke up. "I had a brief conversation with his attorney, but she didn't tip her hand at all."

"Will, I'm just thinking out loud here," Michael offered, "but maybe if we left the option of the death penalty on the table a little longer it would force Barnes to take a deal to avoid the death penalty."

Will nodded and took a sip from his coffee. "No, let's play it my way. I need to get out ahead of what the governor is going to do. Look, we haven't had a Republican governor as popular as Neil Rogers since Tom Kean. I helped him get elected, and I'm expecting him to return the favor."

"What do we know about Barnes's lawyer?" Michael asked.

Lee laughed. "You should get a kick out of this. Tom, I'll let you do the honors."

Whitick was a bull of a man. He was completely bald, which only made him look more intimidating. He had spent five years as an MP in the army before joining the Ocean County Prosecutor's Office as an investigator in 1975. Over the next twenty-five years he had risen through the ranks until he had become Chief of Detectives five years earlier. Opening a file folder, he put on his glasses.

"There are actually two lawyers. Let's start with the easy one," he began, "Duane Abraham Swisher. African-American, thirty-five years old, married to Corrine Swisher, née Butler. Lives in Scotch Plains and they have one child, a two-year-old son named Austin. Swisher grew up in Elizabeth, New Jersey, high school basketball star at St. Cecilia's, which, at that time, was a national powerhouse. Went to Brown on a full academic scholarship. Played basketball at Brown, where he was All-Ivy two years. Apparently tried out for several NBA teams but was not drafted, and then went to Columbia Law School. After Columbia, he joined the FBI. He was there for seven years. Here's where things get a little murky with Mr. Swisher. Apparently, he voluntarily resigned in good standing from the FBI three years ago, but through our sources, we have some information that he left because he was the subject of an internal investigation that may still be ongoing."

"What kind of investigation?" Michael interrupted.

"Again, we are not certain, but from what our sources tell us, there may be an ongoing criminal investigation over a leak of confidential information concerning the wiretapping of Muslims following 9/11." Whitick looked up at Michael. "We are certainly trying to get additional information."

Michael nodded. "Thank you. Please continue."

"After he left the FBI, he began a law practice with Ian McCabe, forming the law firm of McCabe & Swisher three years ago."

"Wait. I thought Barnes's lawyer, this McCabe, was a woman," Will asked.

"I told you you'd get a kick out of this," Lee responded, grinning and rolling his eyes. Lee gestured for Whitick to continue.

"The law firm of McCabe & Swisher is located in Cranford and does primarily criminal defense. Any other questions on Swisher before I move on to McCabe?"

No one said anything until Michael said, "Go ahead."

"Erin Bridget McCabe was formerly known as Ian Patrick McCabe."

Will squinted, trying to process this information, but nodded for Whitick to continue.

"Ian Patrick McCabe, Caucasian, thirty-five years old, divorced, formerly married to Lauren Schmidt, no children. Lives in Cranford, grew up in Union, New Jersey, attended Cardinal O'Hara High School, where he was an All-County soccer player. Went to Stonehill College in North Easton, Massachusetts. Attended Temple Law School and clerked for the Honorable Miles Foreman in Monmouth County. After his clerkship, he went to work for the Union County Public Defender's Office. He was there for five plus years, then left to start his own firm and shortly after that he formed the firm with Swisher.

"As I said, about two years ago, he legally changed his name to Erin Bridget McCabe and started practicing law as a woman. Apparently, all his legal documents have been changed to reflect his new name and gender. Since then he has continued to practice law, but generally has kept a low profile concerning his sex change." He looked up at Michael and Will. "Seems to me there is plenty of fodder here to deflect attention away from the parts of this case that are not exactly favorable to your son, Mr. Townsend. You have one lawyer under investigation, and the other's just as crazy as the defendant."

"Thank you, Tom; that is indeed very interesting information," Will said slowly, rubbing his chin with his thumb and forefinger. "We will need to think about how we use this to our best advantage."

"Assuming the suspect doesn't plead guilty, how do you think they'll defend this case?"

Barbara looked toward Lee, but he simply nodded at her because if the case went to trial, she'd be the one to handle it. "The only logical defense would appear to be self-defense. In other words, claim that Bill freaked out when he discovered that Barnes was not a woman, and in defending himself, Barnes stabbed Bill."

"But if I remember correctly," Michael responded, "there was no evidence of a struggle in the room. Correct?" Before anyone could respond, he continued. "And Bill died of a single stab wound to the chest. Again, not indicative of a struggle."

"You are correct on both counts, Michael," she responded. "So even if that is the defense he goes with, we believe the evidence is much more consistent with a robbery."

"Thank you, Barbara," Will said. "I think we have the picture," he added, cutting off any further conversation. "I'll have my communications director work on a statement for you, Lee—Friday the eighth, right?"

"Yes," Lee replied. "If you want maximum impact, I'll need to issue it right after the arraignment."

"I'll make sure you have it a few days before that in case you have any questions. I appreciate all the hard work that your office has put into solving this. Hopefully after this bastard has been convicted it will help Sheila and I find some peace."

After Will had walked them out, he returned to the kitchen and poured himself another cup of coffee. "Fuck," he said, taking a seat opposite Michael at the table. "I swear to God, if Barnes hadn't killed him, I would have. Where do we stand?"

Michael stared across the table. "Don't worry. I told you, everything has been taken care of and no laws have been broken. Several friends of Mr. Barnes who worked in the same neighborhood have found wonderful new careers outside of Atlantic City, while his pimp was arrested on drug and prostitution charges, and is no longer in circulation. Assuming there is a trial, Mr. Barnes will have to try to convince a jury he acted in self-defense. And why would Bill attack him? Because he flipped out when he learned the truth about Mr. Barnes? That's our worst-case scenario. There is no evidence to support anything else—none."

Will got up and looked out the kitchen window, sipping his coffee. "I don't know if Sheila will survive if this case goes to trial. The testimony about her Billy picking up a drag queen hooker could kill her." He leaned his forehead up against the window. "And if the other scenario turned out to be true . . ." He took a deep breath and turned around, his eyes narrowing as he looked at Michael. "And this sure as hell isn't what I need politically at this point. What I need is this case over quickly. The longer this drags on, the greater the risk something could go wrong," he said, his anger and exasperation growing as he spoke. "Let's see where this goes, but if Barnes doesn't plea quickly, we'll have to reconsider our options. To everyone else the governor's race may look like it's three years away, but I need to line up my ducks now." He let out a guttural groan. "I don't need this crap right now. As long as I'm the poor grieving father, no one wants to fuck with me, but if this goes to trial, who knows . . . Fuck!" he spit out.

"You take care of what you need to do and let me deal with this shit," Michael said. "I still have a lot of sources in Justice. I'll find out what's going on with Swisher. I'll also check to see if there's any other dirt on McCabe, but as it is, we already have enough to have a field day in the press with him. Don't worry. I'll make life miserable for both of them. The more focused they are on their own problems, the less time they have to defend Barnes."

Townsend nodded. "Good. Keep close tabs on those two. I want to know what they're up to."

CHAPTER 6

*T*HE BALL ROLLED OUT OF BOUNDS. WHEN IT REACHED WHERE Erin was standing, she flicked it up on her foot and softly bounced it into the air and caught it. The Westfield defender ran toward her and she tossed him the ball. After thanking her while trying to catch his breath, he quickly turned and ran back toward the touchline, only to see the referee indicating it was a Princeton throw-in.

Ten minutes to go, and although they had dominated for most of the game, Patrick and Brennan's team, the Princeton Cobras, were clinging to just a 1–0 advantage.

Erin watched as Patrick came up from his midfield position and received the throw-in. He faced up against the Westfield defender, and then, with a little move Erin had taught him, deftly flicked the ball up over the defender's head, cut to his left, regained control of the ball, and continued down the left sideline, his head up, looking across the field. When he was fifteen yards out he hit a low cross toward the center of the field, where Brennan had made a cut and was heading right down the center of the field.

Erin watched, her mind instantaneously triangulating. She could see that Brennan would get to the ball just a split second before the goalie arrived, but there'd be no time for him to get off a shot. Instead, she watched in amazement as Brennan, running at full speed toward the ball, let it run right between his legs, where, ten yards to his right, there was a teammate running parallel to him. The goalie, reacting to what he thought was going to be a shot from Brennan, was caught totally out of position as Brennan's teammate redirected the ball into the now-empty goal.

GOAL!

The ball hadn't even settled in the back of the net before Brennan and his teammate veered toward Patrick. The three of them jumped into each other's arms as the rest of the team rushed forward to help celebrate. The scrum of players began to break up, but before Patrick and Brennan headed back to midfield they turned toward the sidelines and winked at where Erin stood with a huge smile, clapping. As she watched them celebrate, she felt a tinge of regret. She had missed two years from their lives. Two years in which both had grown several inches. But it was the subtle changes in Patrick's physique that reminded her that he was now teetering on the edge of puberty. The little boy she remembered was now almost a teenager, and she knew that the time she missed could never be recaptured.

After the game was over, she stood back, watching the players and parents head across the road to the parking lot opposite the field. She then started walking in the opposite direction, having parked in a lot on the other side of the park. Three years earlier when she bought the Miata, Sean had teased her about getting a chick car. Now it wasn't the teasing she was concerned about.

Standing in front of her closet, pondering what to wear, the joy of seeing her nephews slowly started to mix with the trepidations of seeing Lauren and her husband. Even though it had been four years since they had separated and three years since their divorce, the regrets were still there. As foolish as it seemed now, Erin had hoped that they would stay together. She had even stored her sperm, deluding herself to the possibility that the fact that they could still have children together would convince Lauren that their relationship could be saved. It hadn't.

Erin finally decided on a tea-colored maxi dress. It had kind of a sixties hippie look, with a smocked neckline, simple tie straps, and apron-style pockets. A pair of brown sandals completed her outfit. She took her hair out of the ponytail she had worn to the game and used the curling iron to give it some body. Studying her face in the mirror, she knew she was luckier than many trans women. She had been able to afford facial surgery that had given her face more feminine contours, and between the hormones and electrolysis, she had a nice complexion that didn't require a lot of makeup to smooth it out. A little blush, some mascara, a light-hued coral lipstick and she was ready to go. On her way out she grabbed a sweater, knowing they'd be outside on Duane and Corrine's deck.

Walking up the driveway, Erin was greeted by the noise of the party wafting out of the backyard. Duane and Corrine lived on a quiet, tree-lined cul-de-sac in Scotch Plains, in a house they'd bought when Duane was still with the Bureau. At the time, their expectation was that it would be the first of many houses they'd live in, as his career would require him to move from place to place around the country. When his career in the Bureau had come to an abrupt end, it suddenly had become home.

She rounded the corner and looked for familiar faces. She didn't relish the inevitable awkwardness that accompanied meeting someone for the first time as Erin, whom she had known as Ian. Generally, old acquaintances quickly found an excuse to end the conversation. As soon as she spotted Duane standing at the grill, beer in one hand, spatula in the other, she headed in his direction.

"Hey, Swish," she said, giving him a hug and a kiss on the cheek.

"You came!" he said, sporting a big smile.

"I told you I would."

"Glad you made it. How'd the boys from Princeton do?"

"They won, two nil," she said proudly.

"Hey, that's great." He studied her. "Any problems?"

"No, Sean and Liz had no idea I was there. All's well."

"Good," he offered, sounding relieved. "Beers are in the red cooler, wine in the blue one, sodas in the tub over there," he said, gesturing with the spatula, "and cups are on the table. I think Corrine is in the kitchen giving the birthday boy something to eat. Food should be ready soon."

"Thanks."

"Hey, E, I mean it. Thanks for coming."

She smiled. "Thanks for having me."

She walked over to the table, grabbed a cup, and poured herself some pinot grigio. Although she'd noted a few familiar faces, from the lack of response she knew she hadn't been recognized. She opened the back door and saw Corrine sitting at the kitchen table talking to a woman whose back was to the door; a split second later it clicked who the second woman was.

"Hey, girl," Corrine let loose before Erin could retreat. "Glad you made it," she said, a twinkle in her soft brown eyes.

Corrine and Lauren had been roommates at Brown and that's how Erin met her. Corrine was petite with a close-cropped Afro, and her wide smile accentuated her high cheekbones. But despite her diminutive stature, she seemed in command of every situation. Apparently recognizing the look on Erin's face and the reality of what was about to occur, Corrine plowed ahead. "Come on in, we were just talking about you."

The other woman swiveled in her chair and turned her head. The blond hair, the blue eyes, the beautiful symmetry of her face—nothing had changed. Erin, frozen in place, managed to smile. "Hi, Lauren," she said in a voice somewhat smaller than she felt. "Nice to see you."

Lauren slowly got up from the table, her sundress showing off her tanned, athletic figure. As she walked toward Erin, a smile slowly spread across her face. "Good thing I checked you out on your firm's website, or I wouldn't have recognized you." She threw her arms around Erin and hugged her. "It is so good to see you. You look great," she whispered in Erin's ear.

Erin was beginning to regret her decision to wear mascara, what with the tears starting to collect. "Thanks," she squeaked. "It's great to see you too."

Lauren broke her embrace and took Erin by the arm. "Come join us."

Erin walked over to Corrine, leaned over, and gave her a hug. "Hey, how you doing?"

"Only thinking happy thoughts today, so I'm great."

"Where's the birthday boy?"

"I don't know. Last time I saw him, his grandmothers were fighting over him," she said with a deep laugh before a sudden wail from another room had her on her feet. "Sounds like the grandmas are taking a Solomonic approach and dividing him in two," she said, rushing out of the kitchen.

"I can't get over how good you look," Lauren finally said, her smile genuine.

"Thanks. You look great, too. How's your family?"

"Everybody's well. Yours?"

It was just one of those throwaway pleasantries, but from the look on Lauren's face it was clear that as soon as she said it, she wished she had it back.

"My mom's good. We try and see each other once a week. Nothing's changed with Sean or my dad."

"I'm sorry, E. I mean Erin."

"You can still call me E. It works."

Lauren gave her a sad smile. "No, think I'd better stick with Erin. E was a different time in our lives."

The back door opened. "Hey, there you are. Been looking for you."

Lauren looked up at the handsome brown-haired, brown-eyed man standing there and waved him over. "Steve, I'd like you to meet my friend Erin. Erin, this is my husband, Steve." Erin couldn't help but notice that Steve and her former incarnation bore little in common. Steve looked to be around six foot, with broad shoulders and a square jaw.

"Hi, Steve Campbell, nice to meet you."

Erin smiled. "Nice to meet you too," she replied, avoiding saying her own last name.

"I'm sorry. I didn't mean to interrupt," Steve said, turning to Lauren.

She smiled politely. "No, I was just getting reacquainted with Erin. We haven't seen each other in a few years."

"Are you one of the Brown contingent?" he asked Erin.

Erin looked up, grateful for the anonymity. "Oh no, I'm not in that league. Lauren and I know each other from way back in high school."

"Steve, can you give Erin and I just a minute, there's something I need to talk to her about."

"Sure. I'll be on the deck. Erin, nice meeting you," he said warmly.

"Nice meeting you too," she replied.

After he left, Erin looked at Lauren. "He seems like a really nice guy—good-looking too," she added with a slight nod. "I'm really happy you found someone."

"Are you really?" Lauren asked, the trepidation clear in her tone.

Erin looked at her, biting her lower lip. "Of course I am, Laure. I hope you know that all I ever wanted was for you to be happy."

"Thanks." She paused. "Um, there is actually something that I need to tell you."

Try as she could, Erin couldn't read Lauren's face—it was a

look she had never seen before. There seemed to be some hesitancy in her eyes, but there was also a joy burning just beneath the surface.

Lauren seemed to steel herself before she spoke. "Erin, I'm going to have a baby. I'm pregnant."

Such a strange sensation, it was almost an out-of-body experience. What was it? It wasn't joy, it wasn't pain; no, it was a flashback to the beginning of the end. They had both wanted children, but Lauren had insisted that Ian see a therapist before they did. "I love you, E," she had said, "but I don't want to start a family and then have you decide you need to transition to survive. Go explore your true feelings before we go ahead with a family."

"Are you okay?" Lauren asked.

Erin wasn't sure. She was still lost. Lost in a world where she and Lauren were husband and wife, planning for their future, planning for their family. She forced a smile onto her face. "Laure, that's wonderful. I'm so happy for you."

The look of concern lingered on Lauren's face. "Honest?"

"My God, of course. I know how much you want a family. I'm thrilled for you." And that was true, mostly. "When are you due?"

"Valentine's Day."

Erin smiled. "You're going to be a great mom."

"Thanks," Lauren said, her voice quivering. "You know . . ." She couldn't get out any more.

"I know," Erin replied. She closed her eyes, a different time and place still painted there. "I know."

They both got up from their chairs and they embraced. "I really am happy for you," Erin whispered. "You know I'll always have a special place in my heart for you."

"I know," she said. "Me too."

"By the way, I guess Steve doesn't know who I am."

"I told him you might be here, but I didn't tell him your name. I guess I thought it might be awkward for all of us if he knew who you were. Trust me, he'll never guess who you were until I tell him."

"Thanks."

"No problem. It'll be interesting to see his reaction," she said with a chuckle.

"What does he do?"

"He's a metro editor for the *New York Times*."

"Good for him. And you . . . how's the publishing world?"

"Crazy, but good. I got promoted about a year ago. I'm an editor now. I love it, and there's a chance that my most recent project could turn out to be a best seller. How about you? How's the law business?"

"Just crazy," she said, shaking her head.

"Cori told me about what's going on with Duane. Is he going to be okay?"

"I honestly don't know."

"Well, I hear he has a great legal team."

"Ahh, at least half of it is," Erin replied with a grin.

They embraced one last time, said their goodbyes, and then Lauren headed outside to find Steve. Erin lingered by the door, watching as her former wife embraced her new husband, trying not to let the what-ifs overwhelm her. Finally, willing herself to move, she pushed open the door to find something to eat.

She grabbed a burger from the table and was pouring herself another cup of wine when she heard "Hey you!" from a familiar voice behind her. She knew her face was lighting up as she turned.

"JJ," she said, walking over to Jamal Johnson. Even though her hands were full, she gave him a kiss on the cheek when he leaned over. At six foot four he had a few inches on Duane. He kept his head shaved and both his arms sported multiple tattoos, creating a rather intimidating look for those who didn't know him. But despite his appearance, his smile was disarming and his demeanor was more Mr. Rogers than the Terminator.

"How you doing, girl?"

"If things were any better, JJ, it would be a sin."

JJ had been point guard at St. Cecilia's High School, a year ahead of Duane. He had been captain his senior year, when they were ranked number two in the country. The plan was he'd do a year at Notre Dame, where he went on a full ride, then the pros, but his freshman year he'd torn his ACL and MCL when going for a ball out of bounds, compounded when one of his fans fell on him and fractured his tibia. It was seven months before he could even walk without a limp. After another six months of intensive rehab and physical therapy, it was clear he had lost a couple of steps, and he never played another game for the Fighting Irish.

"Honey, knowing you, I suspect it is a sin," he said with a wicked grin. "Do you know Mark Simpson?" he asked, nodding to the man standing next to him.

"No," she said, turning her head. Mark appeared to be their age. About six feet, his hair was jet-black and disheveled in the perfect way that suggested he combed it with his fingertips. He had just enough stubble to be sexy, without looking grungy, and his green eyes seemed to sparkle. "Nice to meet you," she offered.

"My pleasure," he responded with a smile that suggested it really was.

Without intending to, she returned his smile. "How's the therapy business, JJ?" she asked, pulling her gaze away from Mark. Following his injury, JJ had gone on to get a master's in social work and had both his own practice as well as a job working at a group home for LGBT homeless kids. JJ had shocked his own little corner of the world when he came out as a gay man his senior year of college. When Erin had finally decided to transition, JJ had been one of the first people she shared her news with, and he had remained a constant source of support as she rocked her own portion of the universe with her news.

"Too busy," he replied. "Especially at the home. Swish tells me you guys just got involved in a murder case."

"Yeah, we did. In fact, we may need an expert on homeless LGBT kids. You've testified as an expert before, haven't you?"

"Yeah, I have. Let me know what I can do to help." He looked at Mark. "I'm going to grab myself a beer. You want one?"

"No, thanks. I'm good."

"Erin, you need anything?"

"Another hand," she said, holding up in one hand the paper plate, which looked like it was about to bend in two from the weight of a burger and potato salad, and her cup of wine in the other.

"There's a table over there," offered Mark, pointing in the direction of several empty tables set up in the backyard. "Can I help?"

"Thanks," she replied, handing him her cup of wine. "Lead on."

"Are you going to make me eat alone?" she asked when they'd arrived and she'd put her plate on the table. *Why did I say that? Sounds like I'm flirting.*

"Afraid so. Heading over to my mom's for dinner in a little bit," he said, placing her cup in front of her and taking the seat on the other side of the table.

"Where's mom live?"

"Roselle Park."

"Oh, I'm in Cranford."

"Clark," he offered. "So obviously listening to JJ, I figured out you work with Swish."

"Yeah, Duane and I are partners. What about you? How'd you get invited to this shindig?"

"I play ball in a league with Swish and JJ, usually on Tuesday nights."

"If he lets you be on his team you must be good."

"Trust me, we're not in the same league. I think they let me play for comic relief."

She smiled. "I know my partner; when it comes to basketball, there is no such thing as comic relief. Bet you played college ball somewhere."

"NYU."

"See, I know my partner."

"Trust me, I have to bring my A game just to be a sub."

"What do you do when you're not struggling to keep up with Swish on the basketball court?"

"I'm an English teacher at Westfield High School."

"English was always my favorite subject." *Oh God. Did I really just say that?*

"Funny, mine too," he said, his smile stretching across his face. "So how long have you done criminal law?"

"It's really all I've ever done. I clerked for a criminal judge for a year. Then I was with the PD's office for five, and Duane and I started the firm a little over three years ago. What about you? Always been a high school English teacher?"

He shared a warm smile. "No, I've had kind of a checkered past. I worked on Wall Street for a couple of years, and left while I still had a tiny piece of my soul left. Then, I guess as penance, I did two years in the Peace Corps in Nicaragua. Followed by a year backpacking around South America. When I came back six years ago, that's when I went to Westfield."

"Do you enjoy teaching?"

"Yeah, I do. Not crazy about the testing and bureaucratic bull-shit, but I really enjoy the kids." She saw him looking at her left hand. "Um, is there a Mr. McCabe?" he asked somewhat sheepishly.

"Yeah," she immediately responded. "Two actually." She watched the puzzled look growing on his face. "My dad and brother," she added. "I'm divorced. You?" she responded reflexively.

"Never married. Engaged once, but she wasn't crazy about me leaving Wall Street and joining the Peace Corps. We tried again, after I got back, but we had grown apart by that point."

"I don't know . . . a high school English teacher who still dabbles in a serious basketball league sounds more interesting than a

Wall Street tycoon." *Would you please shut up? He's going to get the wrong impression.*

"Well, she didn't think so," he replied with a sad smile. "Listen, Erin, I really do have to go to my mom's, but since we are practically neighbors, can I buy you a cup of coffee at some point and find out more about criminal law?"

"Ah, sure, I guess so."

"Well, that's a ringing endorsement."

"I'm sorry. I'm still trying to find my way post-divorce. But a cup of coffee sounds nice."

"You ever go to Legal Grounds in Cranford?"

"Only every day."

"How about Wednesday, seven p.m.?"

"It sounds nice."

He slowly got up from the table. "Until Wednesday then," he said.

"Okay. Tell Mom I said hello," she said with a laugh. After he left, she sat there. *Okay, tell Mom I said hello—what was I thinking?* She took a bite from her burger and then a sip of her wine. *I think I was actually flirting with a guy. I must be out of my mind.* Her thoughts were interrupted by JJ plopping down next to her, beer and a hot dog in hand.

"Well, I must say, I am impressed," JJ said.

"What's that supposed to mean?"

"Oh, don't play coy with me, Ms. McCabe. I'm immune to your charms. But my friend Mr. Simpson, I think he's been overcome by your feminine wiles."

"JJ! I did no such thing. I was just being nice to a friend of yours and Duane's."

"Really? That's funny because he seemed pretty stoked about having coffee with you Wednesday evening."

"How do you know that?"

"Because he asked me on his way out if I thought you might be interested in someone like him."

She looked at JJ. "Oh shit. Really? JJ, what am I going to do?"

He looked perplexed. "What's the matter?"

"JJ, he doesn't know my history. Besides, I'm not even attracted to men. Shit, what am I going to do?"

JJ smiled. "You're having coffee with him, not eloping. There's plenty of time to tell him your backstory, if you want to. And as far as the not being attracted to men part, well, girl, you may want to reevaluate your position on that because you sure looked like you were interested."

Later, driving home, Erin's mind wouldn't let go of what a curious afternoon it had been. The conflicting emotions on seeing Lauren again, then learning Lauren was pregnant. And then there was her interplay with Mark. *What the hell was I thinking? Flirting with a guy—am I losing my mind? But he was cute. Cute, listen to you. Since when did men become cute?*

She found herself trying to make sense of her own emotions. Why had she suddenly found Mark attractive? She had never been attracted to men before. But, if she was honest with herself, it wasn't like she had a lot of experiences with women either— one exactly. She and Lauren had met in high school and fallen in love. At that point in her life, even though Erin secretly felt that she should have been a woman, she was determined to be a guy's guy, sure that her love for Lauren would keep the feelings of being a woman at bay. *Well, we know how well that worked out*, she thought. In the four years following their divorce, Erin had rarely dated, but the few times she did, it had always been with a woman. Which made her feelings toward Mark even harder to wrap her head around. It was as if her emotions had been thrown into a blender and swirled into some new concoction. Whatever it was, she couldn't deny that there was part of her that was actually curious about what it would be like to be kissed by him. She snapped herself back to reality. Life was complicated enough right now; there was really no need to make it even crazier by dating a guy. But, as JJ observed, it was only a cup of coffee.

CHAPTER 7

"YOUR HAIR'S GETTING LONG. I LIKE IT LIKE THAT."

"Thanks. I'm still learning how to do things with it," Erin said, smiling at her mom. Peggy McCabe returned the smile. The creases that formed at the corners of her mouth as she smiled were the only lines on her face. For someone who had celebrated her sixty-fifth birthday three months earlier, she could easily pass for someone in her early fifties.

"Yeah, well, when you master the curling iron, come give me lessons," her mother laughed, brushing her own short light brown hair off her forehead. "You must be busy, moving our breakfast up to seven thirty."

"More coffee, ladies?" the waitress asked as she passed by.

"Yes, please!" they said simultaneously.

After the waitress had moved on, Erin said, "Actually, Mom, we are busy, and that's one of the things we need to talk about—a new case Swish and I are going to be involved in."

Peggy studied her daughter across the table and ran her finger around the rim of her coffee cup, looking afraid to hear what was coming. "I'm listening," she said, her tone suddenly cautious.

"It's a murder case."

Her mother frowned. "You've handled murder cases before. Why would I be concerned about that?"

I'm concerned because you'll bear the brunt of whatever reaction Sean and Dad have to the case. Just like you've had to bear the brunt of everything for me since I've come out, and yet somehow managed to do it with quiet grace and dignity.

"It happened a little over four months ago," Erin said, fixing her eyes on her mother. "The victim was the twenty-eight-year-old son of a very prominent figure in South Jersey. The son's name was William Townsend, Jr. He was allegedly killed by a prostitute that he had picked up in Atlantic City."

"So I take it that what you're trying to tell me is that this case is going to generate some publicity—some publicity that may involve you."

Erin felt foolish. Why was she beating around the bush? Just tell her.

"Mom, the prostitute in question—"

"Your client," her mother offered.

"Yes, Mom, my client. My client is a transgender woman. So given the prominence of the victim . . . well, if the press find out that I'm transgender, then yes, I'm concerned that there may be some publicity."

Her mother laughed. "I'm sorry," she said quickly. "There's nothing funny about the case. What's funny is that you're concerned there 'may be some publicity,'" she said, mimicking Erin's phrasing. "Erin, my dear, what you're trying to tell me is that this is going to be all over the place and if"—she paused to look at her daughter—"or *when* your past gets out, you'll figure prominently in the shit storm that will follow. Do I have that right?" she asked, cocking her head.

Erin looked down at her coffee. "Pretty much."

"And when all of this happens, your father's and brother's heads will explode, and I will have to deal with the mess. Yes?"

Erin nodded, raising her gaze slowly to meet her mother's hazel eyes. "Something like that," she whispered.

"You couldn't go into corporate or tax law? Something where you wouldn't wind up on the front page of the *Star Ledger*?"

Erin shrugged. "I'm not trying to make your life miserable."

Peggy shook her head. "So when is this all going to break? Knowing you, probably this afternoon."

Erin offered a weak smile. "No, Friday. So you have some notice."

"The things you do to your poor mother. And I used to think I hadn't a care in the world. A good husband, two perfect children, financially well off . . . and then . . ."

"Something happen with Sean?" Erin deadpanned, watching her mother's reaction.

"You used to be such a nice child," her mother offered in return. "So . . . seriously, how bad—" She stopped in mid-sentence. "Never mind. I can visualize the headlines. Okay, I'll let them know what's probably coming."

"How you going to handle it with Dad?"

Peggy frowned. "I don't know, probably beer and sex."

"Mom!"

"What? The beer is for him. The sex is for me. I have to get something out of this." She looked up at her daughter and read her expression. "Don't worry, dear, he'll come around at some point, as will your brother. We'll get through this."

The waitress slid their plates down in front of them, asked if they needed anything else, and was gone.

"So what else is happening?" her mother asked.

Erin paused, her fork midway to her mouth. "Uh, speaking of Sean, I got an e-mail from Patrick and Brennan."

Her mother laid her fork down on her plate. "You got an e-mail from your nephews?"

"Uh-huh."

Her mother lowered her voice. "To their uncle Ian?"

Erin shook her head. "Actually, to their aunt Erin." She reached into her purse and handed her mother a copy of the three e-mails they'd exchanged.

Peggy picked her glasses up from the table, put them in place, and began reading the e-mails. When she was done, she refolded the paper and handed it back to Erin. "Did you go to the game?"

"I did."

"Did Sean or Liz see you?"

"I don't think so. I really was as far away as I could get. And remember, neither of them have seen me since."

"Yes, but like their children, I'm sure they've looked at your picture on your website. In fact, I know Liz has because she commented to me one day how good you looked. I also wouldn't underestimate your brother," she added.

Erin had never underestimated her brother. She had grown up idolizing Sean, who, four years older, had always been the fair-haired son, literally and figuratively. He was just a shade over six feet, with sandy hair, an angular jaw, and hazel eyes that made women swoon. He was also always at the top of his class, which included Princeton undergraduate and the University of Pennsylvania Medical School. He was now considered one of New Jersey's preeminent orthopedic surgeons, and his reputation grew every year.

Liz, his wife, was tall and thin, with long blond hair that framed a stunningly beautiful face. Like her husband, she was Ivy educated and independent, running her own public relations firm.

Like everyone else in her life, Sean had been shocked when she first came out to him. "But you're such a normal guy," he said. "You're married to a great woman. You've always been a jock. Are you sure you have to do this? Have you tried therapy?"

She had patiently explained to him that she had been in therapy for over a year, but therapy couldn't change that she had always felt like she was a woman. She had tried to make him understand that no matter how much she loved Lauren, she couldn't survive if it meant continuing to live as everyone else saw her—as a guy.

To his credit, unlike most of the guys she had been friends with who, after she came out to them, simply never spoke to her again, Sean seemed to, if not totally accept what was going to happen, at least be understanding of the situation. So Erin had been stunned when Sean had suddenly stopped communicating with her six months later, right after she had facial surgery and started living as Erin. Sean's explanation to their mother had been that he needed to protect Patrick and Brennan from what had happened. Because the boys had been so close to their uncle Ian, he wasn't sure how they'd react to the news their uncle was now their aunt. When Erin learned from their mom what Sean's rationale was, she was devastated. Protect the boys from her? It was as if she were contagious, or worse, some type of sexual predator. But, despite how much it hurt, she clung to the hope that someday things would return to normal between her and Sean. She had no choice but to hang on to that hope because the alternative, a life without him, Liz, and the boys, was too painful for her to imagine.

"I really don't think they saw me, Mom. They had no reason to even suspect I'd be there."

"Did the boys see you?"

"Yeah, they did."

"How do you know?"

"Because Princeton scored with about ten minutes left, and when Patrick and Brennan celebrated, they looked over at me and winked."

"Those boys are too much. Do you want me to say anything to Sean or Liz?"

Erin shook her head. "No, let's let it play out and see what happens." She paused, unsure whether to continue. "By the way, I saw Lauren."

"Oh," her mother said casually. "How's she doing?"

"She's doing well." Erin hesitated. "Um, actually, she's pregnant."

Her mother nodded. "I know," she said with a gentle smile.

"How?"

"We still talk occasionally. I always thought of Lauren as the daughter I never had—that is, until you came along, of course, you being the daughter I didn't know I had. Lauren and I were always close, and I guess given the reason for your marriage falling apart, we remained close. I mean, it was a very sad time for both of you. You loved each other very much. So in that respect it wasn't your typical breakup."

Erin smiled. "I'm glad to hear that."

Erin took a sip of her coffee and marveled at her mom, who was one of the most genuine people she knew. There was no pretense about her. Erin recalled how her mother had initially struggled with the news that her child was transgender, wondering if there had been something she had done to cause it. But over time, as they talked through things, her mother had come to realize that Erin didn't choose to be transgender, it was just who she was, and she had become Erin's rock—always there for her. Just before Erin's facial surgery, she and her mother had gone out to dinner. Sitting there, talking about the journey Erin was about to embark on, her mother had reached across the table, taken Erin's hand in hers, and said, "I really don't understand this, and I worry about you and what will happen. But I want you to know that you're my child, and I will always love you." And even after Sean and her father had stopped talking to her, her mother never wavered in her love and support. Now, as Erin looked at her mom, she was happy that of all the things that had changed in her life, her relationship with her mom had grown into something special—a bond between mother and daughter.

After breakfast, Erin walked over to the office, arriving right at eight thirty. Cheryl, their receptionist, secretary, and paralegal all rolled into one, greeted her with a cheerful hello as she did every morning. As she walked by Duane's office, she saw him hard at work. Standing in his doorway, she said, "Good morning. How you doing?"

When he looked up, his expression baffled her.

"Is everything all right?" she asked.

"I don't know," he replied.

"Swish, what's wrong?"

He looked down at his desk. "Ah, we had a game last night," he said. "And after the game Mark came up to me and told me he was going to meet you for coffee tonight . . ."

"Yeah. Is that a problem?"

"I don't know. I didn't think you . . . men . . . you know," he stammered. "I thought you liked girls. Shit, he's a friend of mine."

Her eyes narrowed and she cocked her head slightly. "So, what are you saying? I can't have coffee with a friend of yours? Is that it?"

"No, I mean, of course you can. But . . . well, he's looking at it from the perspective of a guy having coffee with a woman." He hesitated. "Come on, you know what I mean. He thinks you're hot."

She stared at her partner. "And . . . ?"

"Come on, man, you know what I mean. How do you think he's going to feel when he finds out? I don't want him to be pissed at me for not telling him about you."

"No, *man*, I don't know how he'll feel," she said. "My bad, didn't know I needed your permission to have coffee with someone you know."

She quickly turned and walked to her office and slammed the door. She put her purse in the desk drawer and plopped down into her chair. The tears started before she could even start to process what had happened.

She wasn't sure which stung worse, Swish's words or the fact that they resonated so deeply with her own sense that she was a faux woman—a woman born with a penis. She'd never be just a *woman*. She'd always be a *transgender* woman, with an adjective before the noun. Why was she even meeting him for coffee? What the hell was she thinking? Why lead him on like this?

There was a gentle knock on her door, and it opened a crack. "E, can I please come in?"

"No," she squeaked, still trying to stem the flow of tears.

He gently pushed the door open and stood there. "E, I'm sorry. Please believe me, you are one of the last people in the world I'd ever want to hurt. I swear I didn't mean that the way it came out. I wasn't trying to insult you. I hope you believe me. I guess I'm just confused."

She waved her hands in front of her. "Forget it. You're right. I don't know what I was thinking." She grabbed some tissues from a box on her credenza and blew her nose. "I was just being stupid, pretending like I was a real woman."

"Please don't ever say you're not a real woman. You are. I get that. It's just that a lot of men wouldn't feel that way if they knew your past. Shit, you're the one who told me about trans panic and how guys can flip out. I mean . . . uh, well, I just don't want you to get hurt."

"You're right," she said softly. "I don't know what I was thinking. I don't want to hurt your friend."

He made his way slowly across the room until he was standing next to her chair. He bent over and gently wrapped his arms around her. "I just worry about you."

She looked up at him and wiped her eyes. "I get it, Swish. I don't know, it just made me feel kind of nice that a guy found me attractive and I just wondered what it would be like to . . ." She took a deep breath. "Don't worry. I'll tell him and get it over with quickly. No reason not to."

Look, Mark, there's something I have to tell you, I can't have children. Oh God, that's a great place to start. The guy invites you for coffee and you're discussing not being able to have his children. If that doesn't scare him away, finding out you're transgender should be a piece of cake.

She studied herself in the full-length mirror hung on the back of her bedroom door. She had decided to go casual, changing from her business suit into jeans and a light-blue peasant top. It made no sense that she was worried how she looked while contemplating how to tell the guy she was trying to impress that she was transgender. She could show up in a string bikini; once he heard her backstory, he wouldn't care if she looked like Angelina Jolie.

Heading down the steps of her building, she was still locked in a furious internal debate about if and how to tell him. Mark was a good-looking guy who, based on what Duane had told her, found her attractive. As strange as she found that, what was even harder for her to wrap her head around was that she found herself attracted to him, which was all new to her. She had dated a few women since her transition, but had always found herself comparing them to Lauren. None had measured up. She had also never felt obligated to tell any of them about her past. So why was this different? Why did she feel like she would be deceiving Mark if she didn't tell him as soon as possible?

Who was she kidding? She knew the reason why. Just ask Sharise. In the eyes of many men, she wasn't truly a woman, and once they learned the truth, all hell could break loose. Not that she worried about Mark getting violent; he didn't strike her as that kind of guy. But she still felt it would be wrong not to tell him.

She walked out into the warm late-September evening still lost in her thoughts. Legal Grounds was only about thirty yards from her apartment door, so she had no time left to come up with a plan. *Oh well, let's get this over with.*

She took a deep breath, pushed open the door, and walked in. She gave a quick hello to Donna, the evening barista, and looked around. There, sitting in the back corner of the shop, was Mark. He gave her a slight wave as she made her way back to his table.

"Hey, nice to see you," he offered.

She slid into the booth opposite him. "Nice to see you too."

"What can I get you?"

She was caught off guard by his warm smile. "A decaf cappuccino would be great. Thanks."

"Coming up," he said. "Do you want to split something for dessert?" he asked as he stood up.

"Sure, I guess. Surprise me."

She stared at the back wall trying to sort out her emotions. *Don't tell him. It isn't a date. Have a cup of coffee, chitchat, no big deal. No reason to even mention it.*

"Hope you're a chocolate person," he said, sliding a plate with a brownie cut into two pieces toward the center of the table before heading back to the counter for their drinks.

No, you have to tell him. He's a friend of Duane's. You have to be honest. So what's not honest about just being yourself? Are you a woman or aren't you?

"Here you go—one decaf cappuccino," he said as he put down the tall mug brimming with whipped cream and cinnamon. He placed his own mug of coffee on the table in front of his chair and sat down.

"Thank you," she said. "And yes, I am a chocolate person, so good choice," she added. She sat looking at her cappuccino, furrowing her brow, still struggling with what to do.

"For someone who likes chocolate, you don't seem too excited by my choice. Is something wrong?"

She looked across the table at him and stammered, "N-no, honest. It's just been a while since I . . ." *Don't say date*, a voice in her head screamed. *It's not a date. It's just coffee!* "No, everything's good."

"Really? Because it seems like you're uncomfortable," he offered.

"No, it's not that at all." *Oh, the hell with it. Just be blunt and tell him.* "I'm sorry, Mark. It really has nothing to do with you. It's me."

Now it was his turn to look perplexed.

"Look," she said as she drew in a deep breath. "There's something you need to know about me."

"Okay," he replied, taking a sip of his coffee.

"Are you familiar with the word *transgender*?"

"Sure," he replied, seemingly unsure where this was going.

"Do you know anyone who's transgender?"

"I don't think so. Why?"

She looked up from her cappuccino and somehow found it within herself to smile. "You do now. I'm a transgender woman," she said with a bit more conviction than she felt.

He cocked his head to one side. "Okay. I didn't see that coming. Does that mean you want to be a guy?" he asked hesitantly.

A small laugh escaped before she could stop it. "Er, not exactly," she said, her voice rising at the end so it sounded like a question. "In my case, it means that even though I was assigned male at birth and lived part of my life as a guy, I always felt I was a woman."

He sat quietly for what seemed like an eternity.

She looked at him and put on a brave smile. "Honest, Mark, I apologize. I should have told you when you suggested coffee."

He looked at her, a puzzled expression creeping across his face. Then, he started to laugh. "Erin, I suspect that your history is not something you generally bring up in casual conversation. 'Hi, my name's Erin, but I wasn't born a girl.' So I'm not upset you didn't tell me in the five minutes we talked at the party on Saturday. It's just kind of all new to me, so I'm trying to process the fact that this beautiful woman sitting across from me wasn't always a woman. But I guess that's not right either," he continued before she could say anything. "You probably always knew who you were."

He surprised her. Did he really get it?

"Yeah, I always knew," she said almost in a whisper.

"That must have been hard."

She nodded. "It was."

They both sat quietly.

"Are you okay?" she finally asked.

"Yeah, I think so."

"We can go if you want to," she offered.

"Why?" he said, surprised. "I invited you for a cup of coffee so you could tell me about your practice. You do still practice criminal law?" he asked with a smile that was warm and genuine.

"Uh, yeah, of course I do. Sorry, what would you like to know?" she asked, flustered by his smile.

"Erin," he began softly, "how about we get what you're worried about out of the way. Maybe that would make this a little less awkward for you."

She nodded, lowering her head, as if it would soften the blow to not be looking into his green eyes.

He reached across the table and lifted up her chin with his finger. "Like I said, this is all new to me. I don't know anyone who's transgender, or at least I didn't before now. And if you hadn't told me, I never would have guessed. You're a very attractive woman and you seem like an interesting person. Why wouldn't I try to get to know you better?"

"I don't know," she replied. "A lot of men wouldn't."

"I'm not a lot of men," he said with a goofy smile. "Have some brownie."

They sat and talked about the practice of law and then about the Peace Corps. She had never known anyone who had been in the Peace Corps, and she was fascinated by his take on the good and not so good things that resulted when the Peace Corps set up shop in a country. His smile came easily, and his laugh was soft and smooth. She felt like she was being hypnotized. And, as it did when she met him on Saturday, her brain broke into an internal debate trying to reconcile her previous attraction to women with this sudden curiosity as to what it would be like to be kissed by him.

"Hey, Erin," she heard from over her left shoulder. "We're going to be closing in ten minutes. You guys need anything else?"

She stole a glance at her watch—ten minutes to nine. Had

they really been sitting here for two hours? She looked at Mark and he shook his head no.

"Thanks, Donna, we're good."

When she turned back, he was studying her face. "Can I ask you one question before we go?" he asked.

"Sure."

"Do you have any plans for Saturday night?"

She smiled. "I don't know, do I?" But before he could even respond, her smile faded.

"Something wrong?" he asked.

"No . . . well, yeah, maybe. Saturday is the day after the arraignment in the murder case Duane and I are involved in and . . . well, let's just say, as much as I hope it won't, my status may become an issue because our client is a transgender woman. So . . ."

"You worry too much," he said, his grin reassuring. "How about we go to a movie and grab something to eat afterward and you can tell me all about this new case?"

She inhaled and turned her head to the side, trying to figure out if he really was this cool with her. "Sounds nice," she replied.

"Great. Pick you up at seven."

CHAPTER 8

"COUNSEL IN *STATE V. BARNES*, THE JUDGE WOULD LIKE TO see you in chambers," the court clerk announced.

Duane and Erin rose from their seats in the still-empty court-room and joined Barbara and Roger in following the court clerk as she led the way to the judge's chambers.

Judge Anita Reynolds was already standing when they entered. Reynolds was a tall woman who wore almost no makeup and appeared to be counting on her judge's robes to cover her lack of fashion sense. She greeted Barbara and Roger by name as they entered. When Erin and Duane walked in, she extended her hand and, with a warm smile, exchanged introductions before indicating the four chairs in front of her desk. "Thank you all for coming in so early. I figured if I could get you in to talk by eight fifteen, the courtroom would still be empty and we'd have some time to discuss preliminary issues in chambers."

"Thank you, Judge," Erin replied.

"So, Ms. Taylor," Judge Reynolds continued, "I guess we're

all waiting to find out whether or not the State is going to seek the death penalty in this matter. What's the State's position?"

"Your Honor, the prosecutor will be holding a press conference after the arraignment is over, but I can tell you and defense counsel that we will not be seeking the death penalty."

Erin raised an eyebrow and looked at Duane, who could only shrug.

"That's something of a surprise, Ms. Taylor, especially given the prominence of the victim's family."

"Judge, again, Prosecutor Gehrity will have more to say on this later, but obviously, whenever making a decision in a potential capital case, we always seek input from the victim's family. While their feelings are not dispositive, we do give their position great deference, and in this matter, despite the feeling in the office that this case warranted the death penalty, we are abiding by the family's wish not to pursue it."

"Well, as surprised as I am by the decision," Judge Reynolds offered, "it certainly makes the case a little easier to manage from my standpoint."

"Judge, I will give counsel the formal plea offer in the courtroom, but it's a plea of first-degree intentional murder, with a sentence of thirty years to life imprisonment. So after thirty years the defendant would become parole eligible."

Judge Reynolds turned her gaze to Erin and Duane.

"Judge, I am fairly certain there will be a trial in this matter," Erin said. "But in light of what we've heard so far this morning, we obviously have to have a serious discussion with our client."

Reynolds returned her attention to Taylor. "Has all discovery been made available, Ms. Taylor?"

"Yes, Judge. Ms. McCabe picked up a box of discovery earlier in the week, and I have another box, mainly of photographs and forensic materials, fingerprints, DNA, etcetera, that I have outside."

"Ms. McCabe, Mr. Swisher, I know you haven't seen all the

discovery yet, but will there be any motions that you anticipate at this point."

"Yes, Judge," Duane offered, "there will be a motion to change venue. And we're also hoping we can get Ms. Taylor's consent to allow our client to be examined by several medical experts."

"What type of experts?" Taylor asked.

"Concerning our client's gender dysphoria."

"Your client's what?" Judge Reynolds asked.

Duane turned to Erin, who took her cue. "Judge, our client is a transgender woman," Erin said softly. "In other words, even though she was assigned male at birth, she has a female gender identity and has lived as a woman since she was fifteen. Her gender identity issues will be part of our defense. We will also need that diagnosis as part of a motion we will be filing to have her transferred to the women's jail facility and to receive the proper medical treatment consistent with her diagnosis."

Barbara rolled her eyes. "Judge, this case is about whether Samuel Barnes murdered William Townsend, Jr. There's no reason to turn this case into some cause célèbre over transgender rights."

Reynolds turned to Erin. "Ms. McCabe?"

Having no prior experience with Reynolds, Erin wasn't sure where this was going. "Judge," she began, "we're just trying to represent our client. Part of our representation entails trying to protect her safety and get her the appropriate medical treatment for her medical condition. Our client is currently being held in protective custody, which means she is locked up twenty-three hours a day. This is being done, at least in part, because after three years on female hormones, her body has certain feminine attributes that make it unsafe for her to be held with male inmates. And given her condition, being taken off hormones is causing negative physical and emotional issues for our client. And to be clear, we are not trying to turn this case into some cause célèbre, far from it. However, the fact that my client is a transgender woman is extremely relevant to the defense of this case."

"See, Judge?" Barbara said.

Reynolds turned to Barbara. "Ms. Taylor, while I'll be the first to admit I don't have the foggiest idea what all this transgender stuff means, if it is a recognized medical condition, and if in fact the defendant suffers from this medical condition, then he is entitled to treatment. I'm not touching the issue of jail transfer at this point, but every defendant, even one charged with murder, is entitled to be medically cared for while in custody. So I would be inclined to sign an order allowing the defendant to be examined by the appropriate experts, subject of course to satisfying all security concerns. If you feel strongly that you want to oppose this request, we can do it on the record, but that is my inclination sitting here."

Barbara glanced over at Erin. "Judge, we will not oppose the request, assuming of course that if we wish to have the defendant examined concerning this quote unquote 'medical condition,' we will be permitted to have that done."

"Good. Ms. McCabe, provide me with the appropriate order for my signature. Next issue?"

"Judge," Barbara said, "I realize counsel have only recently come into the case, but I would ask Your Honor, as part of any scheduling order, to set a deadline for the filing of notice of a defense."

"Absolutely," Reynolds replied.

"Judge," Duane responded, "we can have written notice to the prosecutor by next week. We will be relying on self-defense."

"That's fine, Judge. Thank you," Barbara said.

"What about the change of venue motion you mentioned, Mr. Swisher? How much time do you think you'll need to file that?"

"Candidly, Judge, I don't know yet. Obviously, a change of venue motion is fact sensitive. Normally I'd say ninety days, but that will put us right around the holidays, so perhaps right at the beginning of January. If I can file it sooner I will, or if we need more time, I will advise."

"Exactly what are you concerned about, Mr. Swisher? Why don't you think Mr. Barnes can get a fair trial in Ocean County?"

"Judge, it's not just Ocean County. My initial thoughts are that it is from Mercer and Monmouth Counties heading south. It's not exactly a secret that Mr. Townsend, Sr., is a very powerful man in this area of the state. I suspect there are probably very few judges in southern New Jersey, be they Democrats, Republicans, or Independents, who weren't vetted in some fashion by Mr. Townsend. In addition, the death of his son has been a huge story, and it's hard to conceive that potential jurors will not have already formed opinions about our client, especially how she's been portrayed in the press. Even here, everyone is referring to the deceased as the victim. As we've disclosed this morning, we will be relying on self-defense, so I think it's safe to assume we will be arguing that the actions of Mr. Townsend's son led to his own death. As a result, we believe it will be impossible to obtain a fair and impartial jury." He did not say "or impartial judge" out loud, but it was silently implied.

Reynolds shifted uncomfortably in her chair. "Ms. Taylor?"

Barbara leaned over and whispered something to Roger.

"Judge, while we think the motion is absolutely without merit, we have no objection to the timing, as long as we can have thirty days to respond," Roger responded.

"May I address one other thing?" Barbara continued. "Several times now, Ms. McCabe and Mr. Swisher have utilized feminine pronouns when referring to their client. I want to be clear—the defendant, Samuel Barnes, is a man, and the State is not going to be forced into addressing him as a female. I don't know if counsel's reasons are based on some strange notion of political correctness or an overall defense strategy to get the jury to think of their client as a woman. But the State is not going to permit Mr. Barnes, a man with an extensive criminal record, to be portrayed as a weak and defenseless woman."

The judge shifted her focus to Erin.

"Judge, if, as I believe they will, our experts opine that the defendant is a transgender woman, then I see no reason why she wouldn't be addressed consistent with who she is."

"Here we go, Judge. I told you that Ms. McCabe was going to try and turn this case into some politically correct sideshow."

"Ms. Taylor," Reynolds interrupted, "I haven't gotten the impression that Ms. McCabe is trying to do anything except protect her client. As I said earlier, I have no notion of how to handle these issues correctly, but I will certainly have my law clerk do some research. Until then, and until I have some legal or medical justification to proceed otherwise, the defendant will be addressed as Mr. Barnes. When, and if, there is a formal application in front of me to change how I address the defendant, I will take it up at that point." Reynolds paused and looked over at Erin. "I also think that, even absent a motion, I will allow counsel to refer to their client in the manner the client prefers until we get to jury selection. I see no harm in allowing counsel to do that."

"Thank you, Judge," Erin said with a small grin.

"So there is no confusion, counsel, I assume your client in addition to feminine pronouns also utilizes a female name."

"Yes, Judge, her name is Sharise Barnes. S-H-A-R-I-S-E."

"Thank you, counsel," Reynolds said, writing Sharise's name on her legal pad. "Anything else?" Reynolds asked, looking first at Barbara and then at Erin.

"No, Your Honor," they replied in unison.

"Good. It's about eight forty. Ms. McCabe and Mr. Swisher, if you'd like to see your client in the holding cell, I will have my court clerk get you in to see him. I will have them come get you and your client before I take the bench."

"Thank you, Judge."

"Two other housekeeping matters," Reynolds said. "There

have been numerous media requests to both film and photograph the proceedings in this case. Two days ago, I had a conference with all the media outlets that requested coverage. Pursuant to the Supreme Court's guidelines, there will be one video camera operating today and two photographers. Based on the conference, I don't think any television outlet intends to provide complete coverage of the trial, and trust me, I did nothing to encourage coverage. My sense was that given who the victim—sorry, who the deceased—was, most of the media will be very deferential to the family.

"Last but not least, especially since counsel have indicated they will be filing a motion to change venue, I remind all of you about the Rules of Professional Conduct concerning pretrial publicity. If I get up Monday morning and see you on *Good Morning America*, Ms. McCabe, you will have a problem with me when it comes to your motion. Likewise, Ms. Taylor, I know you said Mr. Gehrity would be holding a press conference this morning about your office's death penalty decision. If he does anything to prejudice the jury pool, I will take note of that as well. In other words, everyone be on your best behavior. I don't feel like I have to put a gag order in place, but I will if I have to. Understood?"

"Yes, Judge," they all intoned.

As the judge's clerk led Duane and Erin to the holding area, they passed a door where they could look out into the courtroom. Erin's heart raced when she saw the packed courtroom, with two photographers and one television camera already well positioned to record the arraignment. And there in the front row, immediately behind the prosecutor's counsel table, was William Townsend.

Oh shit! What have you gotten yourself into?

CHAPTER 9

*T*HE BAY VIEW MOTEL WASN'T ON THE BAY AND IT HAD NO view, but it was the last place William E. Townsend, Jr., visited on his abbreviated journey through life. Tucked away on a side road just off of Route 9, it was almost invisible from the highway, so chances were if you found your way there, you probably knew where you were going. At some point in its history, the strip of eleven rooms and a small, unattached office building had been painted white with green trim. Now they looked like the color of oatmeal, and the trim was chipped so badly you could hardly tell what color it had once been.

Duane pulled his car in front of the room and parked. Opening the trunk, they both retrieved their gym bags and headed for the faded green door with the number eight. Slightly askew, the eight flirted with becoming an infinity symbol.

"So what did you tell him?" Erin asked.

"I said that the woman I was with was into numerology and wanted room eight—it was her lucky number." Duane smiled. "He handed me the key and said, 'Well, I guess now it will be your lucky number too.'" Duane motioned to her bag. "I hope you brought something sexy to wear."

"You into women wearing black leather and stilettos?"

"Who isn't?"

"Me," she replied. "Just jeans and running shoes. If we're walking around AC after we leave here, at least I want to be comfortable." She turned and looked back at him. "Guess you're not going to get lucky after all, big guy."

Duane gave her a crooked grin and pushed open the door.

The first thing that struck Erin's senses was the odor of new carpet. They walked in, letting the sunlight from the open doorway guide them until she found a light switch and flipped it on while Duane closed the door and pulled the curtains all the way closed.

"Not exactly the Ritz-Carlton," she suggested.

"More like a Ritz Cracker," he replied. "It's tiny."

She rolled her eyes and began looking around. The room was truly small. The queen-size bed ran three-quarters of the way across the width of the room, and while there was a night table on the left side of the bed, there wasn't enough room for one on the right. Straight ahead was a little alcove, and to the right of that, the bathroom.

Duane opened his gym bag and took out his camera, a tape measure, and copies of the crime scene photos that had been provided in discovery.

"Hold this," he asked, running the tape measure from one wall to the other and then switching to do the other dimension. "Wow, ten by twenty. This place is tiny."

"Mind if I change out of my court clothes?"

"Be my guest," he said.

She laughed. "By the way, I'm secretly recording this and I'm going to play it back for Corrine later."

"Be careful. If she throws me out, the only place I'd have to stay would be yours."

"Guess you'll be homeless," she said, closing the door to the bathroom. When she came out of the bathroom, he'd laid some of the crime scene photos across the bed.

"Look at this photo," he said, pointing to one that appeared to have been taken with a wide-angle lens to display the entire room.

"What do you see?" Duane asked.

"The room."

He sighed. "What do you notice about the room?"

"Nothing except the bloody handprints along the wall, which appear to be headed in the direction of the bathroom."

"That's it, right?"

"Yeah, you can't see Townsend because he's hidden by the bed."

"That's my point. If Townsend lost his mind when he found out Sharise wasn't a . . . that she wasn't a natural-born woman . . ." He stopped and looked at Erin.

"Assigned female at birth," she suggested.

"Right, that she wasn't assigned female, don't you think there would have been some sign of struggle?"

"But Sharise said he was on top of her, reached down between her legs, discovered the truth, and then pulled out a knife. You have a better scenario?"

"I'm not sure it's a better scenario. I'm just not sure her story is what actually happened." He shook his head. "Something doesn't add up."

"Listen, J. Edgar, we're not trying to figure out who did it. We already know."

"I know, but there's something off. I mean, how many twenty-eight-year-old white guys carry a switchblade? That's how Sharise described the knife, a switchblade."

"I have no idea. I live a very sedate life in the suburbs."

"Exactly, so did Mr. Townsend."

"Your point?"

"Twenty-eight-year-old white guys from the suburbs don't carry switchblades—sex workers working in the inner city do, for protection. Also, why did he drive to an out-of-the-way fleabag motel that you'd miss if you didn't already know where to find it? He purposely brought her to Ocean County. How many shithole hotels do you think there are in and around AC—twenty, thirty? Why bring her here? Maybe because it's isolated, and it's in daddy's backyard."

"But why? Even if he was planning a thrill killing, what does he do with her body? And if he's a cold-blooded murderer, then he's no longer a sedate white kid from the suburbs, so maybe he did have the knife. But if he didn't have a knife, then how was he going to kill her? Where's the weapon?"

Duane pointed to a picture on the bed of Townsend's body. "There. His hands. He was going to strangle her. Not an unusual MO for a thrill killer. Then, take her body, put it in the car, and dump her in the wetlands."

"So let's say you're right. Mr. Townsend brings her here to murder her. He's going to strangle her. Somehow, from somewhere, our client manages to retrieve a switchblade and stabs him to death in self-defense. The son of one of the most prominent men in the state is a murderous psychopath, and our nineteen-year-old transgender sex worker client kills him in self-defense. Sure, works for me. Shouldn't have any problem selling that to the jury," she said sarcastically, then walked over and sat on the one chair in the corner of the room. "Jesus, you know what bothers me more than anything?"

"What?"

"I'm starting to believe you, even though Sharise's version is much easier to sell—dude goes crazy after learning the truth."

He gathered up the pictures that were on the bed. "Not easier if there's holes in it. Lie down," he said.

She raised her eyebrows.

"Stop," he admonished. "Come on, lie down. I want to see something."

She walked over and flopped on the side of the bed nearest the far-right wall. He came over and straddled her body. "Okay, let's reenact what happened as our client described it."

"Go for it," she said. "Just remember, you're the one who winds up dead."

He smiled. "Got it. So I'm furious because I've discovered your secret. First of all, where do I get the knife?"

She looked at him, perplexed. "Your pants?" she said hesitantly.

"Look at this picture. No pants on." He looked around the room, trying to piece things together. "Okay, let's say for argument's sake, I jump off you, grab a knife from my pants pocket, push you down onto the bed, and jump on top of you. You're struggling. I pop the knife, holding it clenched in my left fist. I pull my left arm back to shoulder height." Duane simulated Townsend drawing his arm back. "Then I lunge downward at you." Duane began to bring his arm down toward Erin's body in slow motion. "You manage to get your right arm up—Sharise said she definitely did it right-handed—and you block my arm as it's coming down."

Erin moved her right arm to try to simulate parrying the blow, but as she did she realized that even if she could get her arm across her body, her arm was in an awkward position to deflect anything.

"At the same time you push your arm up with all your might," Duane continued, "which turns the knife around, and as I'm falling forward from the momentum of attempting to stab you, I'm impaled on my own knife."

She looked up at Duane, realizing she couldn't redirect his arm back in the fashion Sharise described. "Shit," she said, pursing her lips and frowning. "But Sharise is bigger than I am, and you're bigger than Townsend was, so it's not . . . it's not conclusive," she said, trying to sound optimistic.

"Really?" he asked. "That's what you're hanging your hopes on?"

"I know Sharise said he was using his left hand, but maybe she got it wrong?"

"No, already checked. He was a 1995 graduate of Moorestown

High School, where he played baseball. He was a pitcher and outfielder."

"Let me guess. He batted and threw left-handed."

Duane nodded.

She shook her head. "I don't know. What else do we have?" She exhaled, trying to process what it all meant. "Uh, by the way, you can get off me now."

"Sorry," Duane said, sliding to the edge of the bed.

"So, what are we left with? She's guilty; she killed him because he was trying to kill her; or, it happened the way she described it, which doesn't look likely."

"Tough case. I agree with you that most folks, especially straight white men, would be willing to accept that the dude flipped out when he discovered her junk. It'll be a lot harder to get them to accept that the son of one of the most prominent men in the state was trying to murder her because he's a psychopath."

"Yeah," she mumbled.

"Okay, time to get up," he said, motioning her off the bed. He picked up his camera from where he'd laid it on the floor and started taking pictures of the room from every conceivable angle. When he was finished, he looked at her. "I think we're done?"

"We're done and I'm left feeling worse than when we started."

"Maybe we should have started the reenactment from right after they arrived in the room?" he suggested, a crooked smile gracing his face.

"Or played it out to the conclusion," she said, her eyes narrowing into a menacing glare.

"Point taken."

"You have your recorder with you?" she asked.

"Does the pope shit in the woods? Of course. Why?"

"Maybe when you return the key you can find out if the clerk knows anything about Townsend or the murder."

He laughed. "Remember, this isn't the Ritz-Carlton. When you pay cash, you don't return the key. We just leave it on the night table and leave."

"Pardon my lack of experience in sleazy motels. You're a trained special agent. Think of some ruse. Who knows, maybe he knows something?"

Erin waited in the car while Duane went back into the office. If Duane was right, it meant that Sharise had lied to them about what happened. Was she lying about other things? Was it really just a robbery gone bad as Barbara Taylor seemed convinced of? Thinking about it, that sure as hell seemed more plausible than that William Townsend, Jr., was a murderer.

"You take good notes?" she asked when he returned to the car.

"Perfect."

"You were in there for almost fifteen minutes. Was the clerk here that night?"

"No, but the clerk, whose name is Ray, and the owner, who *was* here that night, have talked a lot about it. And he was here in the morning when the maid discovered the body."

"Anything good?"

"Probably more tantalizing than good."

"I'm listening."

"Vinny, the owner of this fine establishment, told Ray that he believes Townsend was at the Bay View about a year before. Vinny said he couldn't be sure it was the same guy, but he certainly looked familiar."

"Why would Vinny remember a guy who'd only been here once?"

"Because the cops showed up that night. Apparently, whoever was here had started using the woman he was with as a punching bag. Luckily for her, she managed to get her phone and call nine-one-one. Cops came, but the woman refused to press charges and simply asked that someone pay for her to get a cab back to AC. About fifteen minutes later, a black Town Car pulled up, there was a short conversation with the remaining police officers, and the assailant is whisked away. Later that night, two different guys show up and one of them drives off in the assailant's car."

"Should be a report on the nine-one-one call."

"Maybe. But without a date, it could prove to be the proverbial needle in the haystack."

"Vinny always work the late shift?"

"Pretty much. They have three other people who handle shifts if Ray or Vinny take some time off. Ray generally comes in at six a.m. and works to four p.m., while Vinny works from four p.m. 'til two a.m. From two to six they have some type of automated system. Outside calls go to an answering service. Calls made to the office on a motel phone get forwarded to an employee on call. They have a total of six housekeepers, three who work from six a.m. to two p.m., and three who go from six p.m. to midnight."

"Interesting. That all fits," Erin said.

"Meaning?" he asked.

"They checked in just before two a.m., while there was still someone working the desk. Assuming Townsend knew the hours they work, he would have known that after two there was nobody in the office. So if he's taking a body out of the room at three, there's no risk of being seen by anyone in the office because they're gone until six."

Duane nodded. "Sounds like you're beginning to agree with me."

"It's either that or she murdered him. How'd you get Ray to open up?" she asked.

His smile grew. "I told him that it turned out the crazy broad I was with really wasn't into numerology. Turns out she heard a guy had been murdered in this room and she wanted to have sex where some guy died. So I asked him, 'Did someone really get murdered in room 8?' He lights up like a Christmas tree and we're off to the races. Pretty clever, huh?"

"The crazy broad you're with?" She turned toward him, pouting. "Is that all I am to you?"

"Women!" he said under his breath, shaking his head.

Erin stared out the window as they took the back roads to Atlantic City, her mind slowly processing what was likely to unfold in the next twenty-four hours.

"Why so quiet?" he finally asked.

"You heard the questions the reporters were asking when we left the courtroom. Someone obviously outed me to the press. There were as many questions about me as there were about the case."

"I noticed," he offered. "But you knew it was going to happen sooner or later."

She snorted. "Yeah, can't say you didn't warn me. I guess I just thought it would be more of a gradual thing, a trickle as opposed to a tsunami right from the start." She paused, shaking her head. "This seemed coordinated. The reporters knew everything. It was like they were briefed on me."

"You okay?" he asked.

"I don't know."

She fell silent again, trying to imagine what the coverage was going to be like. Mindful of Judge Reynolds's admonition, she had responded to every question with, "No comment." But the questions alone told her what the stories were going to be like. She felt bad for her mom, knowing that her dad and Sean wouldn't be happy to see her face in the newspapers, especially under these circumstances.

"You want to come over for dinner tomorrow night? Hang out with us? Maybe get your mind off things?"

It suddenly occurred to her that she hadn't told Swish she had a date with Mark. Oh God, how would Mark react if her face was plastered on the front of the local newspapers?

"Thanks, but, um, I have plans for tomorrow night."

"Oh, okay. No problem."

"Ah, yeah, well, just so you know, I actually have a date with Mark tomorrow night," she said somewhat sheepishly. "Yes, I told him," she said when he glanced her way, sounding both defensive and defiant at the same time. "And yes, he still asked me out."

"None of my business," he responded.

"No, you should know. He's your friend and I don't want it to be awkward for you."

"If it's not awkward for him . . ." He stopped to cringe. "Sorry. I think I'll just shut up now."

"Good idea," was all she said as she tried to lose herself in the passing scenery.

Later they wandered the streets of Atlantic City, looking for the location where Sharise said she was working the night Townsend picked her up. *What a weird place*, Erin thought. The front of the casinos all faced the boardwalk. That's the part of the city everyone saw, with its bright lights, fancy hotels, and nightlife dotting the Atlantic Ocean. But on Pacific Avenue, literally in the casinos' shadows, another world existed. A world where people struggled to survive—the homeless, the prostitutes, the throwaway kids whom no one wanted.

Maybe there were tricks to be turned inside the casinos, but at three in the afternoon, on the corner of Pacific and South Providence, there were few signs of life.

"Think I'll have to come back some night after dark," Duane offered.

"You still have a carry permit?"

"Yeah."

"Then carry. This place gives me the creeps and it's a nice afternoon. I can't imagine what it's like at one in the morning."

When they got back to the car, he said, "Look, I'm sorry for what I said before about Mark."

She turned her head to look at him. "It's not that. Look at this place, Swish. I can't imagine what it's like for a sixteen- or seventeen-year-old kid to be out on the street, hooking to make a living. Knowing that whatever you make, some pimp is going to take most of it. Jesus, I was scared standing there in broad daylight. Sharise had to earn her living out there night after night, always worried about some crazy psycho john, or being discovered as a transgender woman or getting busted. What the hell kind of life is that? What were her mother and father thinking? To assign your own kid to that kind of hell because you think who they are is against God's law? Give me a break. They should come here and see how their daughter had to live." She took a tissue from her purse and wiped her eyes. "I hope we can help this kid. Just once she deserves a break."

CHAPTER 10

*S*OONER OR LATER, BITCH, WE'RE GOING TO GET YOU.

Sharise sat on her bunk, trying not to break. If she cried now, she might never stop. How had she gotten to this hell? Was this truly her punishment from God for believing she was a woman? Her momma had warned her that God would have His retribution for her abomination, but this was so far from anything she ever imagined. But then, she never imagined she'd grow up to be a prostitute. Or be in jail. Or kill someone. She missed Lexington; she missed Tonya; she missed her momma and father. How did this happen to her?

Come on, faggot, you know you want it.

The taunts were constant every time she left her cell. It seemed like every inmate knew who she was, and they never missed an opportunity to suggest what was going to happen to her. Sometimes it was even the guards. It didn't matter; guards, inmates, they all mocked her. They'd brush up against her as she was led through the lockup, groping her, grabbing her breasts.

You think you're a girl? We'll show you what it's like for a girl, bitch.

Two days earlier, the guards had dragged her out of her cell, telling her she was being put into the general population. They walked her down to A Wing while a group of inmates called out and asked them to put her in their cell. The guards laughed. After ten minutes, they led her back to her six-by-nine cell, pushed her in, locked the door, and continued laughing. Laughing at her for being terrified that she was going to be assaulted, raped, and killed.

Come on, bitch, don't pretend you don't want it.

It was called protective custody, but it was just another name for solitary confinement, and it certainly wasn't protective. She spent her days alone, staring at the cinder-block walls. There was no television, no radio, nothing to read except some awful paperback novels—there was nothing but the iron door with an opening through which they slid her food tray.

There was no one to talk to. Twenty-three hours a day spent in that cell—alone. One hour, one fucking hour they let her out to walk on a treadmill and take a shower—again, alone. And then back to her cell, back to her bunk—alone.

When she was young she loved to be alone. It gave her a chance to daydream about a world where she was Tonya's little sister. She'd fantasize for hours about what she would wear and all the things they'd do together. Now being alone meant being tormented by a reality she could never change.

Come on out, honey, we'll do the sex change operation on you for free.

And then there was the day she was caught. It was five years ago—five very long years.

His momma had been waiting for him as soon as he walked in the door from school. He had seen her mad before, so he knew he was in trouble, but there was a look in her eyes that he had never seen. A fury there that was truly frightening.

"Upstairs, young man. Now!" she demanded.

Sam had no idea what he did, but he didn't dare ask. He followed her up the stairs, watching as she turned toward his room. After walking in first, she stepped back so he could see.

When he got to the doorway, he was sure his heart was going to stop. There, spread out on his bed, were the clothes he had hidden away in the back corner of his closet. There were two pairs of panties, a pair of pantyhose, a dress, a bra, and a pair of heels. Clothes that he had accumulated over the last two years, some quietly lifted from clothes his mother was donating, some, like the underwear, stolen from his sister. He looked at them lying on the bed and prayed the house would collapse and he would be crushed.

His mother was tapping her foot. "What is the meaning of this?" she said, her eyes piercing him like lasers.

He stood silent, unable to find the voice or the words to respond.

"I asked you a question, young man. What is all of this?"

"I can explain," he offered, trying desperately to come up with anything to explain the clothes lying on his bed.

"I'm waiting."

His mind went blank. He had never prepared for this possibility. His fourteen-year-old brain had told him he was safe, that no one would ever find his stash of clothes. How could he explain this? He couldn't tell the truth. He wasn't sure he knew what would happen, but he was sure it wouldn't be good.

"It was for a prank, at school," he finally blurted out.

"What kind of prank requires girl's clothes?" she shot back. "You never told me about any prank. And why would you need two pairs of underwear?" Her cross-examination was swift and devastating.

"I . . . I didn't want you to get mad at me."

Her open hand caught him on the side of the head. "You're lying to me, boy. And you're just making me madder."

"Momma, please," he said, his pleas suddenly mixing with his tears. "I just wanted to see what it felt like to wear a dress. I'm sorry."

"Oh, you'll be sorry. When your father gets home, you are

going to explain this all to him. And don't think for one minute I believe that story. I think you have the devil in you."

His pained look immediately changed to horror. "Please, Momma. Please don't tell Daddy. Please."

"You should have thought of that before you decided to see what it was like to wear a dress. Now get out of your clothes and put those on so your father can see exactly what type of son he has."

"Oh no, Momma. Please don't . . ."

"Do as I say. Now!" Another smack with the palm of her hand to the back of his head sent him stumbling forward toward the bed. "Now!"

He quickly pulled his T-shirt up over his head. Sitting down on the bed, he untied his sneakers, removing them and placing them by his bed. Next, he undid his belt and lowered his pants, his mother's piercing gaze never leaving him. He picked the dress up off of the bed and prepared to put it on.

"What are you doing?" she asked. "You are going to put on everything."

He wanted to run from the room, run from his home, run and never come back. But he was fourteen; where would he go? Eventually he'd be forced to come back and then the beating would be even worse.

He put the dress down and lowered his boxers, mortified. As quickly as he could, he put on the underwear and bra, making sure he struggled with the bra, trying to hide how often he had put one on before. Next, he put on the pantyhose. Finally, he picked up the dress again and lifted it over his head, putting his arms into each sleeve and then tugging it down into place. His tears were warm on his cheeks, his humiliation almost complete.

"The shoes too," she commanded.

Zombie-like now, he took the shoes off the bed and sat down. He slid one shoe on, then the other.

"Stand and face me," she demanded.

He stood, but he couldn't look at her.

"You had better pray. Pray the Lord forgives you. Pray that I forgive you. And most of all, pray that your father is merciful and gives you another chance to be a man; to be our son." She moved behind him and guided him over to the mirror that hung above his dresser. "Look at yourself. You are a disgrace. You should be ashamed."

He couldn't even raise his eyes to look.

Suddenly he felt her hand grab the back of his head and pull it up. "Look at yourself!" she shouted. "Look at what a poor excuse for a man you are."

He opened his eyes. There, in the mirror, he didn't see the young woman he so often tried to envision. Today he saw a humiliated boy, a frightened boy; today he saw only a boy in a dress.

"Go sit on your bed and don't move. When your father gets home, he will deal with you."

She turned and walked out of the room, pulling the door closed behind her. Several hours later, he heard his father get home. It was another ten minutes before his door flew open, startling him. His father strode purposely into the room, a belt he'd folded in two in one hand, which he was gently slapping against the other's palm.

"Get up," he ordered.

Sam stood. His father drew nearer. The first blow from the belt caught the bare flesh of Sam's arm.

"If I ever catch you or find out that you are defiling yourself by wearing women's clothes, I will throw you out. Do you understand me?"

The blows started raining down. Sam got his arms up, trying to protect his face, so his father aimed lower, stinging the flesh on his legs. His father grabbed him by the arm, dragging him up, and flipped the dress up over his head. The belt then whipped the back of his thighs and his buttocks, the welts rising even as the blows continued.

Sam screamed, the pain tearing through him. "Please, Daddy."

"Don't"—*smack*—"you"—*smack*—"please"—*smack*—"Daddy"—*smack*—"me"—*smack*.

"Stop! Please!"

He swung the belt undeterred. "I will make a man out of you, boy, or you will rue the day you were born. No son of mine will be a faggot. Do you understand me?" He landed a few more blows and then stopped.

Sam was lying half on and half off his bed, whimpering, unable to move.

"Get out of those clothes, put them in that bag, and put them in the trash. I swear to you, Samuel, if anything like this ever happens again, I will disown you. Do you understand me?"

"Yes," he whispered between the sobs.

After his father left, he slumped to the floor. He wasn't sure which was more painful, the welts left by the belt, or the humiliation of having his secret discovered and knowing there could never be acceptance here.

He instinctively tensed when his sister touched him gently on the top of his head. "It's okay, Sam. It's me," Tonya said. She sat down on the floor next to him and pulled his head into her lap, all the while touching him softly. "I'm so sorry, Sammy, I didn't know," she said, her Southern drawl giving her voice a soothing cadence. "I should have known. You are such a kindred spirit. Not like the other boys," she said, rocking him gently. "Let's get you cleaned up and put some salve on those welts."

He finally turned his head and looked up at her. "Thank you," he choked out.

"Do you want me to talk to them for you?"

"No! No, please don't," he said. "No, I'll never do this again. Never."

"Oh, Sam, you should be free to be whoever you are."

He straightened himself into a sitting position so he was looking into her eyes. "No, they'll never understand. I'll be okay. They're right. God made me a man and that's the way things are."

She reached out and pulled him into an embrace. "Sammy,

God didn't make you the way you are to punish you. Maybe he made you this way to help other people learn about acceptance and love." She kissed the top of his head. "I'll always be here for you, sister, brother—it doesn't matter to me. I love you, Sammy. Always."

Why so quiet, honey? Trying to make yourself look pretty?

But she hadn't stopped. And then came the day she was caught for the second time. Her father probably would have killed her. Only her momma stepping between them saved her life. It would have been better if he had killed her. No, it would have been better if she had killed herself. Who was she to think she could live her life as a woman? What a fool. What a mother-fucking fool. Now, here she was paying for her sins.

You killed the wrong guy, honey, there's a bounty for your dead ass.

No one would ever believe her about what happened. She didn't believe what had happened. And there was no way these two crazy lawyers would be able to convince a jury of what happened. She was destined to rot in jail. No, that wasn't true either. One way or another her life in jail would be short. The inmates would get her, or she'd get herself. It was a death sentence, just by another name.

CHAPTER 11

Wiping the sleep from her eyes, Erin grabbed her chirping cell phone from the night table and checked the outside display before flipping it open. "Must be bad if you're calling me at seven a.m. on a Saturday."

"Yeah, all that and more," Duane replied.

"Shit," she said, suddenly wide-awake. "You okay?"

"Yeah, I'm fine, but pretty sure you won't be."

"Thanks. Guess I better go take a look for myself." She closed her phone and climbed out of bed, knowing there was no point in trying to fall back to sleep now.

When she got out of the shower, the light was flashing on her answering machine. She walked over and hit play.

"Erin, it's your mother. I don't know if you've seen this morning's papers yet, but nothing like walking into the local 7-Eleven and seeing your daughter's picture under the headline A TRANNIE LAWYER FOR A TRANNIE MURDERER. At least the *Jersey Post-Dispatch* was kinder in its description of you. But I'm sure your father and brother are not going to be happy. I tried to talk to your father last night, but despite both of us falling asleep happy, we made no progress on you. Call me on my cell phone when you get your lazy behind out of bed. Love ya."

She shook her head and wondered if she was doing Sharise any favors. Most lawyers wouldn't worry about issues related to their client being transgender, they'd just defend the case. And maybe, if some other lawyer was handling the case, it wouldn't be plastered all over the front page of the papers.

With her mind now working overtime second-guessing herself, Erin threw on a pair of jeans and a top, pulled her hair back into a ponytail, and found a hat and a pair of sunglasses to act as a disguise. She looked at herself in the mirror and laughed. As if Max, who worked the counter at the local deli where she always bought her papers, wouldn't recognize her. She grabbed her wallet and keys from her purse, put them in her backpack, and headed out.

"Morning, Max," she said as she handed him a ten-dollar bill to pay for the *Times*, the *Mirror*, the *Jersey Post-Dispatch*, and the *Ledger*.

She wasn't sure if it was her paranoia or not, but the usually gregarious Max seemed fairly subdued. "Morning," was all he said, handing her the change.

She ambled across North Avenue and felt fortunate that Legal Grounds was almost deserted. She took her large breakfast blend coffee over to the same table that she and Mark had shared a few nights earlier, dropped the papers on the table, and sat down, once again facing the back wall, the memories of that evening still fresh. *Wonder how Mark is going to react to my fifteen minutes of fame.*

She quickly tried to banish those thoughts by opening the *Post-Dispatch*, correctly divining that its story would be the most sensational of the lot. In terms of column inches, the biggest story was in the *Ledger*, which downplayed the fact that Erin was transgender. Unfortunately, even when downplayed, it was still there. She took little solace in the fact that her status was not mentioned in the *Times* article; the damage had already been done in the other papers.

When she was finished reading, she collected the papers and threw them in her backpack. Legal Grounds was starting to fill up, so she ordered another cup of coffee to go and decided to head over to the office, where she called her mom's cell.

"Hello," her mother answered.

"Hi, Mom, it's me."

"Oh, Beth, how are you? I'm making Pat some breakfast right now. Can I call you back in ten or fifteen minutes?"

"Sure, Mom. Call my cell," she said, afraid that even though it was a Saturday, there might be reporters calling the office number.

"Great. Talk to you in a few."

Wonderful. Things were so bad that her mother had to pretend it was someone else on the phone when her dad was in the room.

She looked at her office phone and saw that the voice mail message light was on. She entered her extension and password, and began listening to the twenty-six messages, breaking them into categories as she went: reporters, outraged citizens, television stations, legal publications, her therapist, and death threats. She copied down the names and numbers from all the press-related calls, and saved the irate citizens and death threats—for what purpose, she wasn't sure.

She walked over to the corner of her office, where she had placed the second box of discovery they had picked up yesterday. She flipped through the various manila envelopes until she found the one labeled "DNA." As she suspected, numerous blood samples were submitted in an effort to see if all the blood was from the victim. Additional samples were taken from the vomit on the corpse and several hair samples located on the bedding. Two semen samples were located on a pair of women's underwear; both were contaminated, but still tested. A known sample of blood was also taken from the victim for comparison purposes.

All of the blood belonged to the victim. One set of DNA

found from the seminal fluid on the underwear was consistent with Samuel E. Barnes; the other, which was also substantially degraded with only seven loci present, was consistent with the victim's. The DNA from the hair and vomit came back to Barnes.

She now knew what she needed to know. The DNA of William Townsend, Jr., was in the New Jersey database as a victim, which meant it was not available to other law enforcement agencies. She could only imagine the reaction they'd receive when they tried to have the known sample run through CODIS, the joint state and federal database operated by the Department of Justice, to see if young Mr. Townsend's DNA was also in the database as an unknown perpetrator.

Erin was about to retrieve another envelope when her cell phone rang. "Hi, Mom," she answered.

"Hello, dear. Have you gone into hiding yet?"

"Not yet. My application for the Witness Protection Program has been rejected—I'm too hot to handle."

"It's a good thing your father was hungover this morning, otherwise I think he would have had a stroke."

In spite of herself, Erin giggled. "Better get word out to the medical community that hangovers prevent stroke. Not sure that has been widely reported in medical literature."

"Be a smartass, Ms. Trannie Lawyer."

Erin cringed. "Can I ask you a favor? Please don't use the word *trannie*. It's sort of like using the N-word; it's offensive."

"Oh . . ." Her mother hesitated. "I'm sorry. I didn't know that. But I saw it on the front page of a newspaper this morning—the *Mirror*, I think? Why would they use that term?"

"I'm not sure I'd elevate the status of that rag to a newspaper. Let's just say, that paper has a certain image to uphold, and it did."

"I'm sorry. How are you? I'm sure this isn't fun for you."

"No, it's not. I can't say I fully appreciated what I was getting myself into."

"Do you want to meet somewhere and talk?"

"No, thanks. I'm in the office trying to get some work done

and later I'm going to drive down to Princeton. The boys e-mailed me the other day; they have a game at two p.m. that I'm going to try and get to."

"Do you think that's wise? I mean, your picture is on the front of several newspapers."

"I'll tuck my hair under a hat, wear a bulky sweatshirt, and hide behind big sunglasses. I should be okay."

"Well, your brother won't be there this week; he's off doing something with Doctors Without Borders."

"He's a good man."

"Yes, he is. Now if I could only get him to take his head out of his behind and accept you, we'd be fine."

"We still have Dad to contend with."

"I keep telling you, your father will come around. Once we get Sean on board, then I'll just cut your father off. He'll change his tune quickly then."

Erin laughed. "You make it sound like you can get whatever you want from Dad with sex."

"You sound surprised."

"I am."

"Sounds like we need to have a mother-daughter talk. There are two ways to a man's heart, and only one of them is through his stomach."

"Thanks for the tip," she said, chuckling. "Actually, speaking of men . . ." Her voice cracked, betraying her nerves. "I have a date tonight."

There was a momentary pause. "Wait, you have a date with a guy?"

"Yeah."

"That's interesting. I thought you were into women?"

"I am . . . or was . . . or—I don't know, Mom, I'm finding this whole thing really confusing."

"You're finding it confusing? Join the crowd."

"Really."

"I'm just teasing . . . You're an attractive woman. Why not see what the rest of us have to put up with? You may go back to women." She paused for a moment. "Can I ask a delicate question?"

"He knows about me."

"What makes you think I was going to ask you that?"

"Weren't you?"

"Well, yes. And he still wants to go out with you?"

"Thanks, Mom."

"Sorry. I just kind of imagine for a lot of men that might be a deal breaker."

"It often is. I guess we'll see what happens."

It was five o'clock when Erin dashed up the steps to her apartment. Princeton had won 5–2, and Patrick had a goal and Brennan an assist. She loved watching them play. Even though she didn't have many good memories of high school, she had always loved playing soccer. Driving back from her nephews' game, she entertained the thought of finding out if there were any adult coed leagues. There were a couple of indoor soccer places that had opened up recently; maybe she'd check them out—*after* Sharise's case was over.

She still had a couple of hours before Mark picked her up, but she really wanted to look nice. She peeled off her sweatshirt and jeans, and threw them on the bed, then turned on the shower because it needed at least three minutes for the hot water to arrive. The good thing was, once it got hot, she could take a half-hour shower and have plenty of hot water to spare. As she unhooked her bra, she looked over at the answering machine and saw that the light was blinking. She hit play as she went to grab two towels from the linen closet.

"Hi, Erin, it's Mark. Listen, I'm really sorry, but something's come up and I need to cancel tonight. Hopefully you'll give me a rain check. I'll give you a call and we'll set up a new date. Have a nice night. Bye."

She stood in the doorway, towels in hand, staring dumbly at the machine on her night table. She slowly walked over and hit play again. The message was still the same.

She dropped to the bed and sat there, trying not to fall apart. *Something's probably come up with his mom.* Yeah, so why didn't he say that? *He said he'd call.* You don't really believe that, do you? *He knew about me, it's not that.* Sure, he knew about you, the difference is now everybody knows about you—you're the trannie lawyer, front-page news. *But that doesn't matter to him, he's his own man.* Honey, he's a man who has to look other men in the eye. His buddies will never let him live it down. *No!* Yeah, that's what it is. *Oh Jesus, how could I be so stupid to think any man would want to go out with me?*

She rolled to one side, morphing to a fetal position in slow motion. As she lay there, curled up in a ball, not moving, she could hear the sound of the shower running in the background. At first there were no tears, just an enveloping numbness. If she had been able to shut her brain down, she would have just fallen asleep. But her brain was never that nice to her. It loved to taunt her with her failings.

The tears came next. Mark had stood her up. Lauren was pregnant. Her picture was now all over the place. She would forever be the trannie lawyer. She was a pariah.

She wasn't sure how long she cried. At some point she dragged herself off the bed and turned off the shower. She was alone. She had no one to call. No shoulder to cry on. Other than Duane, all her guy friends had disappeared when she transitioned, and she really hadn't made any close female friends yet. The only thing that she could latch on to, the only thing that kept her from falling over the edge, was Sharise. Erin had to hold on. Sharise had it worse, and if Sharise could hold on, she had to hold on too.

Sharise needed her. And she needed Sharise.

CHAPTER 12

SHARISE LEANED BACK ON HER BUNK AND PROPPED HERSELF up against the cold cinder-block wall of her cell. It had been so good to see Tonya, but the fact that they had been separated by a glass partition the whole time only reinforced the distance between their lives. The realization that she'd probably spend the rest of her life in jail and never have the opportunity to spend time with her sister made Sharise wonder why she was even trying to survive.

She reached down and picked up the papers her lawyers had sent. She wasn't sure how she felt about what her lawyers wanted to file. Then again, she wasn't sure how she felt about her lawyers. Maybe she'd have been better off with a public defender, or maybe she should just take the deal and be done with it. Yeah, thirty years in a men's prison—she'd be done with it all right. How long could she last? No, the better question was how long would she last? Sooner or later some punk would put a shiv in her.

McCabe had told her the motion was a long shot, but if it

turned out that Townsend was in the DNA database as an un-known assailant, it could break her case wide open. Of course, like everything these fucking lawyers told her, there was a down-side too. If there was incriminating evidence out there pointing to Townsend as a murderer, it might cause the fucker's father to try to end the case quickly. And the surest way for the case to end quickly was for Sharise to end quickly. Pissing off the powerful Mr. Townsend—was that something she was willing to risk? It was her decision, they told her.

She laughed to herself. What the fuck was the risk? *Kill me now, kill me later, it doesn't matter, I'll be just as dead.* The only ques-tion was one of timing. And, as it did so often these days, her mind found a dark corner where ending it all seemed like the way to go. Really, what did she have to live for—a life in prison as a man? No, if it came to that, she'd find a way to check out her-self.

Her thoughts returned to the paperwork she was holding. She wasn't sure she understood all the legal mumbo jumbo, but she damn sure understood what they were getting at—young Town-send was a stone-cold murderer. He wasn't there for a blow job; he was there to kill her. But trying to get anyone to believe she acted in self-defense would be somewhat on par with her hopes of going to college someday; nice to fantasize about, but none too likely. She couldn't imagine that there were a whole lot of poten-tial jurors out there who were going to believe that a good-looking, rich white boy tried to kill a nineteen-year-old Black transgender prostitute.

"Let's go, Barnes," Officer Nelson yelled. "Your lawyers are back to see you again."

By now she knew the drill. Place any papers she wanted to take with her on the bed. Turn and face the wall, with her hands held high against the wall. First, they'd shackle her ankles; then they'd turn her around, put the waist belt on her and shackle her hands to it, and run another chain from her ankles to the waist belt.

Her lawyers were already sitting in the room when the guards led her into the holding cell and threw her paperwork on the table. After some pleasantries, McCabe got to the point of their visit.

"Have you had a chance to review the motion?"

Sharise nodded.

"What do you think?"

"File it," she replied without emotion.

"Are you okay with the risk?" McCabe asked.

"You crack me up, girl. I be sitting here in a man's jail, awaiting trial for killing the son of one of the most powerful men in the state, and you acting like this motion is risky. Honey, give me a break. Every day I last without being dead is a miracle. File the fucking thing. All it mean is my chances of winding up dead go from ninety-nine percent to ninety-nine point five percent. So go at it, girl."

"You know who Lenore Fredericks is?" Swisher asked.

Sharise's eyes narrowed as she looked across the table at her lawyers. Finally, she nodded. "Yeah. Why you want to know?"

"I need you to read this. Then we need to talk."

He took the papers out of a manila folder and placed them on the table in front of her. The heading at the top read: "Transcript of call with Lenore Fredericks." She lifted up her shackled hands and placed them on the table so she could turn the pages.

LF: Hello, is this Duane Swisher?

DS: Yes, it is.

LF: Mr. Swisher, my name is Lenore Fredericks. I got your name from someone I know in Atlantic City. I'm calling about Tamiqua, at least that was her street name. I know her as Sharise. I hear you're looking for people who know her.

DS: I am. Do you know Sharise?

LF: (laughter) Yeah, we known each other. We worked together . . . (long pause) we also friends. I know she's in a shitload of trouble.

DS: Where are you now? Can we meet and talk?

LF: Not unless you want to get on a plane. I'm in Vegas.

DS: Oh.

*LF: Listen, I don't have a lot of time, so let me tell you straight out
what I know. I know Sharise since she show up at the homeless shelter 'bout three years back. She was kind of in between, you know
what I mean. Not really Sharise yet, but not her old self either. I was
about twenty then and full time for about two years. So I kinda took
her under my wing and showed her the ropes. She was just a kid—I
don't know, maybe she was sixteen, I think. She tried to get a job,
McDonald's, the boardwalk, but nobody would fucking hire her because she had no papers. So eventually, my pimp takes her on and
she start working the street. I know some of the girls out there, and
we all helped her. Got her some clothes, taught her how to spot the
law, tried to show her how to stay the fuck alive. Suave, he was my
fucking pimp, he was a motherfucker to her. Treated her worse than
the rest of us. Not sure why. Anyway, she survived and we became
friends. Sometime about a week before Easter, she gets this trick
who's driving one of them fancy BMWs. Later when I see her, I ask
her what's with the fucking guy in the BMW and she says apparently
he likes the fact that she still has her dick.*

DS: Wait, he knew she was trans and hadn't had the surgery yet?

*LF: You sound surprised. (laughter) There are a lot of men out there,
Mr. Swisher, who enjoy a girl with a little something extra. You
know what I mean?*

DS: Sorry. Go on.

*LF: Anyway. I remember it was Easter and I couldn't believe Suave
sent us out on the street on fucking Easter. It was late and we was
getting ready to go home when up pulls Mr. BMW looking for
Sharise.*

DS: You sure it's the same one?

*LF: I ain't positive about nothing. But ain't that many dudes in
BMWs come back looking for someone. So I'm pretty sure it's the
same motherfucker.*

DS: Okay.

LF: So Sharise go and gets in the car and that's the last time I see her.

Next morning about ten or eleven, Suave is going fucking crazy looking for Sharise. Then this fucking SWAT team comes in and bust us all. Only later, when I'm locked up, that I hear they saying Sharise killed the guy.

DS: *Did the police interview you?*

LF: *Sure. I told them I don't know her. But Suave must have told them that me and Sharise, we friends, because they keep hassling me. Finally, I told them that I didn't know where she was, which was the truth, and I told them that Mr. BMW been around at least once before. At that point, one of the cops smacked me and call me a fucking liar. So I just shut up after that.*

DS: *You know where the cops were from? Local Atlantic City or from the prosecutor's office?*

LF: *A cop's a cop. They don't wear no uniforms. I don't know where they from.*

DS: *When did you go to Vegas?*

LF: *Couple days after I'm busted, some pastor come in from some church saying he wants to help me redeem my soul and he got me a job working at a hotel in Vegas. All I got to do is say yes and they going to drop the prostitution charges, fly me to Vegas, give me five hundred dollars, and I can start work as a cleaning lady. Sounds good to me. So I said yes.*

DS: *You still working there?*

LF: *(laughter) No, lasted a month. Back on the street. At least it's not cold here.*

DS: *I'd like to come out and talk with you. How can I reach you?*

LF: *(long pause) Call 702-396-0023 and tell the person who answers to have me call. Why do you want to meet with me? I told you everything I know.*

DS: *You might be helpful to Sharise's case. We may need you as a witness.*

LF: *Um . . . look, Sharise is like a baby sister to me, but I don't think I can help. The pastor who helped me, he warn me not to come back to Jersey.*

DS: *Okay, let's see what happens.*

LF: Listen, tell Sharise I said to take care of herself. I gotta go. Bye.
DS: Thank you. Bye.

Sharise looked up from the papers. They found Lenore, or Lenore had found them. Other than Tonya, Lenore was the only other person in her life whom she had ever trusted.

"She's lying. He didn't know about me."

"Sharise, we're trying to help you. We think she's telling the truth," McCabe added. "Lenore has no reason to lie and it all fits."

"You two are crazy. Whose side are you on? Are you trying to get me locked up forever? I told you what happened. He found out I was trans and he flipped out."

"Why was his semen on your underwear?" Swisher asked. "You said all you did was give him a blow job. Forensics found two sets of seminal fluid on your underwear—yours and his."

"What?" she asked, her eyes narrowing.

"Sharise, more went on in that room than a blow job. He knew about you, and if we get a hit on the DNA, everything makes sense."

"Yeah, and if you don't, what happens then? Lenore ain't ever coming in as a witness. The girl's no fool. You heard her. She be told to stay away from Jersey."

"You don't know that. Duane is going to go out and meet with her. She may come."

Sharise laughed. "Great, then we have two Black trans whores against one dead rich white boy. I still don't like those odds." She slid the papers back in Duane's direction. "Let's see what happens with your motion. Until then, he found out and he tried to kill me. That's what happened."

"We have a problem."

"What's wrong?"

"One of the coworkers is talking to Swisher."

"You told me all the coworkers were out of the picture."

"I was assured they were."

"Do we know which one is talking?"

"Yes."

"So . . ."

"It will be taken care of."

"Thank you."

CHAPTER 13

"WHAT THE FUCK ARE THEY UP TO?" LEE DEMANDED, snatching the reading glasses off his face and throwing them on his desk. "This is bullshit!"

Barbara knew better than to interrupt him when he was on one of his rants. She also suspected that his current diatribe had more to do with the fact that he would have to let Will Townsend know about the motion rather than with its potential merits. Lee, after all, was a politician, not a career prosecutor, and upsetting Will Townsend was not something he could afford to do.

Finally, after several more expletive-laced sentences, he paused. "Well?"

"It's framed as a discovery motion, but what they're really asking the court to do is order that Bill Townsend's DNA, which was collected at the scene, be run through the CODIS system to determine if his DNA is already in the system as an unknown perpetrator."

"Jesus Christ, Barbara, put that in English, please."

"What they're claiming is that Townsend attacked Barnes.

Based on that, and the fact that the owner of the motel allegedly said Bill may have been involved in a previous attack on a prostitute, they want Townsend's DNA run through the system as a potential suspect in other crimes."

"Wait? They're claiming Townsend may be in the system because he was a criminal?"

She nodded.

He sat there shaking his head. "We can't let that happen," he said, his voice so soft that she wasn't sure if he was talking to her or himself. "Do you think there's any chance Reynolds will allow this?"

"I don't know, Lee. In an attempt to be fair, she might order us to submit Townsend's DNA as a potential suspect to see if there are any hits."

"I can't let that happen. You know what's going to happen when Will finds out about this motion; he'll go batshit crazy. Sweet Jesus, my career will be over if that happens."

"Lee, even if she granted the motion, I can't imagine there's anything to worry about."

He studied her for several seconds before reaching over and picking up his reading glasses from where they had landed on the desk, his demeanor suddenly calm and deliberate. "You're right," he said, pursing his lips, "but Will and Sheila shouldn't have to put up with this crap. It's not bad enough they lost their son, now they have to have these two suggesting he's a criminal? It's wrong. Go ahead and have the appropriate response prepared and I'll deal with the rest."

God, there are times when I hate this job, Bob Redman thought, resigned to what he had to do. He needed the Barnes case like he needed a hole in the head. After all, he was the presiding judge of the Criminal Division of the Ocean County court, and had certainly earned his battle stripes over the years.

Still, he knew better than to argue with Carol Clarke, the top judge in the county, who had told him that a few private phone calls had been made to her "suggesting" that Judge Reynolds might not be the right judge to handle the case and he should take over.

When his clerk announced that Anita Reynolds had arrived, he pasted a smile on his face and walked to the door of his chambers to greet her.

"Morning, Bob," she said, giving him a small hug. "Happy Friday. How are things this morning?"

He walked back behind his desk. "No complaints," he said, not meaning a word of it.

"What's up? You don't generally invite me down unless I've messed something up," she offered with a small laugh.

"Anita, I'm probably going to make your day. I just met with Carol, and she suggested to me that I take over the Barnes case." He held up his hand to stop her from saying anything. "Hear me out," he said firmly. "You are one of my best judges. You consistently get good ratings from lawyers and litigants alike, which is pretty hard to do on the criminal bench. You've been on the bench for six years, which means next year you're up for reappointment and tenure. I know you're a Republican, you haven't caused any major problems, you're highly rated, which means the governor will look to his fellow Republican senators to see if any of them object to you being reappointed. And who's every one of them going to look to? Senator William Townsend. Anita, you make one decision he doesn't like in this case, and your chances for reappointment vanish. I can't afford to lose you. You're a good judge. You're what, forty-four?"

"Forty-seven," she answered with a grin, suspecting he missed on purpose.

"My point is, you have a long judicial career ahead of you. Presiding judge or even the Appellate Division is almost certainly in your future. But I know you, and you're not going to bend over backward to rule the way Senator Townsend wants you to rule. You're going to call it exactly the way you see it. And you know that sooner or later Townsend is going to be unhappy with one of those rulings and there goes your career," he said, snapping his fingers for emphasis.

"Bob, I appreciate what you're telling me. It's not like I haven't thought about the scenario you describe—I piss off Senator Townsend and my career is over. But I'm a judge. If I'm any good at this job, I have to call them the way I see them, and if that ends my career, it ends my career."

"And that's exactly why I'm pulling this case from you. I have tenure. Will Townsend can't end my career. In another year, you'll get reappointed, get your tenure, and you won't have to worry about the Townsends of the world. If I'm still the PJ then, I'll give you all the hard cases. How's that? But for now, trust me, I'm doing you a favor."

"Jesus, Bob—I haven't even had time to screw this one up. We only did the arraignment a little over a month ago." She paused and looked at him, a quizzical look on her face. "Did Carol get a call on the CODIS motion?"

He nodded.

"We got it on Wednesday and I looked at it last night. I have to give these two lawyers credit. Interesting motion."

"You know how you'd rule on it?" Redman asked.

"No, I haven't had time for Cara, my law clerk, to do any research on it. It's not scheduled until mid-November. It may be a stretch based on one alleged incident to put the victim's DNA into CODIS, but if the victim had been a twenty-eight-year-old convenience store clerk, wouldn't we just say, 'What the hell, why not?' Or if the victim was Black and the defendant white . . ." She let that hang in the air. "I don't know, Bob. I'd hate to think I'd come up with a different result because of who the victim's father is."

"That's why I have to get you off this case. You wouldn't change your mind based on who the victim's father is."

"We can't do that, Bob. The defendant is entitled to a fair trial."

"And I'll give him a fair trial."

"Her."

"Her?"

Anita chuckled. "You better get used to it. The defendant thinks she's a woman; her lawyer thinks she's a woman too. It's a whole new world out there, Robert. You still sure you want this case?"

He inhaled deeply. "I never said I wanted this case. I said I was taking it to prevent you from ending your career. Trust me, if Carol hadn't insisted that I take it myself, there are one or two of our colleagues I'd happily give the case to and watch them end their careers."

"Now, now."

"I'm joking, of course," he said with a wink. He stood, signaling their meeting was over. He walked her toward the door of his chambers. "Someday, you'll thank me for this," he offered with a half smile.

She returned the smile. "I do appreciate you thinking of my career, Bob. Honestly, I do. I wish you didn't have to, but I do understand how things work."

As she walked out, he turned to his law clerk. "Greg, I'm taking over the Barnes case. Here's a motion requesting the victim's DNA be run through the database to see if he was involved in any other crimes. First, do an order sua sponte, sealing the record on this. Then call defense counsel and Barbara Taylor over at the prosecutor's office and tell them I'm scheduling oral argument on the motion on Friday, November 17 at three p.m. Then I want you to prepare a bench memo for me denying the motion."

"Yes, Judge. Um, are there any particular grounds that you have in mind for denying it?"

"That's why I hire bright young lawyers like you, Gregory. I give you the result I want, you find me the way to get there without being reversed by my distinguished colleagues on the Appellate Division. Any other questions?"

"No, Judge. Got it."

"Oh, there's one other motion. Defense counsel wants me to

move the defendant, who's a man, to the women's correctional institution. I don't think you'll have to do too much heavy lifting to deny that one."

Greg chuckled. "No, Judge. I think I can handle that one."

"Lee faxed this over to me this morning."

Townsend handed the papers to Michael, who read through them.

"Do you believe these idiots didn't take the plea offer? For Christ's sake, we actually offered him a chance at parole, not that he ever would have gotten it. What the hell are they trying to prove?" Will turned and snatched the papers back from Michael and began pacing his office. "I don't like where this is going." He stopped pacing and turned so he was facing Michael. "This is different from what Whitick got the call on, correct?"

"Yes, that dealt with a partial match. What they're seeking in this motion is to have Bill's complete DNA profile put into the system."

"Whitick took care of the partial?"

"Yes, I'm assured by both him and Lee that it was pulled out of the system and the particulars were not disclosed to anyone."

"Good."

"How do you want to handle this?" Michael asked.

"Lee and I agree we need a new judge, someone a little more seasoned. Bob Redman is going to take it over."

Townsend plopped down behind his desk and stared at Michael. They had been through a lot together all the way back to 'Nam, when he had saved Gardner's career. Gardner had been leading a couple of platoons to a village to pick up some suspected Viet Cong. It was supposed to be a walk in the park. Just outside the village they were ambushed and Gardner lost five men. From what Townsend later learned, Gardner lost it and ordered the village burned to the ground. The final count of enemy killed was over seventy-five. Townsend had risked his own career to make sure that it was never reported that fifty of the Viet Cong killed were actually women and children. After he left the military, Gardner had gone to law school and then went to work for the government; first at the CIA and then the NSA. Throughout Townsend had stayed in touch and when Gardner retired, Townsend had taken him on as his attorney and fixer. Not only could he be trusted, but his years at the CIA and NSA had taught him how to read between the lines.

"Look, we need to get these two pains in the ass off the case and have Barnes take the fucking deal. Obviously, all the press about McCabe being transgendered hasn't deterred them. Let's exploit the investigation of the other one and put a little of the fear of God into them. Nothing extreme at this point, but I trust your discretion."

Michael nodded. "Understood."

"Is the other situation resolved?"

"In the works."

"Good. Thanks."

CHAPTER 14

*E*RIN HAD MISSED HER NEPHEWS' GAMES THE PAST TWO WEEKS, but in her absence the Cobras had continued their winning ways. Today, with them playing only five miles from home, she had carved out time to get to their quarterfinal game against the Colonia FC Cannon at Colonia's home fields.

She had positioned herself amongst the Colonia fans, hoping to avoid being spotted by Liz or Sean. The game was evenly matched from the start, so it was no surprise when it ended tied at nil-nil. The winner of the match would now be decided by penalty kicks.

The tension was almost unbearable as each player walked to the spot to take their shot. Standing with the Colonia crowd, she could only breathe a sigh of relief when both Patrick and Brennan made their PKs. The score stood at 4–3 as the Princeton player walked up to take his PK. If he missed, game over. If he made it, the PKs would continue. When he hit the ball it looked perfect, but whether it just had too much spin on it, or it hit something on the ground—it was hard to tell—the decided clang of the ball hitting the metal post was audible across the field, and all the Princeton players and fans watched in horror as the ball bounced off the post away from the goal. Game over. The Cannon players raced out onto the field, whooping and hollering, knowing next week they'd be playing in the semifinal of the State Cup. All the Princeton player could do was hang his head and head back to his teammates gathered at midfield.

Looking down the sidelines, she quickly determined that to try to walk out now past the Princeton fans would be risking being spotted by Sean or Liz, so she decided to wait, concealed amongst the celebrating Colonia fans.

Slowly the Princeton fans and players began the tedious trek to their cars, parents hugging players, players gesturing, probably complaining about a call that didn't go their way, a missed opportunity. She waited, lingering amongst the Colonia fans.

When it appeared that the entire Princeton contingent had made it to the parking lot, she felt safe to take her leave. She was about halfway to the parking lot when she saw her nephews coming back through the gates of the complex, heading toward her. *What are they doing?* She stopped, preparing to turn and head back to the safety of the Colonia crowd, when both Brennan and Patrick started running toward her. "Aunt Erin," Patrick called out.

Their pace quickened, and they started waving to her. "Aunt Erin," they called in unison.

She froze. Standing there, she watched, baffled by what was unfolding in front of her. Their tempo slowed as they grew closer, smiles apparent on both of their faces. As they reached her they threw their arms around her, each taking a different side to hug.

"Guys, what are you doing? Where are your mom and dad?"

Patrick spoke up. "We told them that you were at the game, and since we didn't know when we'd see you again, we said we were coming back to see you."

"We don't care if you're our aunt now, you've always been at our soccer games. We missed you, Aunt Erin," Brennan added.

She bent down and wrapped her arms around both of them, and she found herself choking back tears. "Guys, it's so great to see you, but I don't want you to get in trouble with your parents."

"Don't worry, they're not in trouble," a familiar woman's voice responded.

She looked up to see Liz and Sean standing about ten feet away, taking in the family reunion happening in front of them. She tried not to stare at her brother, the brother she had always idolized, the brother she knew she could never match.

Her nephews each grabbed an arm and began herding Erin forward. When only a few feet separated them, she smiled sheepishly. "Hi, Liz. Hi, Sean," she said.

Liz took a few steps forward and gave her a hug. "Hi, Erin. Nice to finally see you."

Brennan left Erin's side and scooted over to his dad; taking his hand, he began tugging him toward the others.

"Hello," he offered.

"Hi," she replied.

"Looks like my kids are a lot more resilient than I gave them credit for."

"You shouldn't be surprised; they have pretty special parents," she said with a crooked grin.

He shrugged. "How are you?"

"I'm good. You?"

"Good. I'm good." He hesitated. He looked down at his sons, both of them staring intently at him. "Nice to see you," he finally offered.

"Thanks," she said, the tears sliding down her cheeks, "it's good to see all of you too."

"Does this mean Aunt Erin can come have lunch with us?" Brennan asked with a mix of youthful exuberance and innocence.

Liz looked at her husband and then down at her son and smiled. "If she'd like to. We'd love to have her join us. And maybe while we're there, you and your brother can explain to your dad how Aunt Erin knew where you were playing today," she responded, but with a look that betrayed she already knew the answer.

They all turned their attention to Sean. "Umm, would you like to join us?" he finally asked. "There's a little pizza place right in the strip mall around the front near Home Depot. We were just going to grab something there."

She looked down at her nephews, their faces displaying their pleas, and then up at her brother. "You sure it's okay?"

Sean nodded.

"I'd love to," she answered with a tentative smile. "And I hope both of you," she continued, her gaze falling back on Brennan and Patrick, "will tell me how you learned to take PKs the way you did. You guys were awesome."

They slowly began making their way toward the pizzeria. "Why don't you guys run ahead and get us a table for five. I think it could get crowded," Sean said to his sons.

After they took off, Sean turned to Erin. "How did you know about the game?"

Erin hesitated, not wanting to get the boys in trouble. But before she could say anything, Liz interjected. "It's okay, Erin, I know the boys reached out to you."

Erin couldn't hide her surprise. "You do?"

"Yeah, despite the boys' confidence that they're better on computers than their parents, they're only half right," she said with a chuckle, looking in Sean's direction.

"I'm totally confused," Sean offered.

Erin looked at Liz, who nodded. "Back before the first game, the boys e-mailed me and invited me. I've been at two other games before today."

"The boys invited you?" Sean asked.

"Yeah, they found my firm and e-mailed me, asking me to come."

Sean looked at Liz. "You knew he . . . umm, sorry," he said, giving Erin a quick glance, "she was at the games and you didn't tell me? Why?"

Liz raised her eyebrows. "Because you were being such an idiot about the whole thing, I figured I'd let it play out."

"I guess I deserve that," he mumbled.

Erin smiled at Liz. They had always gotten along, but now she had a feeling she was going to have a much closer relationship with her. "Do you mind if I ask how you knew?" she asked Liz.

Liz suddenly had a very sheepish look. "I was the one who set up their e-mail accounts and when I did, I had it send me a blind CC of all their e-mails. I mean, you can't be too careful. There're all kinds of whacky people out there."

They walked along in silence, when suddenly Sean stopped and grabbed Liz's arm. "You set up my e-mail account too. Do you get copies of my e-mails?"

Liz gave him a devilish grin. "Do you really think I'd do that to you?" she said innocently.

Erin looked at her older brother and wasn't sure she had ever seen him as flummoxed as he appeared at that moment, and the best part was it appeared to have distracted him from being with her. Reaching back into their past, she pulled out a line that they would sometimes use when a conversation became awkward. "So, how about those Yankees," she said innocently.

CHAPTER 15

*A*NDREW BARONE'S HAND INSTINCTIVELY REACHED OUT AND hit the snooze button before he realized it wasn't the alarm, it was the phone ringing. "Hello?" he answered as he wrestled the headset up to his mouth.

"Sounds like I woke you."

"No," he said, recognizing Ed Champion's voice on the other end. "I had to get up to answer the phone. What time is it?"

"Six thirty."

"Six thirty? It's fucking Sunday morning. Somebody better be dead. What's going on?"

"You need to get up and go buy the Sunday papers."

"I get them delivered. Why? What's happening?"

"I'll just read you the headline: LAWYER FOR MURDER SUSPECT UNDER JUSTICE DEPARTMENT INVESTIGATION FOR ESPIONAGE LEAK."

He was suddenly awake. "What? About Swisher?"

"Uh-huh."

"Who ran that article?"

"That one is in the *Times*."

"What do you mean that one? There's more than one?"

"Yup, there are articles in three other papers."

"Fuck! Where the hell did they get that story?"

"Don't know. But apparently your leak investigation has a leak."

"Any indication Swisher is the source?"

"Nah, the article is designed to embarrass Swisher. It talks about how Swisher was believed to be the source of the leak concerning the FBI secretly wiretapping Muslims after 9/11 and that's why he left the FBI."

"Fuck. Can't anybody keep a fucking secret?"

"Apparently not."

"Perna didn't write the *Times* article, did he?"

"No, Cynthia Neill. Don't know her. You?"

"No. Any thoughts on who the source is?"

He laughed. "You're joking, right? I mean, I know you boys in Justice like to think you're conducting this quiet little clandestine investigation of Swisher, but nearly everybody in Newark knows something's going on. Christ, three years ago you guys turned our office and the Bureau's Newark office upside down. Most people thought Swisher was a good agent who was railroaded. And it's no secret that your guys began sniffing around again when Perna's book came out. So it could be anybody."

"So why the article? Obviously someone doesn't like him."

"The murder case that's referred to in the article . . ."

"Yeah."

"The victim was the son of a very prominent New Jersey politician."

"Wait! The case involving Will Townsend's kid who was murdered by a prostitute."

"That would be the one."

"I don't follow. What's the connection between the murder case and the leak investigation?"

"Not sure there is one. But Swisher is one of the lawyers representing the murder suspect, and Townsend is not someone to mess with."

"Tell me about it," he replied, his tone betraying his weariness. "So what are you suggesting, Townsend is trying to neutralize Swisher?"

"No idea. I haven't followed the murder case at all. Spending most of my time on Jersey Sting, seeing how many politicians we can nail on corruption charges. I know they've tried to hook Townsend into that. Even had a snitch approach him while wearing a wire."

"Any luck on that?"

"Not yet, but not for want of trying. I mean, what better way for the boss to clear the road to the statehouse than by knee-capping the biggest pol in your own party? One way to eliminate competition."

"A word of advice, don't stick your neck out on that one. Mr. Townsend has plenty of friends in this town. He was campaign chair in New Jersey and almost delivered the state."

"Oh, trust me, I know. He has plenty of friends up here too."

"Okay, back to our friend Mr. Swisher. Let me check with OPR. They have a wire up on him. I'll see if they've picked up any chatter."

"Sounds like a plan."

"And just a heads-up, once I tell the Deputy Attorney General about the leak of the leak investigation, I'm sure he'll tell me to bust Swisher's balls."

"Thanks. I'll expect a call."

"Good. I'll be in touch."

"You want me to do anything else?"

"No, sit tight until you hear from me."

"You got it. I can do nothing with the best of them."

Erin sped toward Scotch Plains. Corrine had called just before nine a.m., her voice vacillating somewhere between concern and full-blown panic. Duane had gone out for bagels and the Sunday papers at seven thirty, and he wasn't back or answering his cell. Then, fifteen minutes ago, Ben had called and told Corrine that it was important Duane call back as soon as possible.

Erin had called Ben as soon as she got to her car, and they compared notes as she drove. The whole thing seemed crazy to her, but Ben's best guess was that the FBI had picked Duane up to question him about the article. They agreed that Ben would reach out to Ed Champion, the First Assistant United States Attorney, whom Ben knew, and Erin would see what she could find out in Scotch Plains.

She found Duane's car parked on a side street a few blocks from the house. She called Corrine to let her know Ben's theory, then stopped at the store to pick up the *Times* so she could read the article. After skimming, she called Ben.

"I found the car," she said.

"I found Duane," Ben replied.

"Where?"

"Exactly where I thought he was. I'm on my way to get him now."

"You want me to meet you someplace?"

"No, I'm meeting Champion at the FBI office in Newark. Once I get Duane, I'll meet you at his house. You go and let Corrine know what's going on and make sure she's okay."

Two hours later, Ben and Duane walked through the back door into the kitchen, where Corrine and Erin were sitting at the table. Corrine immediately jumped up and hugged him. When they finally broke their embrace, he looked over at Erin and shook his head.

"Hey, big guy," Erin said before he could say anything. "Since you got lost going for bagels, I picked some up. Help yourself," she added, pointing to the bag on the counter. "I also picked you up a copy of the *Times*, *Mirror*, and *Herald*. Not every day your partner is the top of page six in the *Times*. Guess you weren't happy that I was the only one getting all the bad publicity in this case. Wanted to share in the limelight." She paused, looking at both Duane and Ben, waiting for them to say something. Finally, tired of their silence, she said, "So . . ."

"Honest, E," Duane began while pouring himself a cup of coffee, "Ben and I have been discussing it the whole way here. I guess we all know who had the stories planted, but why?"

"He's trying to run us off so he can get someone in who will be just looking to plead her out."

Duane cocked his head to the side. "Don't you think you're giving us too much credit? I mean we're not exactly the dream team. Why get rid of us? There are plenty of other good lawyers out there."

"The motion. I think your gut was right. Young Mr. Townsend went there to kill her, and we just kicked the hornet's nest with our motion."

"Do you mind if I ask what the hell you're talking about?" interjected Ben. "If I'm hearing you right, you think Bill Townsend picked up your client with the intent of killing hi—er, killing her?"

Erin looked at Duane and they both shrugged. "Yeah, that's our theory," she finally replied. "We want his DNA run through CODIS."

Ben studied both of them. "I'm sorry, Corrine, please don't take this the wrong way, but I'd like to speak to Duane and Erin privately. Is there someplace we can talk?" he asked Duane.

"No, you stay here," Corrine responded. "I'm going to take Austin upstairs for his nap."

After Corrine left the room, Ben stared at them, rubbing his hand across his forehead. "You filed a motion claiming Townsend attempted to murder your client and that he's murdered before?"

Erin inhaled, her stomach churning. Ben was the best criminal defense lawyer she knew and she did not like the way he sounded. "Yeah," she replied, a catch in her voice.

"You realize Townsend is one of the most powerful men in the state. If you're right, or even if he's worried that you may be right about his son, he will stop at nothing to make sure the truth never surfaces."

"Ben, I'm not sure what you're suggesting we should have done," she said. "I mean, what if we're right and Townsend tried to kill our client? She's looking at thirty years. Are we just supposed to tell her to plead guilty?"

"No," he replied softly. "I would never tell you that. You absolutely have to do everything you can to save your client. I get that. But I know Townsend." Ben stopped and took a deep breath. "Don't underestimate what this man is capable of, and watch your backs. I'm worried for both of you." He paused. "And for your client. You've seen that Townsend can get what he wants in the papers, and I'm sure you know there's more than a few members of the judiciary that owe their spot on the bench to his largesse. But bad press and bad judges aren't what worry me. You're both good lawyers with your whole careers ahead of you, and you're poking one very big bear with one very short stick."

It was late when Erin finally got back to her building. After Ben left, she hung out with Swish, Cori, and Austin, watching the Giants lose on a last-minute field goal, and then stayed for some take-out Chinese.

Climbing the stairs, she replayed the events of the day—weird, even by her standards. As she reached the top of the stairs she stopped abruptly. She reached in her purse and pulled out her cell phone and pepper spray, her hand shaking.

"Nine-one-one, what's the emergency?"

"Yes, operator. My name is Erin McCabe. I live at 27A North Avenue." She paused. "I just arrived at my apartment and there is a threatening note pinned to my apartment door with a knife."

"Is there anyone in the apartment now?"

"I don't know, but based on the note on the door, I doubt it. But I won't go in until there's an officer here with me."

"Where are you now, Ms. McCabe?"

"Standing just outside the apartment door."

"All right. Perhaps you should move outside the building. I'll have an officer there momentarily to check it out for you."

"Thank you."

She studied the note stuck to the door with a switchblade, a switchblade similar to the one Sharise had described. There was also a substance that appeared to be blood both on the blade of the knife and on the paper itself. The note was typed and printed. It was in all capital letters.

SORRY I MISSED YOU
BUT DON'T WORRY I'LL BE BACK
I WANT TO FIND OUT IF YOU HAVE A CUNT NOW
AND IF YOU DO
WANT TO MAKE SURE IT GETS SOME USE

Before she put the phone away, she switched it to camera mode and took several pictures of the note. She knew the note itself would be confiscated as evidence, so she wanted to be able to show Swish. When she was finished, she turned and headed back down the steps as fast as she could. By the time she got to the outside door, a police car was pulling up to the curb, its lights flashing. She stepped outside and the officer got out and walked up onto the sidewalk.

"You just call nine-one-one?" the officer inquired.

"Yes, Officer," Erin replied, pleasantly surprised by the fact that the officer was a woman who, at about five foot seven, looked like she could take care of herself. "My name's Erin McCabe. There's a threatening note on my apartment door."

"Have you gone into the apartment?"

"No," Erin responded. "But when you see the apartment door, I suspect you'll understand why."

"Okay. Where is the apartment?"

"Two flights up"—Erin hesitated, looking at the officer's name tag—"Officer Montinelli."

"Can I see some ID, Ms. McCabe, to confirm you live here?" After writing down some information from the license, Montinelli handed it back to Erin. "Okay, wait here and I'll check it out. Is the door locked?"

"It should be, but I didn't try it." She reached into her purse and handed Montinelli the key.

"Any pets?" Montinelli asked.

"No," Erin replied.

About ten minutes later, Montinelli returned and handed Erin her key. "No one's in there now," Montinelli said, "but your apartment was definitely broken into. Let me call it in and then we can go back up together so you can look around; just don't touch anything."

Erin looked on as Montinelli radioed headquarters. "Dispatch, 302."

"Yeah, 302, this is Crammer. What do you have?"

"Looks like a B and E with a threatening note pinned to the door with a six-inch switchblade."

"What's your 10-20?"

"27 North Avenue, third floor. Better get a forensics team over here to take a look at the place and the note."

"Okay, I'll get some help over there."

"Ten-four."

"Hi, Swish, it's Erin. Sorry to bother you, but someone paid my apartment a visit today while I was with you and I need a place to stay tonight . . . No, I'm okay. I'll explain when I get there. But between what happened to you today and this, we need to talk, because they're really starting to piss me off."

CHAPTER 16

*E*RIN COULDN'T HELP BUT WONDER IF HER NEWFOUND sense of vulnerability was some type of karmic payback for all the years she spent cross-examining the victims of her clients' crimes. How many times had she tried to impugn their testimony that the feelings of being violated had lasted long after the crime was over? Now, she understood how someone invading your space warped your sense of security, instilling fear in the exact place where you should feel the most secure—your own home.

Sunday night she stayed with Swish and Cori as the police searched her apartment for clues. Monday afternoon she met with two detectives, one from Cranford PD and the other from the Union County Prosecutor's Office. She knew the guy from the county, Nick Conti, from her days as a public defender. Of course, she had been Ian then, and Detective Conti had not seemed real enthused about becoming reacquainted.

Other than determining that whoever had broken in had come up the fire escape and entered by breaking her bedroom window, they found nothing—no fingerprints, no hair, no nothing, which suggested it was done by a pro. Not that it was that hard to get into her place. The fire escape was off a deserted back alley filled with Dumpsters, and it certainly wasn't hard to get up the fire escape without being seen or heard, especially since the other apartment in the building was currently vacant.

She told them that it had to be related to the Barnes case, if for no other reason than the note was pinned to the door with a switchblade that was almost identical to the one that killed Townsend. They listened politely and then condescendingly dismissed her "theory," arguing that it was more likely someone who had read one of the newspaper articles had been demented enough to assault her. When she pointed out that they thought the person who did it was a pro, they appeared unimpressed by her logic. When she finally realized that they weren't going to do any further investigation, Erin had them make her copies of the police reports and left.

Following her interview with the detectives, Swish prevailed on her to stay with them Monday night, to give her landlord time on Tuesday to install alarms and a new tempered glass window. As she was getting ready to head home on Tuesday, Duane stopped by her office. "Why don't you find a new place? You're welcome to stay with us while you look."

She gave her partner a sardonic grin. "If whoever did this comes looking for me again, they'll just come at me a different way. We're always protecting against the last threat, while the bad guys are already working on a different plan. I'll be okay. But I think we need to get a security system installed at the office."

"Agreed."

"And I'm worried about you and Cori. I don't know how crazy this bastard is, but you heard Ben. 'He'll stop at nothing.' You have Austin to think about."

"We're okay. Cori got a carry permit back when I was with the Bureau, and truth be told, she's a better shot than I am." Swish ran his lower lip between his thumb and forefinger. "Listen, I know how you feel about handguns, but you may want to think about looking into one."

"Swish, you and I both know that a handgun is going to do squat for me. By the time I actually got to a gun, I'd be toast."

His brow wrinkled as he closed his eyes, but he didn't argue with her. "You headed home now?" he finally asked.

"Yeah."

"I'm coming with you. Just let me grab something and I'll meet you out front."

"What's that?" she asked as they walked toward her apartment.

"It will let me know if there're any listening devices in your apartment."

"Really?" she said with a look of disbelief.

As they walked up the stairs, he told her to look around to see if anything was amiss, something the police wouldn't notice, but to carry on a normal conversation. As he did a sweep of her room looking for listening devices, she began looking around.

"Oh my God, what a sick fuck!" she said, her voice tinged with disgust and anger.

"What?"

She held up a large dildo for Swish to see. "This is not mine," she said. "Jesus Christ, what sick bastards. They not only break into my apartment, but they go into my underwear drawer and leave me a dildo."

Duane nodded and continued using the device in his hand, moving from her bathroom to the living room and then into the bedroom. As he approached the phone on her night table, the lights on the gadget began to flash. He motioned for her to keep talking as he unscrewed the headset. He then straightened up, checked out a lamp, and made his way to the kitchen. This time he took the wall phone off of the base unit and watched as the meter on his device lit up like a Christmas tree.

When he finished walking around the apartment, he pointed to the door and said, "I don't see anything other than your new sex toy. How about we grab a cup of coffee? I still think you should stay with us tonight."

She nodded to indicate she understood. "No to a continued stay at Chez Swisher, but coffee's on me as thanks for your hospitality."

They walked across the street and settled into her now-familiar table in the back.

"There are two, both on your phones. They're activated when you're on the phone. They won't pick up conversations in the apartment. So just be careful and don't use your landline, unless you want someone to listen in."

"Why bug my phones?" she asked, taking a sip from her coffee.

"I guess just to keep tabs on you." He suddenly stopped, and his expression showed equal amounts anger and concern.

"What?" she asked.

"Shit, how fucking stupid can I be?"

"The office," she said.

"If they bugged your phones, I'm sure they have the office wired."

"Oh shit . . ."

"Lenore," he said, finishing her thought. "She called me at the office."

"You have the number she gave you?"

He flipped open his phone, scrolling his contacts. "Got it," he said.

The call went straight to a generic voice mail. "Yeah, my name is Duane Swisher. I'm an attorney in New Jersey. Lenore Fredericks gave me this number to call if I ever needed to reach her. I need to speak to her. It's urgent. Please have her call me at 908-555-0137 as soon as possible. That's my cell number. Please tell her not to call my office number. Thank you."

"Fuck," he mumbled under his breath when he hung up. "Why the hell didn't I think of this earlier?"

"Swish, don't beat yourself up. We don't even know if there are any bugs in the office. I've been doing this for almost ten years and would never think of someone tapping me. It's un-heard of. So let's not jump to any conclusions."

"Yeah, but we're playing a different game in this case."

"How long ago since you talked to her?"

He paused for a moment. "We filed the motion ten days ago, so a week before that . . . two and a half weeks."

"Look, they only broke in and bugged me on Sunday, so maybe we're okay."

"Maybe, but my guess is bugging you was an afterthought. We both know the main reason was to scare the shit out of you."

"Mission accomplished," she said.

He pushed his chair back from the table. "If the office is bugged, I need to know and find a way to reach Lenore as quickly as possible."

"I'll go with you," she offered, and followed him out of Legal Grounds.

Two hours later, they sat in Ben's office, Duane having swept it as soon as they got there following the discovery of bugs in their own offices and phones.

Ben laced his hands together behind his head and leaned back in his chair. "Look, you're assuming the bugs in your office are in connection with the Townsend case. There is the possibility that the feds are listening as part of the leak case."

"You know better, Ben," Duane replied. "If it was pursuant to a court order, they wouldn't have put bugs in the phone. They'd just go to the phone company and listen in on a wire. We had bugs in the phone headset, in each of our offices, and in the con-ference room."

"Yeah, but you're assuming that your buddies at DOJ are play-ing by the rules."

Duane shook his head. "No, the leak investigation is being handled out of DC. They may be pricks, but they generally play by the rules."

"Ben, do me a favor, search Lenore Fredericks and see if you get any hits," Erin asked.

Ben turned around and typed her name into Yahoo and waited. He scrolled down the list of results and shook his head. "Nothing."

"Thanks," she said, relieved.

"I need to try and find Lenore," Duane said. "Ben, is it okay if I make a call from your conference room? Right now your office is the only place I know that's clean."

"Sure."

Erin was brushing her teeth when she heard her cell phone ring. "Hey, what's up?"

"She's dead."

"What?"

"Lenore's dead."

Erin slowly slid down the wall until she was sitting on the bathroom floor. "How do you know?"

"Spoke to an agent I know at the Vegas field office. He's the one I called from Ben's. He just called me back. Came in as a Jane Doe, two weeks ago. Vegas PD were able to ID her through her fingerprints."

"Cause of death?"

"A fall from the roof of a twenty-story building."

"Oh shit," she said slowly, almost silently. She inhaled deeply and tried to collect her thoughts. "Any suspects?"

"Vegas PD ruled it a suicide."

"What!" she screamed. "How can that be? That's wrong."

"From what my friend told me, there were no witnesses and the ME did a quickie on her and didn't see any visible signs of foul play."

"How the hell could they find signs of foul play if she was just thrown off a twenty-story building?"

"It'll be another fifteen to twenty days before they get a toxicology report, but I'm willing to bet it comes back positive for heroin. Juice her up, take her up to the roof, and throw her off. End of witness."

Erin started to cry. She didn't know Lenore, had never even spoken to her, but now she was dead and the only thing she had done to end up dead was call Swish to help Sharise. All Erin could picture was this helpless woman, arms flailing as she tried desperately to fly before she hit the ground.

"I'm sorry, Swish. I don't know what to say." She reached up and pulled some toilet paper off the roll and blew her nose.

"We're overmatched, E. They're playing us. They're in the pros and we're the high school JV. And if somehow we manage to keep the score close, they'll just end the game. Sharise will end up just like Lenore—dead. And what really sucks is that there's not a fucking thing we can do to stop it."

"We need a plan."

"Yeah, well, good luck with that one. Kind of hard to have a plan when the other guy has all the cards and makes all the rules."

After they hung up, Erin couldn't find the willpower to get off the bathroom floor. The exhaust fan continued to hum as she sat with her arms propped against her knees, holding her head in her hands. The pieces were there—she was just too exhausted to figure out how to put them all together. The phone taps, Lenore's death, the newspaper articles, it was all there, but if she went to the prosecutor, it would go nowhere or, worse, directly to Townsend.

CHAPTER 17

"**Y**OU LOOK LIKE HELL," ERIN'S MOTHER OFFERED.

She grimaced; her mother's directness was never in short supply. "Thanks, Mom. It's been a long few weeks."

"I guess so. You canceled breakfast two weeks in a row, and you show up this morning looking like you got three hours sleep."

"Two, but who's counting?"

Her mother's expression shifted, her eyes crinkling at the corners in concern. "I'm worried about you. What's going on?"

"We've been busy on the case, and we've run into some other issues, but before we go there, have you spoken to my brother recently?"

"Briefly. He called Sunday night to say hello."

"And?"

"And he said he saw you at the boys' soccer game and that the boys were fine with you. In fact, he said the boys were really happy to see you and brought him and Liz over to you after the game. He said he was surprised by how you looked, but you seemed to be doing well. My impression was that it was a little weird for him to see you as Erin, but that eventually he'd be fine."

"Really. What gave you that impression?"

"He said it was a little weird seeing you as Erin, but eventually he thought he'd be fine."

Erin closed her eyes and inhaled. "You're too much."

"Oh, leave me alone. I did talk to Liz for a long time and she was really happy to see you too. She said once your brother saw how easily the kids accepted you, he was actually a little embarrassed by the way he's acted. She said he's going to be fine."

"I'm glad to hear that."

"Me too. It will make Thanksgiving easier."

Erin stared quizzically at her mother. "What about Thanksgiving?"

"It will be the first time we're all together since you transitioned."

"When were you going to tell me we're doing Thanksgiving?"

"I just did."

"Maybe I have other plans," she offered, not sure if she was ready to face her father. Two years ago, he had made it painfully clear he didn't want to see her, and even if he was ready now, which she doubted, she wasn't sure if she was.

Her mother gave her the evil eye.

"What's Dad's reaction to this family reunion?" Erin inquired, still hoping there was a way out.

"No reaction. I haven't told him yet."

"Are you going to, or am I just going to show up and surprise him?"

Her mother paused momentarily, causing Erin to think she was actually contemplating that possibility. "All in good time, my dear."

"Mom, I don't want to rush you, but Thanksgiving is two weeks away."

Peg just smiled at her daughter. "Dinner's at six. Come around five for cocktails."

"So how you going to get Dad on board, beer and sex again?"

Her mother paused for a moment. "Perhaps tequila and sex."

"I didn't know Dad drank tequila."

"He doesn't. It's for me." She smiled at her daughter. "By the way, how did your date go?"

Erin dropped her head. "It didn't," she replied softly. "He canceled."

She didn't look up, but she could feel her mother looking at her. "I'm sorry, I didn't know."

"No need to apologize," Erin said, trying to sell her grimace as a grin. "You didn't know because I didn't tell you. I guess I understand why he canceled. I mean, who wants to date someone everyone knows is trans? I get it."

Her mother reached across the table and gently took her hand. "You're a beautiful woman, inside and out. And whether it's with a man or a woman, I hope with all my heart that you find someone who doesn't care about any of the other crap and loves you for who you are."

Erin bit her lip, trying to hold it together. After everything she'd been through over the last four years, she prided herself on the fact that she could deal with anything; now she wasn't so sure. Between the lack of sleep, the stress of the case, and all the bullshit going on around her, Erin felt like pieces of her were starting to crack off and fall away. Her stone façade suddenly felt like hardened clay, dissolving more every second.

She was so lost in her thoughts that she hadn't even noticed that her mother had slid into her booth. Her mother gently wrapped her arms around Erin, pulling her into her shoulder. "Seems like there's a lot more on your plate than you've been letting on. Talk to me . . . please."

Slowly, Erin began describing what had taken place over the last few weeks, sugarcoating the break-in as best she could by leaving out the note. Ultimately, she decided not to tell her about

Lenore's fall from a twenty-story building; she gave her mother enough agita as it was.

"It's been a tough few weeks," she finished. "Oh, and by the way, only call my cell. All my other phones are tapped."

Her mother stared at her long enough that Erin began to feel uncomfortable. "I'm sorry you're going through all of this," she finally said. "I'm guessing there's more than what you've told me."

"Thanks, Mom. It'll be okay."

"I suspect neither of us believe that."

"I don't think either of us has a choice," Erin replied.

Later, as Erin walked the two blocks from the restaurant to the office, she racked her brain again for options that wouldn't harm them or Sharise. If they went to the State Attorney General or the Prosecutor's Office, Townsend would likely find out, and he'd already proven himself capable of having someone murdered. So if he'd have Lenore killed, why not Sharise?

The feds didn't look like a viable alternative either. For starters, they were investigating Duane, which didn't exactly make them an attractive partner. Not to mention that the U.S. Attorney, Jim Giles, was a Republican like Townsend. But even if they could get their foot in the door, the only federal crimes she could come up with were violating Sharise's civil rights. Since Giles was a well-known social conservative, she couldn't imagine his office being bent out of shape by the sufferings of a transgender prostitute, especially when she was facing murder charges. If Townsend had them bugged, there was always the chance they could get him on violating the wiretap statute, but would Giles use it to go after Townsend? Not likely.

She had only one other idea, and to call it a long shot was charitable.

"Hey," she said, walking into Duane's office.

He looked up, his eyes vacant from lack of sleep. "Hey," he replied. "You look like shit."

"Seems to be the consensus of opinion. But talk about the pot calling the kettle. You look a little worse for wear yourself."

He tried his best to grin, but it appeared that his spirit didn't want to cooperate. "I feel worse than I look," he said, his tone both sullen and resigned.

"Come up with anything?" she asked.

"Nada," he replied. "You?"

"A long shot that requires a lot of effort on your part, but it's all I got."

"I'm listening," he offered.

"So remember the fact that there were two partial semen samples, one consistent with Sharise and the other consistent with Townsend?"

"Yeah . . ."

"Well, suppose they both went into the database as unknown samples."

A small grin formed on his face. "You're right, it would require some legwork, but . . ." He started to chuckle. "Jesus Christ, talk about long shots."

"How many murders near where he lived?"

"Six over the last five years." He turned around to his computer and brought up the spreadsheet. "Now all we have to do is hope that a suspect's DNA was recovered in one of these investigations."

"And that the DNA matches the semen found on Sharise's underwear," she added. "Because the DNA on the semen is only a partial, it won't be conclusive, but it could be enough to require Townsend's full DNA profile be put into the system. Hey," she added, as she dragged herself out of his chair, "I've always heard you were one of the best on hitting long shots."

CHAPTER 18

*T*HERE WERE TIMES WHEN ERIN WONDERED WHY SHE DECIDED to BEcome a criminal defense lawyer. Maybe it was the dream of inhabiting the world of Atticus Finch and Clarence Darrow, but the reality of being a criminal defense lawyer didn't match the quixotic legal battles conjured up by their fictional and nonfictional courtroom battles.

No, the real world of being a defense lawyer wasn't for the faint of heart, nor was it particularly great for the ego. She could count on one hand the times she had walked into a courtroom expecting to win. The deck always seemed to be stacked against her client. Sure, there were the constitutional "rights" defendants supposedly enjoyed—the right to remain silent, the right to counsel, the presumption of innocence—but did anyone ever really presume a defendant to be innocent? Then there was the matter of resources, the one thing that most of her defendants lacked. And even in a case like Sharise's, where she had resources, there were the intangibles, like judges who had been prosecutors early in their careers or who were beholden to politicians who helped get them appointed to the bench.

Just once Erin wanted to know what it felt like to have the field tilted in her favor. Looking down at her notes one last time before Judge Redman took the bench, she knew that today was not going to be that day.

Sharise was sitting next to her in her standard-issue orange jumpsuit. If they ever got to trial, Sharise would be allowed to wear normal clothes, but until then she came to court in the orange jumpsuit with *S Barnes* sewn on the back. As Erin looked at her client, she noticed that Sharise was nervously bouncing her right leg up and down, as if keeping time to a song only she could hear.

She had decided not to tell Sharise about Lenore. What good would it do? Given Sharise's feelings on her odds of surviving, why give her even more reason to think her days were numbered? Let her cling to what little hope she had that there might be a way to walk out of jail alive.

"All rise. The Superior Court of New Jersey is now in session, the Honorable Robert Redman presiding."

Redman, balding and overweight, ambled out onto the bench carrying a stack of papers. "Be seated," he intoned before he even reached the top step. He plopped the papers on the bench and slowly sat down. "Is there anyone in the courtroom that is neither an attorney nor party in *State v. Samuel Barnes?*"

Erin turned and looked over her shoulder, and noticed a very stern-looking individual sitting in the first row behind Taylor and Carmichael.

"Your Honor," Taylor began, rising to her feet. "Directly behind me is Michael Gardner. He is personal counsel for William Townsend, the victim's father. Mr. Townsend could not be here today, but he asked that his counsel be permitted to attend."

"That's fine, Ms. Taylor. All right, Bailiff, please lock the courtroom door. As counsel is aware, I previously entered an order sealing the record on this motion, and this hearing will be closed to the public, as I find that the need to protect the privacy of the victim's family from this frivolous motion far outweighs the public's right to know."

"Frivolous motion" felt like a smack in the face, yet Erin's facial expression never changed. *Make the best appellate record you can*, she reminded herself, waiting for Redman to say more.

"Appearances, please."

"Barbara Taylor and Roger Carmichael for the State, Your Honor."

"Erin McCabe for the defendant, who now goes by the name Sharise Barnes, Your Honor."

Redman removed his glasses and looked down at Erin. "Has Mr. Barnes legally changed his name, counsel?"

"No, Your Honor, not yet. We've started that process. But Judge Reynolds had agreed that, at least outside the presence of the jury, she would honor *Ms.* Barnes's new name."

"Well, counsel, in case you haven't noticed, Judge Reynolds is no longer assigned this matter, I am."

Oh, I've noticed.

"And," he continued, "it is my practice to refer to defendants by their legal name, and the one used in the indictment. So in front of me, I have Mr. Samuel Emmanuel Barnes, and that is how he will be referred to in my courtroom. Am I clear, counsel?"

"Oh, you're perfectly clear, Judge," she replied, hoping her disdain was not too obvious.

Erin sat down as Redman continued. "I have two motions. The first is to compel the prosecutor's office to submit samples of the victim's blood taken from the scene of his murder to the Combined DNA Index System, to see if the victim is in the system as a perpetrator of any offenses. The defendant has proffered that he acted in self-defense; a statement of a motel clerk, who says the victim was at the motel before; and, finally, an analysis of unsolved murders of"—he paused and indicated quotation marks with his fingers—"'transgender prostitutes' who were murdered over the last five years in locations near where the victim of this crime lived.

"The second motion is to transfer the defendant, a nineteen-year-old male, to the women's correctional facility. Defendant also asked to receive medical treatment by providing him with access to female hormones. Defendant has submitted reports from a Dr. Mary O'Connor, a medical doctor, and a Jamal Johnson, a social worker, alleging that the defendant is suffering from 'gender dysphoria' and is really a woman despite having been 'assigned male at birth.' In opposition, the State has filed a report from Dr. Sydney Singer, who examined the defendant and found him to be a biological male and delusional, in that the defendant believes he is a female despite the fact that he is, in all respects, a man. Having found the defendant to be a biological man, Dr. Singer opines that it would be inappropriate to house the defendant in a female jail, and that providing female hormones to a male would be malpractice and is neither medically necessary nor appropriate.

"First, a procedural question. Ms. Taylor, for purposes of this motion, are you representing the sheriff's office?"

"Yes, Your Honor."

"Thank you. Ms. McCabe, as I said, I have recently taken over this case, so I was not handling it early on. However, I did read press accounts at the time of the arraignment which indicated that you are also a transgender. Is that accurate?"

She hoped her sigh was not audible. She stood and looked directly at Redman. "I'm not sure why it's relevant, but yes, I am a transgender woman, Judge. The word *transgender* being an adjective, Your Honor, not a noun."

"Thank you. I want to be clear. I understand you have legally changed your name, your law license, and whatever else. So you are entitled to be addressed in this courtroom as Ms. McCabe. However, as far as your client is concerned, according to Dr. Singer, he is a biological man, meaning he has male genitalia. That's all I'm concerned about."

"How do you know that I don't, Your Honor?"

Redman looked both puzzled and annoyed by the interruption. "You don't what?"

"Have male genitalia," Erin replied.

Redman's face began to resemble his name. "What?" he intoned, his voice rising. "It's no business of mine what you have, Ms. McCabe. You are not the one in custody. Your client is a man—end of discussion. Accordingly, even if I had the authority to tell the sheriff where to house your client, which I don't think I have, I could never order the defendant transferred to the women's jail. I also agree with Dr. Singer's finding that the county is under no obligation to foot the bill for your client's delusion and provide hormones to the defendant."

"May I be heard on this, Your Honor?"

"No, I've made my ruling."

"Judge, may I at least make a proffer for purposes of appeal?"

"No, counsel. I've ruled."

"Judge—"

"Counsel, I don't want to hear another word from you, otherwise the sheriff will be deciding what jail you're going to spend the night in. I've ruled. Am I clear?"

She stared at him, her body language showing her contempt.

"Are you going to answer me, counsel?"

"Your Honor directed me not to say another word. I was just trying to follow the court's directions."

Redman glared at Erin. "If you are trying to provoke me, counsel, you're doing a very good job."

"I'm not trying at all." She paused. "Your Honor, I'm just trying to follow what I was told to do." *And fuck you and the horse you rode in on.*

Redman inhaled and then looked down at his notes. "Turning to what I'll call the CODIS motion, counsel, I'll hear you."

"Thank you, Judge," Erin said. "However, before I get to the merits, I would note for the record that in Your Honor's opening remarks, you referred to the death of Mr. Townsend as a murder and referred to him as the victim. With all due respect," she said, knowing she no longer had any respect for him, "whether or not Mr. Townsend was murdered or not is what this case is all about. Likewise, whether or not Mr. Townsend was a victim or not is part of what this motion is about. Finally, you indicated you had to protect the victim's family from this frivolous motion, which certainly seems to indicate that Your Honor has already decided the merits of the motion."

She paused and looked up at him, but he refused to make eye contact with her.

"As I hope Your Honor can appreciate," she continued, knowing there wasn't a chance in the world that he could, "my client contends that she acted in self-defense."

"He," Redman interrupted.

Erin squinted at him, confused by his interruption. "I'm sorry, Judge?"

"You referred to your client as 'she.' I have already ruled your client is a he."

A bemused smile spread across Erin's face. *Let's go at it.* "Judge, I agree you have ruled, but that doesn't change who my client is any more than stating you will treat me as a woman changes who I am. I am just as much a transgender woman as my client is. We were both assigned male at birth. The fact that I may have had the benefit of certain medical interventions doesn't elevate my status over hers. Surgeries do not make a person more or less transgender. It's what's up here," she said, pointing to the side of her head, "not what's between a person's legs that determines their gender. All that surgery can do is alter a person's outward appearance. But other than the societal affectations that we all perform every day, surgeries are unimportant to who I am and to who my client is. We are the same. So how you treat her, you have to treat me the same way. So if you are going to insist that when I refer to my client I use male pronouns that are not reflective of who *she* is, then I will insist that the court refer to me with male pronouns as well, even if it is not reflective of who I am."

Redman ran his fingers through his thinning hair and raised his eyes to the ceiling. "I'm not going to get into this now. Please continue."

Erin looked down at her notes, and as she did she noticed Sharise looking at her, smiling.

"Thank you, Judge. As I indicated, it is my client's contention that she acted in self-defense," Erin said, making sure to pound the word *she*. "Accordingly, I think Your Honor is prejudging the merits of this case. It is the defense's position that Ms. Barnes is the victim of Mr. Townsend's attempt to murder her."

Erin went through her argument with her eyes fixed on Redman, hoping for eye contact, but he made sure to stare intently at the papers in front of him and only occasionally appearing to write a note. She discussed the prior incident at the motel and the fact that wherever Townsend lived, transgender prostitutes turned up murdered.

"I'll be the first to admit that we have no definitive proof that Mr. Townsend's DNA is in CODIS," Erin continued. "But there are many reasons why it may not be. But if the court orders that it be submitted and there is nothing there, no one has suffered any harm. On the other hand, if it is not submitted and if, in fact, his DNA is there as an offender, my client may be denied a key element in establishing her argument of self-defense.

"Finally, Judge, the motion also seeks to compel the prosecutor's office to turn over any information it has regarding any matches of Mr. Townsend's DNA with other crimes. I believe this aspect should not be controversial, as any evidence the prosecutor's office has that Mr. Townsend committed other crimes would be exculpatory material that must be provided to the defense under *Brady v. Maryland*. Thank you, Judge."

"Ms. McCabe, I suspect that if the prosecutor was trying to

put your client's DNA into the database you'd be screaming bloody murder and telling them they needed probable cause. Isn't that right?"

"No, Your Honor. If a person's DNA is discovered at a crime scene, there is no probable cause needed to submit it for analysis. Anything discovered at the scene which is unknown is submitted."

Redman turned in his chair so he was facing Taylor and Car-michael. "Ms. Taylor, do you have anything to add to your papers," he asked, using an expression that was usually shorthand for, "You're going to win, so keep your mouth shut."

Surprisingly, Taylor rose to her feet and argued that the motion was frivolous, that there was no reason to submit the samples, that it was offensive to the victim and his family, and that the motion was nothing more than a fishing expedition—a favorite argument for lawyers worried there might actually be fish out there ready to reel in.

As she watched Taylor arguing, she noticed Michael Gardner staring intently at her, then the judge. There was something disquieting about him, but other than looking incredibly serious, she couldn't put her finger on what it was.

When Taylor was finished with her argument, Erin slowly rose from her chair. "May I briefly respond, Your Honor?"

Redman looked at her, then appeared to look in the direction of Taylor—or Gardner, she wasn't sure which one.

"No, counsel, I've heard enough. I'm ready to decide this matter. As I said at the outset, I find this motion to be frivolous," Redman began, reading off of the papers he had brought to the bench. "This is a classic fishing expedition, as noted by Assistant Prosecutor Taylor in her papers and argument. I find that the defendant has not come forward with any competent evidence that would cause me to invade the vic—Mr. Townsend's privacy by requiring the State to submit his DNA to the database. Even in death, we must respect a person's dignity. I am also directing that if there are any other motions related to this motion, or attacking

Mr. Townsend, they must be prefiled with the court so I may determine if they should be filed under seal."

He looked up from the papers in his hands. "As for counsel's argument that I've prejudged the matter, I misspoke earlier. Clearly, I should have said that the defendant is charged with murder, and of course, as all criminal defendants are, is presumed innocent. So to be clear, I have not prejudged this matter in any way, and if the defendant elects to go to trial, he will get a full and fair trial before me."

Redman continued reading his decision and when he was done said, "Anything further?"

"Judge, neither Ms. Taylor nor Your Honor addressed the issue of matches to the DNA in the prosecutor's office's possession."

The judge, who was in the process of gathering up the papers on the bench, inhaled and ran his hand over his mouth. "Ms. Taylor?"

"Judge, the prosecutor's office is well aware of its obligations under *Brady*."

"Thank you, Ms. Taylor."

"Excuse me, Your Honor, but that's not an answer to whether her office has any such information."

"Ms. McCabe, you may not like the answer; however, I find it responsive to your request. I'll see counsel in chambers, please." He tucked his papers under his arms and started to leave the bench.

"Excuse me, Judge," Erin interjected, causing Redman to pause. "May I just have five minutes to discuss Your Honor's ruling with my client before she returns to the jail?"

Redman's scowl suggested he wanted to say no, but instead he sighed. "Five minutes, counsel." He lumbered off the bench and disappeared into his chambers.

As she was sitting down, she glanced to her left to see Taylor and Carmichael leaning over the rail, speaking with Gardner in the first row.

Turning back, she looked at Sharise. Her face seemed to show so many emotions—disappointment, anger, and something else Erin wasn't sure of.

"Thank you," Sharise said before Erin could say anything. "You the first person in my life who stood up and defended me for who I am. And you a badass lawyer that don't take no shit from the man. You be one fierce bitch."

"Thanks," Erin replied. "When we first met, I told you we had something in common. I don't know what it's like for you in a men's jail, and I won't pretend that I do, but I have to imagine it's not fun. So badass or not, I'm not giving up. And, look, the chances are slim, but I'd like to consider what's called an interlocutory appeal, which just means an appeal before the case is over. Despite what he said, I still think we have a shot."

Sharise tilted her head to the side, her head bobbing ever so slightly. "If you think it has a shot, okay. But please don't go wasting my sister's money. They good people and I don't want them going broke on a loser like me."

Erin leaned in and hugged Sharise. "You aren't a loser, girl. Hang in there. We can win this."

Sharise looked at her and smirked. "I'm glad one of us believe that."

They waited for about fifteen minutes in the area where Redman's secretary sat before he buzzed them in. When they walked into his chambers, Redman was standing behind his desk and greeted both Taylor and Carmichael by their first names, shaking their hands in turn. As Erin approached, he shook her hand as well and said, "Nice to meet you, Ms. McCabe. Have a seat," motioning to an empty chair.

"So let me cut to the chase here, folks. What I understand from Judge Reynolds is that the prosecution's offer is thirty years to life, but that the defendant would become parole eligible after thirty years. That seems to me to be a very reasonable offer, Ms. McCabe. Since your practice is up north, I will also tell you that it is generally this prosecutor's office's position that you get the best offer at the start of the case, and at some point if you continue to file motions, they're going to make it life, no parole. So perhaps your client may want to take the deal while it's still on the table."

"Thank you, Judge. I will certainly let her know that the current offer has a use-by date. But up until now, she has shown no interest in pleading guilty and has insisted she acted in self-defense."

Redman leaned forward ever so slightly in his chair. "Look, Ms. McCabe, stop calling your client she. I don't know a whole lot about this transgender stuff, and I will absolutely afford you the respect every attorney who appears in my court is entitled to, but I am not happy with your little speech out there, and you are not going to goad me into creating an issue concerning your status. As far as I am concerned, you are a woman, your client is a man, and I will treat both of you accordingly."

"Judge, most respectfully, I will continue to make an issue out of it and I'm not doing it to goad you into making a mistake. It's to drive home the point that my client is just like me and deserves to be treated with the same respect. If and when this matter comes to trial, I intend to insist that my client be permitted to dress as the woman she is."

"Ms. McCabe, I remind you this is my courtroom and I will decide how the trial is conducted," Redman said, his tone darkening.

"I understand, Judge, but I assume you would want to conduct it in accordance with the law and not discriminate against my client based on her gender identity."

"I have no idea what you're talking about, Ms. McCabe. Of course I won't discriminate against any defendant."

"I didn't think so, Judge. So that's why you should be aware that there's currently a bill pending in the legislature that would add gender identity to the class of people protected under the New Jersey Law Against Discrimination. So if we do go to trial, since a courtroom is a place of public accommodation, I believe my client will be entitled to present herself in accordance with her gender identity."

Out of the corner of her eye, Erin thought Taylor actually smiled.

Redman looked at Taylor and Carmichael as if he was expecting them to argue, but they didn't. Finally, Redman said, "I'm not going to worry about that now. I strongly suggest, Ms. Mc-Cabe, that your client consider the offer on the table." He looked down at a piece of paper on his desk. "I see that counsel advised Judge Reynolds that you would be filing a motion to change venue. Is that still in the works?"

"Yes, Your Honor. Judge Reynolds gave us until January 5, 2007, to file, and we expect to have it filed on time."

Redman looked at the calendar on his desk. "Okay, I'm going to schedule a status-slash-plea conference for Friday, December 15. If we can dispose of the case before then, that would be great. If not, we'll discuss any remaining motions." He stood up. "Thank you, counsel. Have a nice Thanksgiving."

As they walked out into the empty courtroom and began packing up their papers, Taylor leaned over to Carmichael. "You go ahead, Roger. I want to have a few words with Ms. McCabe." Then Barbara turned to Erin, who had just finished packing up her trial bag. "You're puzzling, you know that?"

"I'm not sure I know what that means, but—"

"Do you really believe he acted in self-defense?"

Erin frowned. "Does it matter what I believe?"

"Yeah, it does. You're going up against one of the most powerful men in the state. You filed a motion that essentially claims his son is a serial murderer. You're going to end up like the proverbial bug on the windshield. Do you understand that?"

"Is that supposed to be a threat?"

Taylor let out a small snort. "Good God, no. Just the opposite. I'm trying to warn you, because you don't seem to get it."

She wasn't sure why she did it, but Erin reached into her brief-case and found the copy of the police report about the break-in at her apartment and handed it to Barbara. Taylor took it, her confusion apparent. "Wait, is this your apartment?"

Erin nodded.

"I don't understand. Why are you showing this to me?"

"Keep reading."

As she got near the end of the report, Taylor let out an audible gasp, covering her mouth with her left hand. When she finished, she looked up at Erin. "Have they found out who broke into your place?"

Erin shook her head. "No."

Barbara ran her hand across her forehead. "And the note was pinned to the door with a switchblade?"

Erin closed her eyes and inhaled. "Yeah, the same type of knife the coroner believes was used to kill Mr. Townsend."

"Why did you show this to me?"

"Because you said you want to warn me about who I was dealing with," she replied, fixing her gaze on Barbara. "I know who I'm dealing with. But I thought I owed you the courtesy of returning the favor."

CHAPTER 19

*H*AVING DECIDED TO KEEP HER APPEARANCE AS LOW-KEY AS possible, Erin dressed very casually—slacks, a sweater, flats, light on the makeup and jewelry. This was going to be hard enough, and she was afraid her father's head might explode if she walked in wearing a dress and heels.

She purposely arrived late, wondering how she was supposed to eat Thanksgiving dinner when her stomach was in her throat. Patrick and Brennan, who were playing with the latest handheld game in the living room, jumped up from the couch. "Aunt Erin's here!" they shouted in unison toward the kitchen.

"Hi, guys," she offered as they came over and hugged her. "Nice to see you again."

Liz walked into the living room and gave her a hug. "How you doing?" Liz asked, the tone in her voice almost foreboding. As if to say, however you were feeling before, it's about to get worse.

Sensing the ominous inflection in Liz's voice, Erin hesitated. "I don't know. How am I doing?"

"I'm not sure. In an effort to get prepared to see you, your father has had a few drinks. Let's just say he's very loquacious."

"My dad? The man whose idea of a dinner conversation is 'Pass the salt, please'?"

"That would be the one," Liz said, raising her eyebrows.

"Uh-oh."

"Hello, dear," Erin's mother interrupted as she walked into the room, wiping her hands on her apron. "Nice of you to join us."

"Thanks," Erin replied, as she leaned in and gave her mother a kiss. "I hear Daddy's feeling no pain."

"I will confess that he has tried to anesthetize himself. All we can do is hope."

She wrapped her arm in Erin's and led her into the kitchen, where Sean was standing by the sink and her father was sitting at the kitchen table, beer in hand.

"Erin's here!" Peg announced as they walked into the kitchen.

Sean took a tentative step forward and extended his hand with a cautious smile. "Hey, good to see you."

Erin, internally cringing at the handshake instead of a hug, reached out and shook her brother's hand. "Good to see you too," she replied, before turning toward the kitchen table. "Hi, Dad," she said, her voice cracking ever so slightly.

Her father looked up from the table but closed his eyes. When he opened his eyes and she was still there, he gave her the once-over from her head down. He closed his eyes again and this time he exhaled. "Whatya want me to say, good to see you? Well, it's not. Not like that," he said, motioning with his arms. He pushed his chair away from the table and walked out to the den.

Erin stood there, red-faced, not sure what to say.

"Well, that went well," Sean mumbled.

Peg turned to Liz. "Do me a favor, love, stir the gravy," she said, handing Liz the spoon and taking Erin by the hand. Peg marched into the den, Erin in tow, closing the door behind them. She practically pushed Erin into the easy chair opposite the sofa where her husband had gone for refuge, then stood in front of him. "Patrick McCabe, you look at me."

He glanced up at the angry face of his wife.

"You listen to me. That is no way to treat our child."

"Peg, this isn't the time—"

"Baloney!" she said, cutting him off. "For over two years now you have ostracized your daughter, and it's time for this nonsense to stop."

"I don't have a daughter," he said defensively.

"I got news for you. Yes, you do. And you are either going to come to terms with that, or you're going to be having Thanksgiving dinner at McDonald's—by yourself!"

"Listen, Peg, you can't browbeat me into accepting this," he said, avoiding looking in Erin's direction.

"Like hell I can't."

"You two do realize I'm sitting right here, right?" Erin interjected.

"You be quiet, young lady. This isn't about you," her mother snapped.

Erin laughed reflexively. "Actually, Mom, I think it is." When both of her parents looked at her, she continued. "Look, both of you, stop. I don't want you to fight over me. I don't want you to fight, period. It's Thanksgiving. This used to be my favorite holiday because it was all about family and being together." She took a breath, hoping her stomach would stop churning. "Honest, I'm not looking to cause problems." She paused and looked at her father. "Truth is, Dad, I didn't think you were ready to see me like this. But Mom really thought it would be okay. Obviously, it's not."

Her father let out an awkward laugh. "I don't know why anyone would think I'd be okay with this. One day my son decides he's a woman and I'm just supposed to go, 'Oh, okay, I'm fine with that.' Well, I'm not fine with that. You want to pretend you're a woman, knock yourself out. Just don't ask me to buy in to your fantasy."

She stared at her father, stung by the lash of his words. "No, Dad," she said softly. "I didn't decide one day to be a woman. This is who I've always been. I was born this way. I don't know why." She lowered her gaze, looking at the floor. "I always tried hard to be the son you wanted me to be; honestly, the son you deserved. I wanted so much to please you, to make you proud of me, to be a man for you. I hated myself for the longest time because I knew I'd disappoint you if you knew the truth. So I pretended to be the person you saw." She wiped a tear off her cheek before making sure she was looking him in the eyes. "I just couldn't be that person. That's when I was pretending, Dad."

She rose from her chair and stood in front of him, a hint of defiance entering her voice.

"Dad, take a good look at me. I'm not pretending now. And more importantly, for the first time in my life, I'm happy with who I am. I didn't choose to be a woman any more than Mom or Liz did. This is just who I am." She smiled at him sadly. "I hope you know, no matter what, I couldn't have asked for a better dad. All I can hope is that maybe one day you'll understand and we can be a family again." She paused, trying desperately to hold it all together. "Happy Thanksgiving, Dad. I love you," she said, giving him one last wistful look before walking out of the room.

She entered the kitchen to the stares of her nephews, Liz, and Sean. "Is everything okay, Aunt Erin?" Patrick asked, even though he seemed to recognize it wasn't.

"Absolutely, Patrick." She looked from him to Sean and Liz. "I was just talking with Nanny and Grandpop. Unfortunately, I can't stay," she said, tussling his hair. "I'll see you soon."

Brennan looked at her, his eyes pleading with her not to go. "But you just got here! Can't you stay and have dinner with us?" he asked, turning to his mom, hoping for her to intercede.

"I'd love to, Bren, but I have an emergency to take care of." Erin bent over and gave her nephew a hug. "I'll talk to your mom and dad about coming down to visit you guys. Promise."

She walked into the living room, followed closely by Liz, to gather her coat and purse.

"Is there anything we can do?" Liz asked.

"No, he's just not ready yet. I didn't think he was, but Mom insisted."

"If you leave, it's going to be miserable. Why don't you stay?"

"Thanks, Liz," she said, wrapping her arms around her sister-in-law. "If I stay it will be even worse."

"Are you going to be okay?" Liz asked as they separated.

Erin nodded unconvincingly.

"What are you going to do?"

"I don't know. Go for a run, I guess. I'll find something. Do me a favor, try to keep the peace here." She hesitated. "I have a feeling World War Three is about to break out. Maybe you can defuse things before it goes nuclear. I don't want your sons to see that."

"I'll try," Liz said, choking back tears. "It'll work out. He just needs time."

Erin's face betrayed her doubt. "I hope so," she said, squeezing Liz's arm. Then she turned and quietly left the house, closing the door behind her.

It was the first Thanksgiving Tonya had shared with her family in four years. What had happened with Sharise had driven a wedge between them, and it was hard for Tonya not to blame her parents. Sharise was their child, their own flesh and blood—that should count for more than pride or religion or whatever was the source of their anger. But with all that was going on, she decided it was important that she try to persuade them they needed to be a family again. Knowing how her father felt about Sharise, she was grateful for Paul's support. She could only hope that his status as an NBA player held some sway with her dad.

The talk at the dinner table had been about everything but the elephant in the room. Finally, as she and her mom started to clear the table, she broached the subject.

"Can we talk about Sam?" she asked tentatively.

Her father, who had walked into the living room to check the score of the football game, tensed. "I prefer not to," he responded coldly.

"Daddy, please don't abandon Sam."

He closed his eyes, his anger percolating close to the surface. "I told you, I would prefer not to talk about this. I have a daughter and I had a son. But my son is dead."

She looked from her father to her mother, who was standing in the doorway. "Mom, Sam is not dead. But he could wind up spending the rest of his life in jail. He needs you and Daddy."

Her mother met her stare and didn't look away. "Samuel is getting what he deserves. Your father and I gave him a chance to repent and turn away from his sinful ways. He chose to turn away from God instead."

"Don't you understand? Sam didn't choose to be this way. Do you really think God made Sam this way just to be miserable?"

Her father stared at her. "Don't you dare question God's reasons for doing things. God gives all of us burdens that we must carry. Your brother has chosen the easy way, the sinful way, to deal with what God has given him. If God had wanted me to have two daughters, He would have given me two daughters."

"Don't you see, Daddy? He did give you two daughters. Maybe God isn't placing the burden on Sam, maybe He just wants to test both of you to see if you could love your child even if he did not conform to your beliefs."

Her father's eyes widened, and she tensed, thinking he was about to slap her. Suddenly her husband stepped between her and her father.

"Don't, Frank," he said in a voice that resonated from every inch of his six-foot-five frame. "We didn't come here for a confrontation. We came to talk about helping Sam."

Franklin Barnes took a step back, the imposing figure of his son-in-law having corralled his anger. "There's nothing to talk about."

"You know Tonya and I have hired lawyers for Sam."

"That's on you."

"We're not asking for your help paying for the lawyers, Frank. But the lawyers think that when the case goes to trial, it would be helpful to have you and Vi there for support, and maybe even to testify about your relationship with Sam."

"No," he replied without hesitation. "I have no intention of being turned into some heartless villain by some lawyer who, from what I read, is just as crazy as Sam."

Tonya and Paul exchanged a look, surprised by the fact that her father was keeping track of the case online.

"Nobody's trying to make you look like anything," Tonya replied. "Sam's lawyers just want the jury to know that Sam has a supportive and loving family."

"Samuel did have a loving and supportive family. But whoever this person is, he is not Samuel."

"Daddy, you know Sammy was only protecting himself. He'd never hurt anyone on purpose."

Again her father's temper flared, his voice becoming stronger and louder. "He is a harlot, a common whore. Do you know that about your brother? He has sex with men for money. Don't tell me how innocent he is. He is suffering the wrath of God for his sins, and I will not lift a finger to help him."

Tonya lowered her head, tears forming in the corners of her eyes. She walked to the closet in the foyer and removed their coats from the hangers. "I think we should go," she said quietly, handing Paul's over to him, then turned to give her mother a peck on the cheek. "Thank you for dinner," she whispered, and then to her father, "I'm sorry, Daddy, but Jesus never treated anyone like you're treating your own son. I don't know what's going to happen, but Paul and I intend to stand by Sammy. He's my brother . . ." She paused. "No, she's my sister, and I won't abandon her. No matter what."

CHAPTER 20

*P*ULLING BACK THE CURTAINS, ERIN SQUINTED AT DOWNTOWN Cranford before searching through her purse for the ibuprofen bottle. Her head felt like there were little demons inside it keeping time on a bass drum, and that last glass of wine, which seemed like such a good idea at the time, didn't feel so good now.

After she had left her parents, she decided to try to replace the pain of Thanksgiving with the pain of a long run. To her dismay, although her run had been painful, it didn't help with the emotional sting. Plan B had been red wine, which had only made her more melancholy, causing her to revisit Thanksgivings past and remember why it was her favorite holiday.

After moping around her apartment for a half hour, she decided to get dressed, grab a coffee, and head to the office, where she decided that she should spend the day devoting time to her other clients, whose cases were falling into disarray with all the time they were putting into Sharise's.

Entering her office, she saw the blinking light on her phone. *Oh, for crying out loud. Who would call the day after Thanksgiving?*

She tried to ignore it, but the annoying light eventually got the better of her.

The voice was deep, but somewhat muffled, as if the caller was trying to disguise his voice. "Ms. McCabe," it began, "you don't know me, but I'm calling because your client Samuel Barnes is being moved out of protective custody and into the general population sometime today—today being Friday, November 24. I don't know any other way to get you a message. I hope you get this before it's too late."

She stared at the phone, momentarily stunned. Then suddenly the realization hit her: Whether this was true or not, others had heard the message too.

She grabbed her purse and cell phone and ran out of the building to start making calls. First, she called Duane to let him know what was happening; then, because it was a court holiday, she started searching for emergency numbers. When she called the prosecutor's office's emergency number and told them she needed to speak with Barbara Taylor, they were dismissive enough that she was startled when her cell phone rang ten minutes later.

"Hello," Erin answered tentatively, not sure who was calling her.

"Is this Ms. McCabe?"

"Yes. Barbara, is that you?"

"Yes, I just got a call from the duty officer telling me that it was imperative I call you immediately. Erin, why are you calling me? What can't wait until Monday?"

Erin took a deep breath. "Barbara, I received an anonymous phone call that my client is being moved today out of protective custody and into the general population. Are you aware of this?"

"Erin, what are you talking about? An anonymous phone call—this sounds crazy. Why would your client be moved? I suspect someone is playing games with you."

"You may be right, but whoever left the message sounded legit. Could you please just call over to the jail and check for me?"

There was a long pause. "Fine. I'll call you right back."

Five minutes later, Taylor called back. "Erin, I don't know

who called you, but whoever it was knew what they were talking about. Your client is scheduled to be moved later this afternoon."

"Barbara, you have to stop this! You know she won't be safe in the general population."

"I hope you believe me—I tried. But the watch commander told me it was a direct order from the sheriff. I don't have the authority to countermand it."

Erin ran through her options quickly. "Barbara, I'm going to find the judge on call and file an emergent application to enjoin the move. When I find out who the judge is, I'll need to file the paperwork. Will you participate if I can get an emergent hearing, and is there a way to get you the papers?"

"Erin, my daughter's home from college. We're supposed to go out shopping." There was a long silence, then a sigh. "Judge Sylvia Wolfe is on call today. You can fax me the papers at this number."

"Thank you, Barbara. I appreciate it."

While Erin reached out to the judge, Duane frantically scurried to put together the papers, mostly doing a cut-and-paste from their motion to have Sharise moved to the women's jail. Some of his argument verged on stream of consciousness about the danger she would be in if she was moved out of protective custody. To their relief, Judge Wolfe agreed to hear the application over the phone at noon and gave Erin a fax number to send her the papers. Erin passed the information on to Barbara, and now all she could do was hope that the move hadn't already happened.

Ed Champion looked at his cell display before he answered. "What's this, payback? I woke you up on a Sunday morning, so you're calling me on Black Friday?"

"Funny. But no," Andrew Barone replied.

"So what's up?"

"Do you guys have your own wire on Swisher or his partner?"

"What? Of course not. Why would we be up on them? Besides,

if we were, you guys at DOJ would know. You told me the other day you were listening to Swisher. I'm confused."

"I just got a call from the agent who is running the leak investigation. He tells me that about an hour ago Swisher got a panicked call from his partner. Apparently a call had come into the office leaving an urgent message that Sharise was being moved out of protective custody."

"Do you want to put that into English?"

"I can't. But then the partner tells Swisher that since the call went to the office, it was on a tapped line, and now Townsend will know that they know about her being moved."

The line was quiet for several seconds. "Look, I have no idea what any of that means. Maybe the State has a wire going on them and Townsend is well connected enough to find out whatever the hell it is they're talking about. We have liaisons with the counties and the AG's office. I can check backchannels next week and see if they have anything going."

"Okay. But there's more. The agent said there had been two other unusual calls about a week ago. One is with an agent Swisher knows in Vegas. The second is with his partner immediately after that call. If you're near a computer, I'll send them to you."

"Sure."

"What's your personal e-mail?"

"EQChampion1952@home.com."

"What the hell does the Q stand for?"

"Quincy."

"Who the hell gives their kid the middle name Quincy?"

"John and Abigail Adams."

"Funny."

"Seriously, my mom was a history professor at Rutgers. She loved Abigail Adams."

"Whatever. Sending them now. Call me back after you read them."

The e-mail popped up in his in-box and he opened the attachments. The first conversation was between Swisher and a Special

Agent Terrance Johnson, whom he didn't know. The second was a call from Swisher to his partner, which happened immediately on him hanging up with Johnson. When he got to the end, he went back and reread it. How was this connected to Townsend? Why were they certain Townsend would know about the call to the office? Even though all he had was a sterile transcript, he could feel the fear in Swisher's voice. He had been there. He knew what it felt like when a key witness suddenly disappeared. There was professional panic, yeah, but if you have an ounce of humanity, there was also fear that something you'd done wrong had cost someone his or her life.

He reread the transcript of the call Swisher had made to Agent Johnson—*She's a hooker in Vegas and I need to find her because I think her life may be in danger. I've tried the number she gave me, but I'm not getting anyone*—then reached for his cell phone and started dialing. As he did, his eyes were focused on another part of the transcript. *We're overmatched, E. . . . And if somehow we manage to keep the score close, they'll just end the game. Sharise will end up just like Lenore—dead.*

"What do you think?" he said, answering on the first ring.

There was a long pause. "Do we know who Lenore is?"

"Yeah, my guys ran it down with Vegas PD before they called me. The person's name was Lenore Fredericks, aka Leonard Fredericks. Apparently he had been busted a few times for solicitation on the strip, and as described, took a Brody off a twenty-story building."

"Okay, I'm not connecting the dots here."

"I pulled his rap sheet. Looks like Fredericks was originally from New Jersey. Was in the same line of work in AC. Busted four times for prostitution in New Jersey, twice for drugs. About five hours before the call between Swisher and Johnson, Swisher made a call to a cell number listed to an L. Fredericks urgently trying to reach him. Swisher left a message telling Fredericks not to call his office, but left his cell number for him to call."

"And you are sharing all of this with me . . . why exactly?"

"My order on Swisher runs out next week and I have no argument to extend it. He hasn't talked to anyone about the leak. Christ Almighty, until this happened, I'm not sure we had any complete calls recorded because they were obviously all unrelated to our investigation. You and I both know we probably should have minimized the calls I sent you, but I can get around that. What I can't get around is there's nothing for me to get an extension on."

"Okay?"

"Look, I know you've hinted about Jersey Sting."

"Yeah. How's that help you?"

"Who's running the investigation?"

"Phil Gabriel, Public Corruption. Reports directly to me and the boss. But the boss is really driving the bus on this one."

"Maybe you can help me stay up on Swisher and in return, I share what I hear is going on that may be helpful in your efforts."

"So what are you saying?"

"See if this works . . ."

After the judge took down their names and who they represented, she immediately asked Barbara Taylor if she had authority to speak for the sheriff's department and the correctional facility. When Taylor hesitated, Judge Wolfe said, "Ms. Taylor, counsel indicated in their papers that during their motion to have their client transferred to the women's facility before Judge Redman, you represented the sheriff and the jail. Is that accurate?"

"Yes, Judge."

"Has anything changed?"

"Well, Judge, I haven't had the opportunity to confer with them on this issue."

"Ms. Taylor, let me see if I can make this easy. This is an emergent application to keep the defendant Samuel Barnes, who also goes by the name Sharise Barnes and who has been diagnosed as being transgender, from being moved out of protective custody and into the general population of a men's prison on the day after Thanksgiving without an opportunity to contest the transfer and—at least according to the paper submitted by Ms. McCabe—at great risk to his physical safety. I'd like to hear if you have any objection to me granting the requested temporary injunction until a full record and hearing can be held. In other words, is there any reason I should not preserve the status quo? Actually, let me ask it another way. What harm will come to the sheriff's office, the corrections department, or your office if Mr. Barnes is not moved until a full record can be developed?"

Erin held her breath, ready to write down every word of Taylor's response.

"None, Your Honor."

Erin exhaled.

"Good," Judge Wolfe replied. "I will sign the order enjoining changing the status of Mr. Barnes and ordering that he remain in protective custody until further order of the court. Ms. Taylor, when we get off this call, I want you to call the ranking officer on duty at the jail—presumably the watch commander—and direct them that Mr. Barnes is not to be moved out of protective custody. If for any reason he has already been placed in the general population, I want him returned to protective custody status immediately. Please tell them they will be getting a copy of my order by fax in the next five minutes. Any questions?"

"No, Judge."

"Very good. Ms. McCabe, anything further?"

"Yes, Your Honor. I'd like permission to visit my client today to make sure she's okay. Since today is a state holiday, I would need an order from Your Honor."

"Any objections, Ms. Taylor?"

"Um, assuming . . . uh—"

"Let me see if I can help. Ms. Taylor, when you call the watch commander, advise him I have ordered that Ms. McCabe can visit today between . . . Ms. McCabe, when are you going?"

"Immediately, Judge. I should be there around two o'clock."

"Fine. She can visit anytime between two and four this afternoon. If the watch commander gives you a hard time, call me back. Otherwise I will assume there will be no problems. Anything else?"

"No, Your Honor," they intoned simultaneously.

"Thank you, ladies. Enjoy the rest of your day."

It was normally an hour drive from Cranford to Toms River, but today the drive seemed to take forever. Erin had told Duane to go home and be with Cori and Austin, but she needed to see Sharise to make sure she was all right.

Later, sitting in the attorney visiting room, she was getting nervous. The sergeant on the front desk had called down for Barnes, but she had been waiting for twenty minutes. She was about to pick up the phone and call the control room when she saw Sharise coming down the hallway escorted by two officers.

The guard who led Sharise into the room glared at Erin. "Well, lookie here, two peas in a pod," he offered as he pushed Sharise down into the chair. "You know the drill," he added, walking out of the cell and locking the door.

"Why you be here today, girl? It's the day after Thanksgiving. Ain't you got better things to do?"

"Just wanted to make sure you're okay."

Sharise tilted her head and frowned. "And why wouldn't I be okay? You have a bad dream or something?"

Erin explained what had taken place earlier in the day, leaving out only the fact that they were being tapped. When she was done, Sharise shook her head. "Who called you to warn you?"

"I have no idea. I really don't. I don't know who could've known you were being moved at nine o'clock in the morning, but someone did and gave it up."

"Must be my guardian angel. She done finally wake up and say, 'Holy shit, that Sharise sure be in a fuck lot of trouble. Better keep her from getting herself killed.'" She let out a sarcastic belly laugh. When she stopped, her expression grew serious. "Thanks," she said.

Sharise looked around the room conspiratorially. "I know we

lost the motion, and I ain't saying what Lenore told your partner is what happened, but do you really think Lenore would come to testify? And if she did, would my chances be any better?"

For a split second Erin hung her head. She quickly looked up, but before she could say anything Sharise knew.

"She dead, ain't she?"

Erin closed her eyes and nodded.

"Oh sweet Jesus, no," Sharise said, slowly rocking back and forth in her chair. "Oh Lord, please no. Not Lenore."

The jail rules forbade her from touching an inmate, but she reached across the table and laid her hand on Sharise's shackled wrist. "Sharise, I'm so sorry."

"How?" Sharise asked through her sobs, no longer able to hold back her emotions.

Erin looked around the jail cell. Was it paranoia if they were really out to get you? She decided that there was at least a fifty-fifty chance someone was listening, so she left out the part about their office being bugged. Erin told her that Duane had a friend in Vegas law enforcement who'd told him about Lenore's death.

Sharise rested her head on her shackled arms and wept. When she finally looked up, her eyes puffy from the tears, she said, "It was because of me, wasn't it?"

"We don't know at this point, Sharise. It is still being investigated," she lied. "It could have been a suicide."

Sharise's head went from side to side. "No, not Lenore. She was the strong one. No, somebody threw her off that building. Ain't no way that girl jumped. She like you, she was a fierce bitch, that Lenore."

Ten minutes later, when Erin went through the final set of locked doors on her way out of the room, Lieutenant Rose was standing there waiting with another officer by his side.

"Lieutenant," she said when she saw him.

"Ms. McCabe, the rules are you are not allowed to touch an inmate. That is a serious infraction of the rules. I could have you barred from visiting with your client."

"Really, Lieutenant. Unless I'm mistaken, I believe the right to counsel still applies in Ocean County." She smiled. "And what makes you think I touched my client? Were you watching, Lieutenant?"

His face reddened. "We are allowed to observe for security purposes," he replied, his tone defiant.

"Really. Does the tape have sound as well? Perhaps I should watch the tape with you, Lieutenant. I have no recollection of touching my client, but if you'd like to show me . . ."

His lips tightened, then slowly morphed into a scowl. "Consider this a warning, *Ms.* McCabe," he said, placing a lot of emphasis on the *Ms.* "The next time, we will pursue disciplinary action against you."

"Thank you, Lieutenant. And please make sure you keep that tape. I may want to watch it in the future."

"Have a nice day," she cooed as she collected her ID from the desk sergeant, making sure she did her best to wiggle her ass as she walked out the door, taking a perverse pleasure in trying to turn on the very transphobic Lieutenant Rose.

She got back to Cranford a little before five. She'd called Duane on her way back to let him know that Sharise was all right, but that she'd had to tell her about Lenore. Now, as she headed up the stairs to her apartment, she decided that the building's solitude had gone from inviting to downright scary. She had purchased timers for the lamps in the living room and bedroom so she wouldn't have to come into a dark apartment, but she was beginning to think Swish was right; as much as she loved walking to her office, maybe it was time to start looking for something a bit safer.

The lights were on when she went in, and as she looked around, pepper spray in hand, everything seemed normal. The phone in the bedroom had three messages. She hit play.

"Message received at 9:28 a.m. Erin, honey, it's Mom. I'm so sorry about yesterday. It's all my fault. I really thought your dad was ready. Please don't hold it against him. Please call me. I'm worried about you."

"Message received at 3:05 p.m. Erin, it's Mom again. Please call me."

"Message received at 4:14 p.m. Erin, it's Mark. Um, look, I know I owe you an apology. I'd really like to see you so I could explain in person what an idiot I am. If you're willing to share another cup of coffee or whatever, please give me a call."

She hung up and dialed Duane's number. "Hey," she said when he answered.

"Is she okay?"

"Yeah, she's fine. Nobody said anything to her about being moved."

"Okay. Listen, Cori and I are just about to have dinner, so can we discuss on Monday?"

"Sure, sounds good. Tell Cori I said hello."

"Will do."

She stared at the phone knowing someone else had been listening as she placed it back in the charger. *Maybe that will buy us some time*, she thought, picking up her cell phone and dialing. "Hi, Mom. I'm fine. It's just been a long day. Um, by the way, Mom, remember how I asked you not to call my landline?"

CHAPTER 21

Mark offered a weak smile as Erin slid into the booth at a restaurant called the Cranford Hotel, one of her local favorites. "Hi," he said, much more reserved than the other two times they had spoken.

"Hi," she said without any emotion, placing her leather jacket and purse on the seat next to her. "Sorry I'm a little late."

"It's okay. I'm glad you came. I thought maybe you had decided not to."

"I thought about it. So, can I ask you why you called?" she said, immediately recognizing it came out a little more strident than she intended. "I mean, thank you for the call, but you really don't have to apologize for anything. I suspect I know what happened."

He looked down at the table, avoiding her knowing look. "I guess the main reason I called is I do feel I owe you an apology. I acted just like everyone else. I wish I hadn't, but I did."

Her smile was weak, and there was a resignation in her tone. "Mark, I really do understand. It's one thing for you to privately know about my past—and honestly, I was surprised that you hung in through that!—but it's quite another thing for you to know that everybody knows about my past. Suddenly, everyone knows the woman you're with is transgender and . . . let's just say I understand what comes next in most people's minds."

"But it shouldn't matter," he responded defiantly.

"But we both know it does. Since I've been on the front page of the papers, there are people at some of the shops in town who suddenly don't talk to me even though I've been going there for two years. So I know it does matter." Erin gave him a sad smile across the table.

"Can I get you guys something?" the waitress interrupted.

She realized it was decision time. If she ordered, she was going to have to stay at least long enough to finish a drink. Or she could just stand up, say "nice seeing you again," and walk for the door.

She looked across the table at him, where his eyes pleaded for her to stay. She drew in a breath and closed her eyes for a split second.

"I'll have a Corona," she said.

His look conveyed both a sense of relief and a thank you. "A Brooklyn Ale," he replied, then rubbed his lower lip between his fingers. "Thanks for staying."

"I'm not sure I made a decision to stay as much as I felt it would have been rude to come and yet not hear you out."

"Fair enough," he said.

They sat in an awkward silence for what seemed like minutes. She brushed her hair back off her face and finally said, "So why are we here? You could have apologized on the phone."

He waited for the nearby waitress to deliver their drinks before replying. "Look, from the moment we were introduced at Swish's, I've wanted to get to know you better. You're a single, smart, attractive woman, and the few times we've talked, I've really enjoyed our conversations." He stopped and took a swallow of his ale, his expression serious and genuine. "All those things are still true."

"Mark, this can't end well for either one of us. I told you when I walked in that I understood why you canceled our date, but that doesn't mean it was easy for me—it wasn't. I cried for a long time that night. Be honest with me—if your family or friends ever found out you went out on a date with me, you'd catch all kinds of crap, right? Some people who know you would probably call you fag or worse. It wouldn't be fun for you. And when you decided it wasn't worth putting up with all the nonsense, it wouldn't be fun for me. So why don't we save ourselves a whole lot of time and aggravation and not even set ourselves up for that to happen."

"I guess because I hope I'm man enough to get past all that crap." He took a longer sip from his beer. "I wish I could swear to you that none of it mattered, but I don't know. Maybe you're right. But I'm here because I want to be. I'm here because I met a woman who I'd really like to get to know better. I'm here because of you."

She shook her head. "Mark, you seem to be a really nice guy, and you deserve to meet a really nice woman who doesn't come with the baggage I do."

"Erin, I screwed up. I admit it." His green eyes bore into her. "And you have every right to say, 'Thanks, Mark, but I'm not interested.' But please just don't make it about protecting me from you. I'm a big boy. I can take care of myself."

She ran her finger along the rim of her beer glass. "Okay," she said. "But I've seen how people react." She closed her eyes and took a deep breath, yesterday still fresh in her mind. "I didn't have Thanksgiving dinner with my family because my dad just can't accept me as his daughter. My brother, who is one of the best guys I know, just started talking to me again after two years. So let's just say my experiences so far with the men close to me have not left me feeling warm and fuzzy about how this plays out."

"I don't know what to say. I only know you this way," he said, gesturing toward her. "I'm sorry you have to deal with that. I can't imagine what that's like for you."

"It's not fun. . . ." She paused. "I don't get it. Why me? There are plenty of women out there. I don't get why you would be interested in me."

"Why do you find it so hard to believe that a man would find you attractive and be interested in getting to know you?"

"Because you know my past, and that changes everything for men."

"You guys want menus?" the waitress interrupted.

"Sure," Mark replied.

As she laid two on the table and walked away, Erin cocked her head to the side. "A little presumptuous?"

"No, we don't have to order. Have you already eaten?"

"No, but I'm not sure how hungry I am."

He gave her a resigned smile. "Let me make a suggestion. Let's have something to eat and just hang out for an hour. If we walk out of here and you never want to see me again, I tried. And if it turns out I never want to see you again, at least you had something to eat. Sound like a plan?"

"Sure," she replied, taking a sip from her beer.

"Good," he said. "I'm sorry about your dad and Thanksgiving. I'm sure that's hard to deal with."

"I feel bad for my mom. She's a great woman and just wants us to be a family again. So I know it's really rough on her. But, anyway, how was your Thanksgiving?"

"It was good. The last few years have been hard. My dad died three years ago from a heart attack out of nowhere. He was only sixty-three. And my mom's still trying to adjust."

"I'm sorry."

"Thanks," he said with a shrug. "He was a good guy and we miss him." He didn't say anything for a while. "Anyway, my older brothers were in with their spouses and kids, and my sister and her friend were there. It was nice."

She was trying to gauge what he had just said without trying to read too much into it. "Can I ask a stupid question?"

He gave her a knowing grin. "My sister's friend is her girl-friend."

"And how is everyone with the fact that your sister is a lesbian and has a girlfriend?" she asked cautiously, afraid what the answer might be.

He winced.

"You have a lousy poker face."

"So I've been told."

"And?"

He looked at her, his eyes betraying his desire to avoid this discussion. "Let's just say coming from a Catholic background, my family wasn't thrilled when Molly came out. I guess it was kind of a shock. Molly was a cheerleader, popular, dated guys, so when she brought Robin home a couple of years ago, there was a bit of an uproar."

Erin laughed.

"I know. I probably just indicated how ignorant I am about lesbians—like they can't be a popular, pretty cheerleader. But I have to confess, that's how everyone felt."

"Even you?" she asked.

"Yeah," he answered sheepishly. "Even me."

"Why?"

He nodded. "It's complicated."

"And you think I'll have a hard time with complicated?"

"Touché," he said with a small snort masquerading as a laugh. He took a long draw from his beer. "Molly's two years younger than me and we've always been close. When I was a senior in high school Molly started dating my best friend, Leo. They dated all through college and the year after she graduated college, they got married. Right after their wedding I left for the Peace Corps and by the time I came back, they had already separated and were getting a divorce. Well, when I found out that the reason was because Molly was a lesbian, I'm sure my reaction wasn't what Molly had hoped for." He paused and took another sip of his beer. "It was shortly after that that I left for a year backpacking. When I got back, Molly had moved to DC and was working for Health and Human Services."

"So what happened between the two of you?"

"On my way home from Chile, I stopped in DC. You can do a lot of soul-searching backpacking for a year, and after about a week of staying there, everything's been cool with us since."

"When did she come out to your family?"

"I guess it was about two years ago. She and Robin moved in together about four years ago while Robin was finishing her post doc at Georgetown. Two years ago, Robin got a job at NYU. That's when my sister told everyone that they weren't just room-mates and that's why they were still living together. They live in Jersey City now."

She raised an eyebrow. "And how's the family with Robin?"

"It was hard at first. I know my mom struggled. And it took Jack and Brian—my brothers—a while. But I think people have started to adjust."

She looked down at her beer.

"I know what you're thinking," he said.

"Isn't it pretty obvious?"

"I know, if they had this much trouble with a lesbian daughter and sister, how will they ever deal with you?"

She sighed.

"You ready for another round?" asked the waitress, who had suddenly materialized at the side of their table. "Food should be out shortly."

Mark conveyed that it was up to her with a motion of his hand.

"Um, sure," she replied.

"Yeah, thanks," Mark replied to the waitress. Then, "I don't know how they'll be, but we're getting too far ahead of ourselves. We haven't even gotten through dinner yet."

She laughed. "Good point."

The tension from earlier started to fade as they chatted, talking about favorite books and restaurants. Like most Friday nights, the Cranford Hotel filled up around nine and the noise became deafening. Looking around the crowded room, Erin made a decision.

"Can I make a suggestion? Maybe we can continue this conversation elsewhere. I don't have Brooklyn Ale, but I have some Sam Adams, or I could make some coffee."

He smiled. "A cup of coffee sounds perfect."

It was a quiet night as they walked the block from the restaurant to her building. The streetlights illuminated his face in short bursts as they walked, and she began to wonder what had gotten into her that she had just invited a cute guy back to her apartment. She shook her head ever so slightly, still slightly mystified as to when she had begun to find men cute.

"So you're the English teacher—what are your favorite novels?"

"I really like a lot of books, but if I have to pick, two of my favorites are *Catch-22* and *Slaughterhouse-Five,*" he responded.

She laughed. "A little on the dark, absurdist side—that explains so much."

"You ever read them?"

"Absolutely. Loved them both."

"So you have a dark, absurdist side too?"

"I am a lawyer," she replied with a wink.

"Right. Anything else I should know about your reading habits?"

"Douglas Adams is a favorite."

It was his turn to study her as they stood on the corner waiting for the light. "You truly are a complex woman."

She raised an eyebrow. "I thought we had established that already."

They crossed North Avenue, and she unlocked the outer door that led upstairs. As they headed up the stairs toward the second floor, Mark said, "Well, now I know why you run. To stay in shape just to be able to get to your apartment."

"Still another flight to go," she responded.

"Well, I hope you like solitude, because this place is really dreary."

"What can I tell you? It was affordable and walking distance to the office."

She unlocked the door, pausing before she opened it. What would he think? She lived a relatively Spartan existence and maybe he'd think it wasn't feminine enough. Was there such a thing as a "woman's" apartment as opposed to a "man's" apartment? She constantly found herself doing battle with stereotypes of femininity that did not seem to match her own sensibilities. Did she have to dress or act a certain way to be a woman? Did she worry about meeting certain standards of femininity because she was transgender, or was she just the victim of societal attitudes that all women had to deal with?

She pushed open the door and flipped on the light. "Be it ever so humble," she offered as she tried to measure his reaction. *Jesus, it's your apartment. Why do you care what he thinks? Relax,* she ordered herself as she put her purse on the desk and turned on another light. "So still feel like coffee, or would you prefer a Sam Adams?"

"Coffee would be great if it's not too much trouble."

"No trouble at all. Come on in," she said as she walked into the kitchen. She opened her cabinet, removed the airtight ceramic container, and poured the beans into the grinder, knowing exactly what she needed for two cups, before turning it on.

"I'm impressed. You grind your own coffee."

"One of my few vices: freshly ground coffee."

"I noticed vinyl is another," he added, nodding toward the turntable.

She smiled. "Yeah, it is. One of the best things about being alone in the building is I can play my music pretty loud before I bother anyone else."

"Do you mind if I take a look?"

"Be my guest," she offered. She walked over and turned on the amp and preamp. "All you have to do is move the arm over and the turntable will start," she said, heading back to the kitchen. "Do you take milk or sugar?"

"No, just black."

Five minutes later, as the opening notes of "Mercy Mercy Me" began floating out of the speakers, she carried two mugs of coffee into the living room and gently placed them on coasters on the coffee table.

He walked over and sat next to her on the couch.

"Good pick," she said.

"I cheated. It was already on the turntable. Although I do like Marvin Gaye," he added with a grin. He picked up his coffee and took a sip. "Nice," he offered.

"Thanks."

They sat there, awkwardly talking about music, sipping their coffee.

"So, can I make an observation?" he said, putting his coffee down and shifting his body on the couch so he was facing her.

She nodded.

"For two thirty-somethings we're both acting as nervous as a couple of high school kids." He stroked the stubble on his chin with his hand. "Why is that?"

She laughed. "Are you serious? Why? Maybe it's because—"

She never got to finish her thought because at that moment he leaned in and kissed her. It wasn't a great kiss, mainly because he caught her in mid-sentence, but it did stop her from talking. And when he kissed her again, she slowly relaxed and let his lips cover hers, putting her arm around his neck so she could pull him closer. She was surprised by how different it was. This wasn't her first kiss. She had loved kissing Lauren and must have kissed her thousands of times, but as she pulled him close, his smell, the feel of his skin on hers, the taste of his lips, all seemed so much more intense. It was as if she had suddenly awakened in the Land of Oz—the world now filled with colors. She closed her eyes and slowly stroked the back of his neck, enjoying his reaction, her own body reacting in a way that she had never experienced, the warmth of his lips spreading throughout her, her body tingling in an unfamiliar but wonderful way.

Later, after he left, she crawled under the duvet, trying to sort out her feelings. They seemed so stereotypically female that she couldn't help but wonder if she was attempting to live out some deeply ingrained fantasy of what it meant to be a woman. How could she have gone from someone sexually attracted to women to feeling so comfortable with the embrace and kiss of a man? Were these feelings always there, lying dormant? No, she was sure she had never felt this way before. The coarseness of his stubble, the strength in his arms, the warmth of his mouth on hers—it was all so new and strange that she felt that somehow her feelings couldn't be real, yet they didn't seem anything else.

CHAPTER 22

*E*RIN HAD HER SUNDAY ROUTINE DOWN TO A SCIENCE: BUY the Sunday *Times*, brew herself a fresh cup of coffee, usually a Costa Rican blend, check her e-mails, and then stretch out on the couch and read the paper. After a leisurely start, she'd go out for a long run.

But this morning was different. She had tried to convince herself that the fact that Mark hadn't called on Saturday was simply him not wanting to appear too eager, but the feeling in the pit of her stomach told her it was something else. Still in her pajamas, she placed her coffee down next to her laptop and opened her e-mail. As soon as she saw msimpson1791@home.com and the subject line—"I need more time"—she closed her eyes and took a deep breath. Then she clicked on it.

> Dear Erin,
> I'm so sorry. I know as you read this you will think you were right; no man could ever want you. But that's not true. You are a beautiful, intelligent woman. The problem is not

with you—it's me and my own insecurities. I know your past shouldn't matter to me, but I'd be less than honest with you if I said that right now it doesn't. I need time to sort out how I feel about all of this. I know this is the second time I hurt you, so I wouldn't blame you if you said good riddance and never wanted to hear from me again, but I hope you won't. Please don't think less of yourself. You are an extraordinary person. I promise to be in touch.

    Mark

She went to the couch, where she picked up one of the throw pillows and hugged it to her chest. She didn't know how she felt, but she was determined not to cry. She wasn't angry. Most surprising, she wasn't even berating herself for thinking anyone could possibly love her. She just felt sad. She liked him. He seemed like a nice guy. She would've liked the opportunity to get to know him better. She would've liked a chance to explore the strange emotions she felt. But what could she do? She was who she was and she couldn't change it.

Finally, she dragged herself off the couch and changed into her running clothes. She needed to clear her head. She needed to let go of all the personal shit going on in her life and stay focused on Sharise and her case. She needed to say fuck you to the rest of the world and live her life.

She locked the door and bounded down the steps. As she stepped out into the cold November morning, she locked the door on the street, took a deep breath, and headed off toward Nomahegan Park.

Sitting in the window of Legal Grounds, two men observed Erin leave. "Let's go."

They walked across the street and the one leading the way took out the keys they had gotten from the real estate agent. He quickly opened the outside door and handed the key to the man behind him.

"If for any reason she heads back before you're done, I'll call you. Get out of her apartment and pretend that you got lost while looking for the apartment for rent."

"Karl, don't worry. I'll be back before you finish your coffee."

Will removed his reading glasses and pinched the bridge of his nose. "This looks normal, but I know you, you wouldn't be here on Sunday of Thanksgiving weekend unless there was something you needed to talk about in person. What's bothering you?"

Michael leaned up against the kitchen island. "Well, for starters, there's the fact that someone tipped them off that Barnes was being moved."

"Any idea who it was?"

"Let's come back to that." He walked over to the table and pointed at the transcript. "This is what's bothering me."

Will turned in his chair. "What, the conversation she had?"

"It's a setup, Will. She's involved all day with keeping Barnes from being moved and when she gets back to her apartment, she has three messages—two from her mom, who sounds pretty upset and is concerned about something, and one from some guy who wants to meet her to apologize. And what's the first call she makes? To Swisher. She never calls mom back from her landline and she doesn't call the guy back either."

"She probably just used her cell."

"Exactly! So the question is why call Swisher on the landline and switch to the cell for Mom and the guy?"

"You think she knows someone's listening."

"I do. When she gets the call tipping her off that Barnes is being moved, there are no calls from the office to Swisher; the only calls are to the judge. We know she called Taylor, but it was from her cell. I went back and listened to what we've gotten from the office over the last week and it's all bullshit. They're not discussing the case. Honestly, they're not doing anything that has to do with this case or any other case."

"How? The only ones that know are you, me, and Joe the plumber."

"Swisher is former FBI. I think he checked out the apartment after the break-in and found our shit, then put two and two together."

Will gritted his teeth and mumbled "fuck" under his breath. "So what else do you think they know?"

"My guess is they know about Vegas. I was told there was a pretty emotional scene in the jail on Friday between Barnes and McCabe, which would be consistent with Barnes learning a friend was dead. But I don't think they have the other stuff. Not yet anyway."

"Who besides Lee knows?"

"Whitick. He's the one who got the call in the first place."

"He's solid."

Michael pulled out the chair across from where Townsend was sitting. "Maybe."

Will's eyes opened wide and his head involuntarily snapped back. "You're worried about Whitick?"

"Will, let's go back to your first question. You asked me who I thought tipped them off about Barnes being moved. Granted, more people knew about it and could have been the source. But I've listened to the tape of the call to McCabe's office, and while I'm not certain it's Whitick, I can't eliminate him as a suspect. And if it was him, then we have a much bigger problem."

Townsend locked eyes with his former XO. "So you're not certain he's the leak. Secondly, I have known Tom Whitick for twenty years. Not the brightest bulb, but a loyal guy. He also happens to be the Chief of Detectives in the county. Michael, I know you're my fixer, but there's got to be another way to fix this. It's one thing for some whore in Vegas to commit suicide . . ."

"Then I think it's time that we find a way for the case to come to a quick end."

Will closed his eyes and rubbed his temples. "How? He's still in protective custody. If we had gotten him into the general population, it would have been easy. Now there's a fucking court order that he can't be moved."

"You need total deniability on this," Michael said. "So let me worry about it. I have some thoughts, but let's leave it at that."

Will nodded. "How that fucking idiot came from my gene pool is beyond me." He looked up and met Gardner's cold brown eyes. "What about going forward? What happens if others are looking?"

"Hopefully it's been taken care of."

"Let's hope so," he said quietly, more as a prayer than a reply.

"I also decided to have everything pulled out of McCabe's apartment and their office. If they know, I don't want any evidence left behind."

"I agree. I don't need more problems; I just need this over."

"There is one more piece of good news. Turns out the DOJ's Office of Professional Responsibility has a wire on Swisher's cell phone."

"Yeah, so?"

Gardner's sneer almost resembled a smile. "I didn't spend all that time in the NSA without developing some sources in DOJ. I've been promised updates."

Will stared at Gardner, shaking his head. "I'm glad you're on my side."

CHAPTER 23

*D*UANE STOOD OUTSIDE THE GLEAMING, ULTRA-MODERN glass and steel Public Safety building, home to the Providence, Rhode Island, Police Department, thinking back to the last time he was in town. He was still with the Bureau and he'd been sent up to interview a "terror" suspect, who it turned out was nothing more than a drunk Muslim student from Johnson & Wales who had shouted "Allahu Akbar!" at the top of his lungs outside a frat house. Except for violating the school's drinking policy, and perhaps some religious tenets, it wasn't the next terrorist wave the campus police had called in to the FBI. Back then, Providence PD was housed in a building more fitting to a Dickens novel than headquarters of a police department. Sixty years old, decrepit, and sorely overcrowded, it was barely functional.

How times have changed.

Standing there, Duane realized there were times when he still missed being part of law enforcement. But he knew there was no way back. He could never clear a background check. To the rest of the world it might look like he left the FBI voluntarily, but anyone hiring from within the world of law enforcement would dig a little deeper, and once they did, they'd get enough of a whiff of the truth to head in a different direction. *C'est la vie.* At least working on the defense side kept him involved in some interesting cases.

He eventually made his way up to the Detective Bureau and went through the paperwork of signing in. About ten minutes later, a tired-looking guy of about fifty, in a rumpled gray suit that on closer inspection was actually the remnants of two rumpled gray suits, approached the counter. "Swisher?" he asked.

"Yeah, that would be me."

"Detective Vince Florio," he offered. "Thanks for coming up. Follow me."

They made their way through a maze of cubicles, and then Florio made a sudden right turn into a good-size office. Surprised Florio had an office and not a cubicle, Duane quickly took in as much as he could: pictures of what looked like the wife, three kids, a number of awards were all hung crookedly and haphazardly on the walls.

"Have a seat," Florio offered, pointing to a chair opposite his desk before unceremoniously plopping down in his own chair. "Brown class of '93, right?"

Duane nodded. "Yeah."

"Yeah, my oldest was about thirteen then. Saw you play, I dunno, maybe a half dozen times. My son was a huge Providence College fan. But you were good for a Bear. We enjoyed watching you play."

"Thanks. Your son play?"

"He did," he responded, a sudden sense of something else entering the conversation hanging in the air. "Died of leukemia in '97. Still miss him."

Duane's mind immediately flashed to Austin as he tried to take in the pain of losing a child. He couldn't. It was unimaginable. "I'm sorry. I know that's totally inadequate, but I am."

"Thanks." Florio seemed momentarily lost, as if the ghost of his son was somewhere nearby. He finally faked a smile and moved on. "So look, I do appreciate you driving up here. Like I told you on the phone. It sounds like I have information you're looking for and you may have info I'm looking for." He paused and gave Duane a small grin. "You want to go first?"

Duane nodded, recognizing the cops' mentality of wanting to know what they were getting before sharing what they had. He knew it wasn't just because he was now a civilian—it had happened when he was an agent too, probably even more then, because local cops generally never trusted the FBI to share anything, usually with good reason. Slowly, methodically, Duane began explaining the case and their suspicions about William Townsend, Jr., including who Townsend's father was, being careful to never say anything that if repeated in a courtroom would incriminate Sharise in any way. Florio showed no emotion as Duane laid everything out; he just sat there, his arms folded across his chest, listening.

When Duane was done, Florio unfolded his arms and rocked forward in his chair. "You really believe Townsend was a serial killer?"

"Not sure," he replied. "But it's the only thing that makes sense."

"How about maybe your client just flat out robbed and murdered the guy?"

"Too many pieces don't fit for that to be true."

"Or maybe you just don't want them to fit. Biggest mistake in this line of work? Come up with a theory of what happened and make the pieces fit the theory."

"Trust me, a lot of other theories offer a better chance for a not guilty, or even a hung jury, than that Townsend was a stone-cold murderer."

Florio's laugh was deep and cynical. "I'm probably not the first to suggest to you that your chances for a not guilty are a little on the skinny side."

"Maybe. But that's why I'm here."

Florio opened a manila folder that was about a half-inch thick. "Anthony DiFiglio, Jr.," he said matter-of-factly. "Date of death was September 19, 2000. Found in a Dumpster off of Valley Street. Nineteen years old, living on the street. Had been thrown out of his house by his dad, who couldn't deal with his 'faggot son'—father's words, not mine. Cause of death, strangulation. Dead approximately five days before the body was found. Body was in pretty bad shape when it was found, no prints. The only evidence recovered was a semen stain on the dress Anthony was wearing."

Duane immediately picked up on the tone and familiarity in Florio's voice. "You know the victim?"

Florio's head nodded ever so slightly, but the words seemed stuck. "Yeah," he said almost in a whisper. He inhaled and then blew it out quickly. "Know his dad well. He's a cop in Pawtucket. We went to the academy together. He started here, then moved up to Pawtucket after about five years on the job. We stayed in touch." He let his eyes slowly close. "Tony junior was out of place right from the start. Not athletic, hung out with the girls . . . drove his dad crazy. Tony, the old man, is a rough-and-tumble kind of guy. Don't get me wrong, he's not a bad guy. But he wanted to play football with his son, go to a ballgame together, you know, do the typical father-son shit. But junior was never that kid and it drove his old man crazy. When he was about seventeen, Tony gave his son an ultimatum: join the army and man up or move it. The kid moved out. I mean really, this kid had about as much chance of making it in the army as Tinker Bell did." He let out a little sigh. "Anyway, after he moved out he was living on the streets as a woman. To look at him you'd never know he was a guy. He got busted a couple times for drugs, prostitution; you know, survival crimes. I made sure people knew who his dad was and tried to make sure he caught some slack. Tried to talk to Tony too. But Jesus, us goombahs can be pretty fucking stubborn, and Tony is nothing if not stubborn."

He looked down at the papers in the file. "I was head of

Homicide when the body was found. There was no ID on the body or around the Dumpster. Detectives who were called to the scene had no idea who it was. Just some poor SOB who wound up in a Dumpster. They figured it was some kid who OD'd, whose friends panicked and dumped him. When I read their reports, I guess I had a bad feeling about who it might be—guy dressed as a woman, the estimated age. When the ME came back with who it was, and cause of death . . ."

He went to continue, but nothing came out. He scratched his eyebrow, his eyes showing the memory hadn't faded.

"I went up to the house to tell Tony. He knew as soon he saw me at the door that it wasn't because the kid had been picked up again. He knew where I was assigned and he knew I was on the job. His knees buckled a little when I told him, but he grabbed on to the door and he steadied himself quickly. After we released the body, he had an undertaker come take the body and had him buried with his mom. No wake, no funeral, no service. Like I said, Tony's not a bad guy, but that was a little cold, even by my standards."

"What'd mom die of?"

"She and Tony divorced when the kid was about four. About three years later she got stage four breast cancer. Don't think she lasted even a year. When she got real sick that's when Tony moved back in with his dad. It was all downhill from there."

"Siblings?"

"No, only child."

Duane made a mental note to play with his son when he got home. "What did the investigation turn up?"

Florio studied Duane before he continued. "After the ME told us it was a homicide, I had forensics go over everything. That's how we found the stain on the dress. But as you might imagine, it was not a pristine crime scene and the sample was pretty degraded. All we had was the stain. No witnesses, no clues, nothing. So we put it into the system. When it came back, there were no matches, but because the sample was so degraded, we were really just looking for a partial from which we could get some leads. About a year after that I got moved out of Homicide."

"You asked to get out?" he asked.

He gave Duane a smirk. "Yeah, I asked to get out of Homicide, just like you asked to get out of the FBI." His eyes seemed to bore into Duane. "No, let's just say I lost my temper one day in the interrogation room."

"Where you assigned now?"

"I'm not on the rubber gun squad, if that's what you're asking. I'm in your old line of work, counterterrorism."

Duane was impressed that Florio had done his homework on him for a simple meeting. "So if you're not in Homicide anymore, why did they give you my call?"

"Anybody who's been in Homicide for any length of time has a case that haunts them—their white whale. I was in Homicide for ten years. Tony DiFiglio, Jr., is my Moby Dick. Even if the old man doesn't care, and I suspect he does, I owe it to both of them to find out who killed him."

Duane gave him a puzzled look. "So what brings us here?"

Florio rubbed the back of his neck. "Every year, I ask the lab folks to run it through CODIS and every year, as a courtesy to me, they do. Like I said, given the state of the sample that we put in, I never thought we'd get anything. So about two months ago, I asked them to run it for me. Couple hours later, Andrea Peters, who runs the lab, knocked on the door and said, 'I have news for you.' She proceeded to tell me about getting a partial match. If you know CODIS, you know there are no identifiers, just the submitting agency. So naturally, I immediately call the submitting agency, the Ocean County Prosecutor's Office, and ask for the chief. Tell him who I am, what I'm looking at, and give him the sample number." He looked down at some handwritten notes in the file. "Guy's name is Whitick, Tom Whitick. You know him?"

Duane shook his head no.

"Anyway, could've been nicer. Told me he'd have his guys run it down and he'd get back to me. About a half hour later, he calls me back, and says there's been a terrible mistake and the sample was from a victim and should never have been in the unknown suspect category.

"I'm, like, what the fuck are you talking about. I don't care if the sample belongs to Mother Teresa, just give me the name. And he said, 'no, it was submitted without following appropriate protocols and so he couldn't release any information to me." Florio frowned, barely hiding his anger. "Look," Florio continued, "I have a pretty good bullshit detector, and what he told me was total bullshit. After I hung up from him, I called a friend of mine in the FBI and asked him if there was any way I could get the info, and he told me that if the submitting agency won't give it up, there was nothing to be done."

Florio let out a small huff. "You know what's funny, after that happened, I spent every night for about two weeks trying to find every murder I could in Ocean County, New Jersey, looking for victims who were transgendered. I never thought that it might be the other way around."

"It's transgender, by the way."

"What?" Florio said, clearly confused.

"You said you were looking for victims who were transgendered. The correct term is *transgender*. It's an adjective."

Florio's expression grew even more perplexed.

"Sorry," Duane offered. "My partner is a transgender woman, and she is constantly schooling me on the correct use of terminology."

Florio shifted uncomfortably in his chair. "Sure. Whatever," he replied.

"So this is what I have on Townsend." Duane reached into his briefcase and pulled out a sheet of paper. "This is his partial DNA profile from a semen stain that was found at the scene. What happened was my client's underwear was left at the scene. So they sent it out to the State Police lab for analysis. Apparently they didn't realize there were semen stains on the underwear; they thought there was just blood. As a result, when the State Police entered everything into the system, the semen stains weren't put in as known victim samples. Like your sample, these were pretty contaminated, so they only got partials on both of them. One stain came back consistent with our client, the second, according to the report, was consistent with Mr. Townsend. But because it hadn't been submitted as a known sample from the victim, it was analyzed as a suspect. I assume that's why when Andrea ran yours it came back with a partial hit. We filed a motion to have Townsend's entire known sample be run through the unsolved section of CODIS. Unfortunately, it was denied."

Florio took the sheet and looked at it. "I can't understand this gibberish. Mind if I see if Andrea can join us?"

"Fine."

After he made his call, his focus returned to Duane. "Can you put Townsend here?"

Duane gave Florio a knowing look. "I've done every search I can on Townsend—postal records, voting records, school records—anything I could get legally. In August 1999 he rented an apartment two blocks from Providence College, where he went from September 1999 until May 2001, when he graduated with an MBA. So I can put him in your city when the murder occurred."

"Did he try to strangle your client?" Florio interjected.

"I can't answer that—you understand that I can't repeat what my client has told me."

Florio nodded.

"After he gets his MBA, he moved to Boston for two years, then moves back to New Jersey, where his parents own homes in Moorestown and Mantoloking. Moorestown is a suburb of Philadelphia, and Mantoloking is not too far from Atlantic City, where my client was plying her trade."

Florio gave him a knowing look. "You have others, don't you?"

Duane took another sheet out of his briefcase. "Funny you mentioned Pawtucket, because there's an unsolved murder of a transgender woman there in March 2001. Unclear if she was a prostitute or not. The others were all transgender prostitutes. There was one in Boston in February 2002 and there were two in Philly; one in January 2003, the other March 2005. The attempt on my client was in April of 2006."

Duane handed the piece of paper to Florio. When he was finished looking at it, he cocked his head to the side. "Interesting. Except for Tony, they were all in the winter."

"Pure guess on my part," Duane offered, "but if Tony was the first, and if they're all related, maybe he learned some lessons— fewer potential witnesses on the street in the winter, and maybe it takes a little longer to realize someone is missing because people aren't out as much. Not sure, but yeah, there does appear to be a pattern."

"You have any DNA info on any of them?"

"No, I met with Detective Bradley in Pawtucket this morning. Not the friendliest sort. Told me from looking at the file that they had no DNA samples. The Massachusetts State Police lab handles Boston, and they wouldn't talk to me. Philly told me they had submitted DNA on the 2005 homicide, with no results, and hadn't collected anything in the 2003 case."

"So you have one potential in Philly and one unknown in Boston." He paused. "I should be able to at least find out if Boston submitted anything. We share a lot of info with Massachusetts. If Boston submitted samples at the time, we may even be able to get them to resubmit it."

There was a gentle rap on the door and an attractive, fortyish African-American woman entered the room. "You looking for me?"

"Andrea, here's our sample on the DiFiglio case and here's a printout on another case. What do you make of it?"

She took a pair of glasses off the top of her head and studied the two documents. After about a minute, she looked up at Florio. "Could be the same. As I explained to you, you need thirteen loci to have a match. Our sample is so degraded the best we're ever going to match is eight, because that's really all we have.

This sample only has seven loci, so it must have been degraded too, but the seven here match the corresponding seven loci on ours. So could be the same guy, but it would never be admissible. This looks like the one I brought to you two months ago."

"It is."

She looked at him over the top of her glasses and then removed them and placed them back on the top of her head.

"Andrea Peters, this is Duane Swisher—Mr. Swisher, Andrea Peters." After they shook hands, she turned her attention back to Florio. "So what gives?"

"Thanks to Mr. Swisher, we have a name and information on our suspect. You deal with State Police Lab in Massachusetts a lot, Swisher has a case out of Boston. Here's the info on it. Think you could see if they collected DNA on the homicide up there and if they've had any hits?" he asked as he handed the paper to her.

She glanced at it without even putting her glasses back on. "Sure. Anything else?"

"No, thanks. Appreciate the help."

After she walked out and closed the door, Florio closed the file on his desk. "She doesn't like me, but she's damn good at what she does." Florio seemed like he was going to leave it there, but then continued without waiting for Duane to ask. "The kid I smacked around in the interrogation room was a Black kid brought in as a suspect in a drive-by that killed a seven-year-old girl who just happened to be in the wrong place at the wrong time. Turned out he was completely innocent and I was a fucking moron. That's why I'm here, and not still in Homicide. The city paid the kid some money to make it go away, but Andrea and others weren't real happy with the racial overtones. Let's say I called him some things I'm not proud of. When the only thing that happened to me was they sat me down for ninety days and transferred me to counterterrorism, some people, Andrea included, were incensed. I tell you that because if you're thinking about using me as a witness, you have to know that there's an Internal Affairs investigation in my file and it ain't pretty."

"Let's talk about the possibility of you as a witness," Duane said. He then proceeded to explain where the case was, the motion the judge had already denied, and how they hoped to use this information. He also suggested that there might be another way for Florio to help, and as they discussed that possibility, Florio seemed genuinely intrigued.

Duane had just gotten onto the Garden State Parkway on his way home when his cell phone rang. "Swisher," he answered.

"Hey, it's Detective Florio. Listen, I have good news and bad news."

"I'm listening."

"Apparently Boston has a good DNA sample. There were skin cells under the fingernails of the victim, who apparently scratched whoever murdered her."

"The bad news?" he asked.

"No matches when they searched today."

"Shit," Duane said.

"There's more. I had our sample rerun today and didn't get the partial match we got two months ago."

"Ocean pulled it out of the system," Duane said.

"Apparently."

Neither of them said anything. Finally, Duane said, "I'll fax you the affidavit tomorrow for you to review. But before we file a new motion, I'd still like to try what we talked about."

"I'll try and call him tomorrow."

He hung up from Florio and immediately called Erin to fill her in. When he finished, he was surprised that she didn't sound more excited. "Is everything okay?"

"No."

"What's wrong?"

"I . . . no, make that we, were broken into again."

"What are you talking about?"

She said nothing for the longest time. "I went out for a run yesterday and after I got back, I felt like there was something off.

I told myself I was just being paranoid, but I still unscrewed the phone in the bedroom to check. The bug was gone. I checked the kitchen and that one was gone too. I immediately ran over to the office and checked the phones and where you told me the other bugs were—all gone."

"Why didn't you call me?"

"I knew you were on your way up to Providence. Besides, what were you going to do?"

"I dunno. You call the police?"

"What, and tell them someone broke into my apartment and took out the illegal listening devices they installed on my phone? I suspect that would have gone well. Maybe I could have put some aluminum foil on my head to make them really think I was nuts."

"You okay?"

"No! Someone broke into my apartment for the second time in, what, three weeks? And by the way, they didn't force their way in. So no, I'm not feeling terribly safe these days."

"Sorry," he offered.

"Me too." She paused. "I really want to fuck these bastards. I just hope we all stay alive long enough to get there."

CHAPTER 24

*T*HEY WERE HUDDLED IN ERIN'S OFFICE CRAFTING THE WORD-
ing of the affidavit for Florio to sign when Cheryl buzzed her.
"Erin, it's First Assistant Prosecutor Taylor and she says it's urgent that she speak with you."

Erin shrugged as she caught Swish's questioning glance.
"Thanks, Cheryl. Put her through."

Erin immediately hit the hands-free button so Duane could
listen in. "Hello, Ms. Taylor. I have you on speaker because I'm
sitting here with my partner."

"That's fine. I'm sorry, I have very limited information right
now, but I received a call from the warden about five minutes
ago. Your client has been rushed to the hospital. Apparently
while being transported this morning to the exercise enclosure,
he fell down a flight of steps and was injured."

"How seriously was she injured?" Erin asked.

"I'm afraid I don't have specific information at this point, but I
was advised by the warden that . . . that she was unconscious and
her injuries appeared to be serious."

Erin exhaled. "What hospital has she been taken to?"

"Bristol General."

"Okay. I'm leaving now for the hospital. Can I ask you to please call me if you get any updates on her condition?"

"Of course." She hesitated. "Um, Erin, I have no information about whether Mr. Barnes has any family, and if so, how to reach them. But you may want to reach out."

As soon as she hung up, Erin called Tonya and filled her in on what they knew. "I'll be on the first plane that I can get on. I'll let you know as soon as I have my tickets," Tonya had replied.

They took separate cars, unsure as to what they were going to need to do. After arriving at the hospital, they were advised that Sharise had been taken to the intensive care unit. As they approached the nurses' station, Barbara Taylor was walking out of one of the rooms accompanied by someone who appeared to be a doctor. When Taylor saw them she waved for them to come over.

"Ms. McCabe, Mr. Swisher, this is Dr. Peter Ogden, he's handling Mr. Barnes's care." They exchanged handshakes and then Taylor continued. "I spoke with Dr. Ogden about the fact that there is no family local and that the two of you are Mr. Barnes's attorneys and how we handle both the dissemination of medical information under HIPAA and the decisions that need to be made concerning the appropriate care for Mr. Barnes. Since Mr. Barnes is in the custody of the county sheriff's department, and they have not only the authority, but the duty, to make appropriate medical decisions on his behalf, I've spoken with the sheriff and he has agreed that under the circumstances, you should be advised of his condition and be part of the decision-making process, unless and until a family member can make the decisions on his behalf. I assume you are okay with that."

Erin was momentarily taken aback by what Taylor had just said. Erin had expected that they would have to fight to get medical information about Sharise.

"Thank you, Barbara. We genuinely appreciate your taking

care of that for us. And Sharise does have a sister in Indianapolis, who we have spoken to, and she's on her way."

Dr. Ogden looked perplexed. "I'm sorry. Who's Sharise?"

Erin gave Taylor a glance. "Long story," she replied to Ogden. "Samuel Barnes also goes by the name Sharise Barnes. Sorry for the confusion."

Ogden nodded. "No problem."

"Doctor, if you don't mind, could you tell Ms. McCabe and Mr. Swisher what you just told me."

"Sure. Mr. Barnes has suffered a basilar skull fracture to his frontal bone as a result of the fall. He was unconscious when he arrived. Given the severity of the fracture, we put him into a drug-induced coma, hoping to minimize any potential swelling of the brain and, if he survives, any long-term traumatic brain injury. He also suffered a broken clavicle, three broken ribs, and other bruises and soft tissue injuries. At this point, he is in critical condition, and we are certainly monitoring him for cerebral edema, which may require us to do further surgery. If he makes it through the next forty-eight to seventy-two hours without any major complications, he has a reasonable chance of surviving. But right now, it's too soon to tell."

"Thank you, Doctor. May we see her?" Erin asked.

"See her?" Ogden replied.

"Like I said, long story," she replied to Ogden.

Ogden looked from Erin to Taylor to Duane. "Sure, okay."

"Can we speak privately?" Taylor asked Erin and Duane.

The three of them walked to the end of the hallway and stood in front of a large window looking out on the hospital parking lot.

"Look," Taylor began, "I'm a prosecutor, so I'm suspicious by nature. Obviously, I know about the attempt to move your client out of protective custody, and that after that didn't take place, he was seriously injured in a fall. I know if I were in your shoes, I'd sure be wondering what was going on. I just want you to know, I share your concerns. I've already spoken with the warden to make sure that all videos are preserved. I don't think any of this changes my opinion about your client, but by the same token, if someone is trying to harm him, it's part of my job to make sure that doesn't happen." She stopped and drew her lower lip between her teeth, seemingly unsure as to what else to say.

"Thank you, Barbara. I . . . we do appreciate that, especially securing the video. All I can say is that there are other things that have happened—things we're not at liberty to discuss—that make us almost certain this was not an accident. Hopefully, she'll pull through. But in the meantime, when she gets here, we'll meet with Sharise's sister to try and figure out how to protect her."

Taylor's expression showed her confusion. "Obviously, she'll be under armed security from the sheriff's office the whole time she is here."

Erin smirked. "I'm sorry, but the scene from *The Godfather*, when they come to kill Don Corleone in the hospital, keeps running through my head. Not to mention the fact that she's being guarded by officers from the same office that were with her when she"—Erin paused to give air quotes—"'fell' down the steps. So please forgive me if I don't feel exactly warm and fuzzy about her safety."

Taylor said nothing.

Finally, Erin said, "I'm sorry. I didn't mean that to be a personal attack on you or what you've done. We really do appreciate the fact that you made it possible for Ogden to talk to us. It's not you we don't trust, it's everybody else that seems to want our client dead."

"I suppose I understand," Taylor said. "I've alerted the sheriff's officers that you and any family members are allowed to be in the room. There will be two guards outside at all times, and when there are visitors in the room, one of the guards will stand inside." She took a deep breath. "Please let me know if you need anything else."

As Taylor indicated, there were two sheriff's officers stationed outside the door to the intensive care room. Inside, Sharise was hooked up to a ventilator, several monitors, and had IVs in both arms. Her face was bruised and swollen. Her hands were handcuffed to the bedrails.

Erin looked at the handcuffs and shook her head in disgust. She grabbed one of the chairs provided for visitors, moved it alongside the bed, and sat down. She bent over and spoke softly to Sharise. "Hey, Sharise. It's Erin and Duane. We're here with you. Your sister is on her way. Hopefully, she'll be here in a few hours. Stay strong, girl. You can make it."

She sat back in the chair and looked up at Duane to say something when she caught sight of the officer within earshot standing by the door. She turned back to Sharise, shaking her head. "Stay strong," she repeated in a whisper.

When they were alone in the hallway, Erin turned to Duane. "I have an idea. Not sure if it will work, but we need Tonya and Paul to buy in."

"I'm listening," he said, his curiosity evident in his tone.

When she finished explaining her idea, he shook his head. "That's crazy. Do you really think they'll go for it?"

"You're the one who told me Paul is making over five million a year, and on year one of a new three-year guaranteed contract."

"Worth a shot," Duane said with a snort.

Shortly before eleven, Tonya called to let them know that the owner of the Pacers was providing them with his company jet to fly them to Atlantic City and a limo to get them to the hospital. While they were on the phone, Erin explained her feeling that Sharise's fall hadn't been an accident, and her plan on how to try to protect her against another attempt.

Throughout the rest of the morning and early afternoon, they took turns sitting by Sharise's bed, talking to her. Around 2:30, there was a knock on the door. "Family here to see Barnes," the sheriff's officer said to the officer sitting in the room watching Erin. "I've checked them, they're okay."

Erin had always been impressed by Duane's size and build—he clearly kept himself in great shape—but when Paul Tillis walked into the room, she suddenly realized just how big NBA players were. Not only was he taller than Duane, but his size was imposing in a way that Duane's wasn't. Tonya, at 5'9", seemed petite in comparison. She was a beautiful dark-skinned woman whose black curly hair fell over her shoulders. Both Erin and Duane had met Tonya when she'd visited Sharise in jail, but neither of them had met Paul.

After some brief introductions, Tonya hurried over to Sharise's bedside. When she looked down on the battered face of her sister, she covered her mouth with her hand, choking back the sobs that desperately wanted to turn into a wail. Paul walked over and rested his hand on Tonya's shoulder and then gently pulled her toward him. She allowed herself to fold into him, overwhelmed by the sight of Sharise's battered body.

She finally lowered herself into the chair and leaned over so she was within inches of Sharise. "Hey, baby. It's Tonya. Paul's here with me too. I know you can hear me. You can get through this. I love you, little sister."

Erin quietly left the room and waited in the hallway with Duane. After about fifteen minutes, Paul came out of the room. "Is there a place where we can get a cup of coffee?" he asked. "Tonya spoke to me about your suggestion and I'd like to discuss it with you."

Well, at least he didn't say no. "Yeah, there's a cafeteria on the first floor."

"Okay, let me just let Tonya know where we'll be. Seeing what I've just seen, I think I want to move on this as soon as possible."

CHAPTER 25

"GOOD MORNING, SHERIFF, WHAT CAN I DO FOR YOU?"

"Barbara, I've been trying to reach Lee, but apparently he's out of the office at a very important meeting. I'm calling because bail was just posted for Samuel Barnes."

"Charlie, what the hell are you talking about?"

"His sister just came in and delivered a certified check for a million dollars. That's his bail."

"What the . . ." She was about to tell him not to release Barnes from custody until she could get to court to raise his bail, when she realized that Barnes was in a coma and wasn't going any-where. What the hell was McCabe doing? "Okay, Charlie, sit tight for now. As you know, Barnes is in the hospital in a coma, so it's not like he's going to suddenly disappear. Let me check into what's going on."

"Uh, will you let Lee know?"

"Sure, Charlie. I'll find him and let him know."

She hung up and buzzed Angela, Lee's executive assistant,

only to be told he was at a meeting with Will Townsend. Angela promised to leave a message that it was urgent he call Barbara.

Barbara picked up her cell phone and scrolled through her contacts.

"Hi, Barbara," Erin answered on the first ring. "I thought I might hear from you."

"Did your client's sister really just post a million-dollar cash bail?"

"She did."

"Erin, what are you up to? You know your client can't go anywhere. Am I really going to have to go to court to stop this?"

"I hope not. Look, my client's sister wants the ability to have her own security team guarding Sharise and her own private nurses taking care of her. Call me crazy, but I'm a little concerned that a nurse might accidentally give Sharise something in her IV that kills her. I don't care if you post guards at the end of every hallway and every exit from the hospital. You know Sharise can't be moved. We just want the ability to make sure she's safe. Something the county has not done a good job at."

There was a long silence.

"Barbara, are you still there?"

She paused. "Yeah, I'm thinking."

"Just so you know, I'm at the hospital and Duane is with Sharise's sister now. We also had her sister appointed as Sharise's temporary guardian. You also may want to let the sheriff know that he will need to reposition his officers, because we will insist that they not be at her door. Not that we don't trust them or anything." Erin paused. "Oh, and by the way, please tell them to remove the handcuffs. As of now, she's on bail."

"Erin, have you thought through the ramifications of what you're doing?"

"To be honest, probably not. But I've thought through the ramifications of not doing it, and there's really no choice."

Barbara sighed. "Okay. I'll be in touch."

Barbara rubbed her eyes and thought about her options. It

wasn't like Barnes was going anywhere. At this point, it wasn't even clear Barnes was going to survive. She picked up the phone and dialed. "Charlie, it's Barbara. Yeah, I confirmed and for now, until I can talk to Lee, just order your men to stand guard at either end of the hallway. Apparently, the sister has hired some private security guards to provide protection. So for now, let's just make nice. It's not like they can move her, or him, or anything. Just keep an eye on things and let me know if anything unusual happens. Oh, and, Charlie, tell the officers to remove the handcuffs. Thanks."

About ten minutes later, Lee called. "Hey, I heard you were looking for me and it's urgent. What's going on?"

"Are you still with Will Townsend?"

"Yeah, we're just wrapping up. Why?"

"Barnes's sister just posted bail for Barnes."

"What?"

"That seems to be the general reaction."

"What's the bail—isn't it a million cash?"

"Correct, and before you ask how, Barnes's brother-in-law plays in the NBA and he is the source of the funds, so we can't even ask for a source hearing—it's legit."

"Barbara, you've got to get into court and stop this immediately. Barnes can't be released."

"Lee, before you lose it, let me remind you that Barnes is in a coma and may not survive. He's not going anywhere. I spoke to McCabe, and the reason they did it is so that they could have their own personal security at the door and bring in their own nurses to handle her care. In other words, they don't trust us."

"I don't give a rat's ass as to whether or not they trust us, I can't allow this to happen."

"Lee, let me suggest that from a liability standpoint, we may want to leave this alone for now."

"What the hell are you talking about? Liability, what liability?"

"Lee, Barnes is lying in a hospital with a fractured skull and may not survive. I've looked at the video from the jail, and while it's inconclusive as to why, there's no question that there was contact between the corrections officer and Barnes, and that causes Barnes, who is handcuffed and shackled, to fall down the steps. The CO says it was accidental, and there's no way to dispute that, but I suspect at some point there will be a lawsuit. If Barnes survives and comes out of the coma, then we can worry about going to court and jacking up the bail. But right now, given the situation, it may look a little mean-spirited. We can always claim we didn't do anything now so he could get the care his family wanted him to get. If we fight the bail now and win, if he doesn't pull through, the county will get blamed."

Lee said nothing for several seconds. "I need to talk to Will and Michael. I'll call you back."

The line went dead, and Barbara was left to wonder why he was meeting with them in the first place. She had been doing this long enough to trust her gut, and her gut was telling her that there was something off. This had started off as an open-and-shut case, but it had slowly morphed into something far more complicated. Lee was acting strange, and the whole series of events leading up to Barnes's fall was eating at her. Her instincts were screaming at her that someone wanted Barnes dead.

She didn't need this complication. She knew that even though she managed to hide it from everyone else, her divorce from Dan and selling their home had taken an emotional toll. So she had secretly hoped that once the case was over Townsend would show his appreciation by helping her to get appointed as a judge. With Vicky set to graduate college in the spring, the timing would be perfect.

She swiveled in her chair and pulled open the file drawer that held *State v. Barnes*, and pulled out Swisher's chart showing the murders of transgender prostitutes near where Townsend lived. She took a deep breath. *Damn it. If word ever gets back to Will that I investigated his son's background, my chances of going to the bench are toast.* But some things were more important than becoming a judge—like looking in the mirror at night. She wasn't convinced that Bill Townsend was a murderer, but she no longer was convinced he wasn't either.

Will paced back and forth. "I told you I needed this case over," he barked. "I can only imagine what will happen if Barnes survives. This case could drag on for months while he recovers. I'm not a happy camper, Michael."

"Well, I'm afraid that I have news that is going to make you even unhappier."

Will lowered his head to one side and eyed him suspiciously.

"I told you I was promised updates on the wire on Swisher's cell phone."

"Yeah."

"He was in Providence, Rhode Island, on Monday meeting with the detective who had called Whitick."

"The one who had the partial match?"

"Yeah, him. Swisher is supposed to be getting an affidavit from this guy about his conversation with Whitick. They haven't put it all together yet, but they're getting dangerously close."

Will closed his eyes and slowly inhaled. "Shit," he muttered. "What do we do now? Do they have the affidavit from this guy?"

"What I'm told is not yet. But I'm guessing they'll have it in the next twenty-four to forty-eight hours."

Will rubbed his face with his hands. "Well, I guess we're done then. If Providence PD knows, it's only a matter of time."

"Maybe not," Michael said.

"Explain."

"What I'm told is that when Swisher called McCabe, he explained that the cop he met with had some internal affairs issues and, as a result, is no longer in Homicide. Apparently, the murder with the partial match is a cold case file that he pursues from time to time. So it's possible that he's the only one who has the information, or, at least, he's the only one who cares about the information. Remember Whitick pulled everything off two months ago and we haven't heard a peep from Providence. So they're not exactly banging down anyone's door over the case."

"This shit show just seems to get worse and worse," Will said, the anger creeping back into his voice.

"Never known you to quit halfway through a mission," Gardner responded.

"I never said anything about quitting," he replied loudly. "I'm just not happy with the mission creep that's going on. If things had gone the way they were supposed to, we wouldn't even be having this conversation."

"Most people wouldn't have survived the fall. He still might not. We just need to deal with all eventualities."

"We? I thought that was your job," Will said.

CHAPTER 26

*I*T HAD BEEN A LATE NIGHT ON WEDNESDAY. OGDEN HAD ADvised Tonya that Sharise was suffering from a brain bleed. They immediately rushed her into surgery, where Ogden performed a craniectomy in an attempt to relieve the pressure on her brain. The surgery had started around four in the afternoon and it was almost five hours before Ogden walked into the waiting area to tell them that things had gone as well as could be expected. Left unsaid in all the discussions was what Sharise's mental condition would be if, in fact, she did survive. By the time Sharise was out of recovery and back in ICU, it was well after eleven.

Erin dragged herself to the office at nine o'clock the next morning. Both she and Duane had been out of the office for most of the last two days, and the work was piling up. As she listened to her messages, she was relieved that there was nothing from Taylor or Carmichael indicating they were going to court to demand that bail be increased.

Around ten, Tonya called to give her an update. Sharise had spiked a fever of 104 and they had increased her IV antibiotics, concerned that there was an infection from the surgery. Despite the setbacks, Ogden felt Sharise had a fifty-fifty chance of surviving. Although when Tonya had asked about the potential that Sharise had suffered long-term brain damage, he had been very evasive.

Duane rolled in around ten thirty, finalized Florio's affidavit, and faxed it off. Afterward, he and Erin sat in his office, just staring at each other. The last forty-eight hours had been so out of control that they barely had time to deal with one crisis when they were on to the next. It had been a whirlwind, and they found themselves physically and mentally exhausted.

"You think she'll make it?" Duane asked.

Erin gave him a small smile. "You know what, I do. She was thrown out of her house and survived on the streets for four years. She's not only tough, I'd say she's pretty damn resilient. So yeah, my money's on her to pull through."

Duane nodded. As she watched him, she couldn't help but notice how uncomfortable he seemed to be. He was actually fidgeting.

"What's up?" she finally asked.

"I played hoops Tuesday night," he responded.

"Great, I'm busting my hump putting the bail papers together in case they move to hike her bail, and you're out playing B-ball," she said, her sarcasm more for effect than real. "So I'm thinking there's more to your confession than just letting me know you have sinned?"

"Yeah, there's more," he responded sheepishly. "After the game, Mark and I talked."

"Yeah, so? He's your friend, you're allowed to talk to each other."

Duane looked down at his lap and slowly raised his head so he was looking her in the eye. "E, this is a little awkward, but look, I know you . . . well, you were attracted to Mark. And I know that things haven't gone exactly the way you wanted. But, I guess, I was just wondering if you still had the ability to remember what it was like to be a guy and see things from a guy's perspective?"

"Swish, what the hell are you talking about?"

"Well, when you were a guy, you found Lauren really attractive, right?"

Erin inhaled, her impatience growing. "Yeah. So?"

"And you told me that before Mark, you never were attracted to a man. Right?"

Her glare provided enough of a response for him to continue. "Well, suppose when you were a guy, you found yourself attracted to this woman, but then you found out she had been assigned male at birth." Duane paused, and it looked like he wanted to smile at getting the terminology right, but her piercing stare dissuaded him. "Anyway, if you found that out, what's the first thing you would wonder?"

She stared at him in disbelief. "Are you for real? Are you trying to tell me that Mark is struggling because he doesn't know what I have between my legs?"

Even with his dark skin, she could see his cheeks redden. "Come on, E, do you really find that hard to understand?" he finally asked.

"Well, thanks for the heads-up. If Mark ever asks me out again, I'll be sure to let him know."

"Look, I was just trying to help. I thought maybe if he understood, you know . . . that, well, everything was normal."

She sighed, shaking her head. "So you told him I had surgery?"

His eyes answered.

Her bemused look suddenly slid off her face. "You know, there is a part of me that does get it. And then there is another part of me that is so fucking offended that I'd like to start throwing things across the room. Basically, what you're saying is that if I hadn't had bottom surgery, and if he was attracted to me, then maybe he'd be revolted by the fact that he kissed a woman who still had a penis. But if I have the right parts, the parts girls are supposed to have, not a girl with a penis, then all's right with the world."

She stood up, grabbed her purse, and headed for the door.

"Wait, E, where you going?"

She stopped and turned to face him. "Look, Swish, I appreciate that you were trying to help. I'm not mad at you—really, I'm not," she said with an air of resignation. "And you know, there really is a part of me that understands why it matters. But Jesus, Swish, it's so demeaning to know that at the end of the day, the only thing that matters to people is what's between my legs.

"I mean, think about it. That's exactly why I can't get the judge or the prosecutor to accept Sharise as a woman. Shit, I can't even get them to *address* her as a woman. But you know what? She's just as much a woman as I am. And maybe there's the rub; people perceive me to be a woman, so they accept me. But as soon as the perception is challenged, then all hell breaks loose. Then, I'm just like Sharise—delusional. Did you know that's what Redman called Sharise on the motion, delusional? He wasn't going to order the county to pay to treat her for her delusion. Well, if she's delusional, then I am too. I'm just some batshit crazy guy who has delusions he's a woman."

She grabbed her coat off the tree in the corner of her office. "I'll be back. We have too much to do. I just need some fresh air," she said as she walked out the door.

"Thanks for coming," Erin said, as her mother leaned over and gave her a hug.

"Least I could do after the Thanksgiving debacle."

Erin waved her off. "I told you, not your fault. Dad will get there when he gets there, or, as I'm discovering, maybe he won't."

"That sounds ominous. Care to explain?"

"Not really. Can I ask you a question?"

"Of course, my dear."

"Okay. Let's suppose that, hypothetically, I hadn't had the surgery I had down below."

Her mother raised her eyebrows. "Okay."

"But I otherwise looked exactly like I do today."

Her mother tilted her head as an indication to continue.

"Would you consider a guy who might be attracted to me gay?"

"You dragged me from the comforts of my office, not to talk about Thanksgiving, or your dad, or how I'm doing, or how you're doing, but to ask me whether or not a man who finds you attractive is gay?"

"Basically, yes."

"I should presume that this has to do with the guy who dumped you not once, but twice."

"Uh-huh."

"My God, if I ever had any doubt that you were a woman, it's gone now."

"What's that supposed to mean? That sounds incredibly—"

"What? Sexist? Stereotypical? It is. As you are discovering, we women can be our own worst enemies at times. We constantly blame ourselves for the faults of the men we're attracted to. If we were only better wives, mothers, girlfriends, lovers, you name it, fill in the blank, then they wouldn't be having whatever problem it is they're having. And that's exactly what you're doing, Erin. If this guy you're attracted to is so hung up on the fact that at one point in your life you lived as a man, that's his problem, not yours. Either you consider yourself a woman or you don't, but it's up to you to be comfortable with who you are, and the hell with everyone else."

Taken aback by her mother's stern tone, Erin said nothing.

"Look," her mother continued, "your father can be an absolute idiot at times, as evidenced by what happened at Thanksgiving. But I'm not sitting here blaming myself because he's an idiot. I'm blaming him. That doesn't change the fact that I love him and I have to learn to deal with his failings. But I can't do that by making his failings my failings. He owns them, not me. Don't get your panties in a knot because some guy is hung up on what's between your legs. It's his problem, not yours."

Erin leaned back, her eyes open wide. "Well, glad I got that off my chest."

Her mother suppressed a laugh. "Sorry. I guess I'm just tired of you beating yourself up. Again, it's generally a thing women do well." She smiled at her daughter and reached out and took her hand. "I'm incredibly proud of who you are. And no surprise, I'm sure that for many straight men, your history may be a deal breaker. You know what? There's not a damn thing you can do about it. So my suggestion is accept it, deal with it, and move on."

Before Erin could respond, her phone started ringing. She looked down and saw it was Duane. She held a finger up to her mom and flipped open her phone. "Hi. I'm just talking to my mom."

"E, get back as soon as you can. Something's happened to Florio."

"What do you mean? He won't sign the affidavit?"

"No, he's been shot."

"Oh shit. I'm on my way."

She looked across the table at her mother. "I'm sorry, Mom. When this nightmare is over, we'll go somewhere and I'll explain."

Peg's concern was written all over her face. "Is Duane all right?"

"Yeah, but a key witness may not be." She slid out from the table, grabbed her things, and gave her mother a hug.

"Be careful," her mother whispered.

"I'll try," she said, rushing out.

She ran up the stairs to the second floor and past Cheryl to Duane's office. "What happened?" she asked without so much as pausing at his door.

"I don't know. I called his office to see if he had gotten the affidavit, and when I asked for Detective Florio, I was put on hold. Then a Sergeant Brown got on the phone and asked why I was calling. When I told him, he told me that Detective Florio had been shot last night, but he wasn't at liberty to give me any more details at this time. I immediately went online and found the website for the *Providence Post*, which said that Florio had received a call about a possible terrorist suspect around five p.m., and he and another officer went to investigate. When they arrived at the location, they were ambushed. The other officer escaped injury, but Florio was taken to the hospital in critical condition."

Erin lowered herself into a chair and cupped her hands behind her head. She wanted to believe it was unrelated, but how was that possible?

"Any arrests?"

"No."

"Do you think it's related to us?" she asked.

Duane nodded.

"Why?"

"The shooting took place a block from where the body of the murder victim in the Providence case, Tony DiFiglio, was found. It's a message to us. No one else will get or believe the connection. But message delivered, loud and clear."

"But wait. It can't be connected. How would they know that you had met with Florio and given him information? And even if they somehow knew, why would murdering one cop change things? There'd be other cops who would follow up."

"I thought about that too. So do you remember when I was driving home from Providence on Monday, I called you and we went over everything?"

"Yeah," she said, confusion wrinkling her brow.

"Well, I remember telling you that Florio was no longer in Homicide and that this was his white whale, the cold case that haunted him."

Her face contorted as the recognition of what he was suggesting slowly spread across her face. "Your cell phone?"

He nodded.

"But how? They'd have to have a wire up on you to get your cell phone. Even Townsend isn't that powerful."

"No, but DOJ is."

"Swish, I'm missing something. Assuming you're right and

DOJ is up on a wire on your cell, presumably on the leak investigation, how's it get from there to Townsend? Maybe we're just seeing shadows."

"You're right, I don't know how it gets from DOJ to him, but I don't believe in coincidences."

Neither one of them said anything for a long time. Finally, Erin said, "I know this is going to sound heartless, but is there anyone else who can sign the affidavit?"

"Maybe," he replied. "I met the woman who runs the lab. I already put a call in to her. She hasn't gotten back to me."

"Do you think Florio called Whitick before he was shot?"

"Don't know. He told me he was going to try and call yesterday. But I don't know if he did."

His computer chimed, alerting him to a new story on the shooting. He quickly turned and refreshed the page. "Shit," he mumbled, resting his fingers on his forehead. "He died." Duane closed his eyes, a pained expression consuming his face. "He had two kids. And I can't help feeling responsible. We're the kiss of death."

She slowly inhaled and nodded, the thought of two kids now without a dad haunting her. Another person was now dead because of them. They sat in silence, allowing it to envelop them, like a shroud.

"Have you wondered why Townsend hasn't come after us?" she finally asked.

"Yeah."

"And?"

"Kind of ironic, but I don't think we're worth the risk." He shrugged. "Lenore looks like a suicide. Sharise has an accidental fall. And now Florio gets killed in the line of duty—all pretty plausible. How do you kill us without it looking suspicious?"

Her look betrayed her weariness. "I don't know, but I hope he doesn't figure it out."

Later, Duane walked into Erin's office as she was getting

ready to leave for the day. "I'm heading back to Providence on Monday."

"Why?" she asked, looking up from her keyboard and rubbing the back of her neck.

"I need to try and convince the head of the lab to sign the affidavit."

"She won't do it."

"Nope. As she said, this case was Florio's lost cause and she doesn't really care if whoever killed the trannie is ever caught."

"Ouch. Would it help if I went with you? Maybe I can make a good presentation on behalf of all trannies," she said with a smirk.

"Yeah, thanks. No offense, but not sure that will help. I'll put in a good word for you, though."

"Thanks. Good luck."

"Thanks. Sounds like I'll need it."

CHAPTER 27

*D*UANE GLANCED AT HIS WATCH FOR THE THIRD TIME. HAD Andrea Peters totally blown him off, or was this her way of getting back at him for going over her head to the chief? He had been waiting for over an hour and his patience was wearing thin. Just as he was about to ask to speak to the chief, a young man in a lab coat, maybe in his late twenties, called his name.

"Hi, I'm Richard Barbieri, one of Dr. Peters's assistants," he said. "She asked me to come get you and to apologize for the wait."

"No problem," Duane lied, noting with interest that Florio had never used her formal title.

When they entered the lab, Barbieri led him past an array of people working at lab tables to the glass door to an office. As they approached, Peters looked up from whatever she was reading and motioned them to come in.

"Thank you, Richard. We'll finalize things after I speak with Mr. Swisher. Please close the door on your way out." Then turning her attention to Duane, she said, "Please have a seat, Mr. Swisher."

Duane nodded. "Thank you for taking the time to see me."

She placed a curled finger up to her mouth, displaying her long crimson fingernails. "I only agreed to because the chief asked me to. Otherwise . . ." She stopped, leaving the rest unsaid.

"I'm terribly sorry about Detective Florio."

Her eyes bore into him. "Mr. Swisher, while I hesitate to speak ill of someone who died in the line of duty, it's no secret that we did not get along."

"He did tell me that. And gave me a very truncated version as to why your relationship was strained."

She let out a sarcastic laugh. "Oh, I'm sure it was truncated—probably sterilized and fabricated as well. Let me give you the unvarnished reason. In my view, Detective Florio was a racist, pure and simple." She paused. "Did he tell you that the man was innocent and that during the interrogation he hit the young man so hard, he broke his jaw and while hitting him, repeatedly called him a nigger? Did he tell you that?"

"Not in that detail, no. He did tell me that the victim in the case was a seven-year-old African-American girl who was caught in the crossfire of a drive-by shooting."

"I'm sure trying to make it sound like he wasn't biased, just lost his temper, right? Good old Florio, incensed at the loss of a poor innocent young Black girl." She stared at him. "Mr. Swisher, I did some research on you, so I know you were with the FBI. I suspect you must know how prejudiced law enforcement can sometimes be. To me, people like Detective Florio are emblematic of that problem."

He nodded slowly. "You're right. There is a lot of bias in law enforcement and I've experienced some of it firsthand. When I was in the FBI, a cop stopped me when I was walking in my own neighborhood. He later told me he stopped me because he was suspicious of a Black guy walking in a white neighborhood. The irony is he's Black. So yeah, I agree with you. But you don't have to be a white Italian-American to pick up biases in this profession."

She pinched her lower lip between her fingers and her eyes

continued to show her wariness of him. "Tony DiFiglio was Florio's white whale, not mine. I honestly don't care about the case, because at the end of the day you and I both know that we are never going to be able to prove based on DNA who killed DiFiglio. You gave Florio a suspect, and that's all we'll ever have: a suspect."

"You know DiFiglio's father is a cop?"

"Please, don't make me laugh. From what I hear out of Pawtucket, he makes Florio look like MLK."

"Look, I can't make you do anything. But my client is a nineteen-year-old African-American transgender prostitute who got thrown out of her house when she was fifteen. She's charged with murdering the twenty-eight-year-old son of one of the most prominent and powerful white politicians in the state of New Jersey. My partner and I are convinced that the guy she's accused of murdering is actually a serial killer. Right now, the only thing we have to go on is the murder of Tony DiFiglio and the DNA profile you hit that's no longer in the system. And as we sit here, I'm not even sure if my client is alive, because when I left last night to drive up here, she was still in a coma, having 'fallen' down a flight of stairs after a prison guard 'accidentally' bumped into her. So honestly, I don't care if Florio was a card-carrying member of the KKK; this isn't about him, and you're right, it's not about Tony DiFiglio either, it's about Sharise Barnes and trying to save her life."

"Well, I wish you well with that, Mr. Swisher, but that's not my job. My job is to assist the state, county, and local police in solving crimes here in Rhode Island. Seems to me it's someone else's job to solve crimes in New Jersey."

He slid the affidavit he had drafted for her across the desk.

"What's this?" she asked.

"It's what I'd like you to review and, if accurate, sign."

She chuckled. "Weren't you listening to me, Mr. Swisher? I have no reason to help you."

His stare was cold. "I think you do."

*   *   *

Later, sitting in his office, Duane beamed like the Cheshire cat as Erin reviewed the signed affidavit. "You got her to contact Massachusetts while you were there?" Her voice rose with excitement. "Holy shit, there's a partial match with Boston too." She looked up from the papers. "Swish, this is unbelievable. There are two partial matches in locations he was living at the time of the murders. Sweet Jesus."

"And Boston has a full DNA profile of their suspect. If we can get Townsend's full DNA profile to Massachusetts, we may have a complete match," he added.

She wiped her eyes. "How did you get this?"

He let out a little huff. "I really thought I was coming back with nothing. She wasn't giving an inch. So I laid everything out for her—Lenore, the break-in to your place and our office, the listening devices, trying to move Sharise out of PC, then her fall, and finally our suspicion that Florio, who she did not like, was murdered because of this case. At first, she just laughed at me, but as I went through everything, I think she began to realize that it was plausible."

"And Boston?"

"She made a deal with me. She said she would call a colleague she knew in the Massachusetts State Police and send up the results from our case. If there was a partial match, she would give us her affidavit and help me get one from Massachusetts."

Erin got up from the chair, went around the desk to where he was sitting, bent over, and gave him a hug. "Great job. Great job. And there's more good news."

"Yeah?"

"Tonya called around three. Sharise's fever broke, and there's been no more swelling or bleeding on the brain. Still too early to tell if there's any permanent damage, but Ogden thinks she's gonna make it."

"Shit, that is great. Maybe her guardian angel is finally looking after her."

"Yeah, let's hope," she replied with a warm smile. "Let's hope."

Neither said anything for a while, just trying to savor a good day—one of the first in a long time.

"So, how do you want to handle this?" he asked. "I mean, it's still only two partials, it's not like game, set, match just yet."

"I know. And with Redman's order in place requiring us to pre-file with him, I'm worried they'll still try and bury it."

She thought for a moment, wondering how to make sure the evidence could be preserved and passed along to the press if those pulling the strings tried to bury it.

"I'll prepare a motion for reconsideration, but rather than ask to have Townsend's full profile entered in the system, we'll just ask to have his full DNA profile provided to Massachusetts so they can see if there's a full match." She thought for a moment. "And Philly too. No reason not to include them. If there's a match, I'd say it's over, we win."

She continued to turn things over in her mind, reflecting on the mutual respect that she felt was developing between her and Taylor.

"What do you think if I give Barbara a call and set up a meeting to discuss some new evidence we have discovered? If we can get her on our side, I don't think even Redman would refuse to provide the DNA to Massachusetts and Philadelphia."

"Works for me."

She reached over and dialed Taylor's direct office line, which she now had memorized. After four rings it went to voice mail. "Hi, Barbara, it's Erin and Duane. We're calling because we'd like to set up a meeting to discuss some new evidence. Give me a call in the office tomorrow. Thanks."

She hung up the phone and looked at her partner. "I know it's cold as hell, but what do you say we go have a beer to . . . I was going to say to celebrate, but that may be premature, and I don't want to jinx anything. How about we have a beer for the hell of it?"

"Sounds good," Duane replied with a wide grin. "My treat."

CHAPTER 28

AS BARBARA MADE HER WAY TO HER CAR, SHE CURSED THE early December cold snap. The last three days had been brutally cold, and today the gale-force winds only made it feel colder. She threw her briefcase behind her seat and started the car, turning the heat up as high as it would go. Even knowing that it would only blow cold air until the car heated up, she still hoped that would be warmer than what currently occupied the inside of her car.

She thought for a moment, trying to figure out what she wanted for dinner. It was Monday night and she didn't feel like cooking. Since the divorce and with Vicky away at school, she rarely felt like cooking. She was trying to generate some heat by rubbing her hands together, while at the same time trying to figure out where she wanted to call for takeout, when her cell phone rang.

"Hi, Tom, what's up?"

"Barbara, where are you? I need to meet with you."

The tone of Whitick's voice confused her. It sounded like he was in a panic. In all the years she had been in the office, the last three as the first assistant, she had never seen Whitick rattled. "Tom, is everything okay? What's the matter?"

"We can't discuss it over the phone. We need to meet tonight, as soon as possible."

"Um, I'm in the parking lot. I haven't left yet. Are you still in the building? We can meet in my office."

"No!" he said excitedly. "We can't meet there. It needs to be private."

She took the phone away from her ear and looked at it, troubled by the strangeness of the conversation. "Okay. Where would you like to meet?"

"Can you come to my house—about twenty minutes?"

She had been to his house many times, both socially and on business, usually to get him to sign off on some investigation the office was involved in. "Sure. Are you sure you're okay?"

"Yeah, see you in twenty minutes."

It was only fifteen minutes from the office to Whitick's house, so she stopped at a 7-Eleven to pick up a cup of coffee, hoping to not only warm up, but to wake up.

Whitick's house was in a development of modest split-level homes built in the 1970s, and they all looked the same except for color. As she pulled up, there didn't appear to be any lights on inside, and none of the outside lights were on. The only illumination came from a nearby streetlamp and the flashing yellow light of a utility truck parked several houses down the street.

As she stepped up to Tom's door, purse and coffee in hand, the porch light came on and the front door opened.

"Come in," Whitick said. As she walked into the foyer, he quickly turned off the outside light.

"Your house was so dark, I thought maybe you had lost electric."

"No, I don't know what it is," he said as he nervously looked out the door, before hurriedly closing it. "They've been working there since yesterday."

"Tom, what's going on?"

"I'm sorry, Barbara. I know you must think I'm crazy, but we need to talk—privately. Please."

They walked through the darkened kitchen and into his den, lit by just a desk lamp. She put her coffee down on the table, took off her coat, and placed it on the back of a chair as he went over to his desk, picked up some papers, and found his way to an easy chair opposite her. "Have you seen this before?" he asked, handing one over.

"Tom, I can barely see my hand, it's so dark in here. Can you turn on a light?"

He walked over and turned on a pole lamp that was on the side of the couch. "Sorry."

She studied the document before looking up. "It looks like a DNA profile? But since I don't know who it's from, I don't know if I've ever seen it."

"Did Lee ever tell you anything about Providence, Rhode Island?"

"Providence? No. Why?"

He took a deep breath. "Did Lee ever tell you about a partial match in the Townsend case?"

"No. Tom, what in God's name are you talking about?" she asked, frustration creeping into her voice.

He took his glasses off and rubbed his right eye. "About two months ago, I received the printout I just handed you from a detective up in Providence. They had matched seven loci with one of our case's semen samples, so he was looking for the name of the suspect so they could start digging to see if they could put the person near the crime scene. Since we had uploaded the data, he was looking to us for help."

It suddenly dawned on her where this was going. "Townsend?"

His head nodded ever so slightly.

"Tom," she almost screamed. "Why didn't I know about this?"

He drew in a deep breath. "I went to Lee. I mean this was . . . is, potentially explosive. I explained what it was, and what it potentially meant. He told me I had to pull this from CODIS and tell the guy in Providence it was a mistake. I told Lee we had to tell you, but he said, 'No, this has to stay with us.'"

She leaned forward on the couch, cupping her hands over her mouth as she tried to sort things out. "Why are you telling me now?"

Even in the dim light, he looked pale. "Last Wednesday, I got a call from the detective in Providence. He told me he had information on Townsend and said he can put him in the city at the time of a murder of a transgender prostitute. He said if I didn't put the sample back in the system, he was going to sue us to get the information."

"Wait, he had information on Townsend? How did he get that?"

"Remember, the semen stain went in as an unknown. It was degraded, but it was in the discovery provided to McCabe and Swisher."

"But how did he connect it to . . . ?" She caught herself in mid-question. "Swisher's exhibit of where Townsend had lived and where there was a murder of a transgender person. Swisher must have talked to the detective in Providence." Her brow furrowed as she connected the dots. "Shit. So McCabe and Swisher may be right. That Townsend may be in the database as a suspect because . . ." She paused. "Because he murdered before."

"There's another piece to Providence that you need to know about," he offered. "I was so shaken by the call, I took off Friday and Monday trying to figure out what I was going to do. When I got back to the office today, on my desk was a national alert on NCIC from Providence PD notifying all law enforcement offices that they were looking for an armed and dangerous suspect who had ambushed and murdered one of their detectives." He paused and closed his eyes. "The murdered detective was the guy who called me."

She shook her head. "You're not saying it's connected, are you?"

"Honestly, I don't know what to think. No one else knew about his call to me, so I want to believe it's just a terrible coincidence, but I'm not sure because there's more."

"Okay?" she said.

He took a deep breath. "I don't think Barnes's fall was an accident. I think they're trying to murder him to stop this information from coming out."

"Why do you think that?" she said in a hushed tone, afraid of betraying her own concerns.

Whitick stared at her. "Barnes is lying in intensive care with a fractured skull. Do you really think that was an accident?"

"I don't know," she said, expressing her own doubts for the first time to someone else. "I read the reports, so I know what the official version is. The officer was taking him from his cell to the exercise area. They paused at the top of the tier steps because he was waiting for his partner to get in place at the bottom. An inmate screaming behind him distracted him and when he turned around, he accidentally knocked into Barnes, causing Barnes to lose his balance and fall down the steps." She studied his face. "But you don't believe that, do you?"

"No, no. Ten days ago they tried to move him out of protective custody and into the general population? And now, after that move was blocked, he falls down the stairs and may not survive. While at the same time, Swisher and McCabe are developing potentially damning evidence. Barbara, those aren't just unrelated coincidences."

She went to speak, but he held up his hand.

"Thanksgiving night I got a call from the warden at the jail," Whitick said. "He told me he had just gotten off the phone with Lee, who wanted Barnes moved into the general population the next day—the day after Thanksgiving, when all courts were closed. The warden was beside himself. He told me Barnes would be dead by Sunday night and he'd be the guy hung out to dry. He begged me to call Lee to see if I could get him to change his mind. So I called Lee. When I started talking to him it was pretty clear he'd been drinking. I told him about the warden's concerns and he started screaming at me, telling me it was none of my fucking business and what the fuck did I know, I didn't have to answer to Townsend. Needless to say, I was kind of shocked, because I never heard Lee behave like that." He looked down at his lap. "The next morning, I did what I could to stop it."

She leaned back in her chair with the recognition of what he just admitted to. "You're the one who called McCabe?"

"I had to. I was convinced . . ." He stopped and took a deep breath. "Look, you know I think Barnes and his lifestyle are totally nuts, but knowing what I did, I believed I would be complicit in his murder if I didn't try to stop it. I can be many things, including a miserable SOB, but I'm not a murderer."

"Why didn't you call me?"

"I was hoping McCabe would get the message and stop it. I also called the warden and told him to delay the move as long as he could, because I was trying to stop it. Fortunately, McCabe did get the message and got it stopped. If she hadn't, I would've called you. But honestly, I've been trying to keep you out of this. I don't want to ruin your career. If things go right for you, maybe Townsend will recommend you for prosecutor or a judgeship. But if you cross him, you'll never have a shot."

A sad smile of appreciation slid across her face. "Thank you, Tom. That's very generous of you. But my oath is to seek justice, not please Will Townsend, and if that means I never get to be prosecutor or a judge, so be it."

"Well, I've got you in the middle of it now. But I didn't think I had a choice. After Barnes's fall, and now this crazy shit up in Providence, I didn't know who else to go to."

She closed her eyes, lost in thought. Her gut had been right. Funny, she thought, she hadn't called Whitick to ask for help in investigating Bill Townsend's past because she hadn't been sure she could trust him, leaving her to do it on her own. Turns out she had underestimated him.

"You okay?" Whitick asked.

She offered him a sad grin. "Yeah, peachy," she said. "We need to talk this through. What happens if we tell Lee and he fires us before we can disclose what we know to McCabe? I mean, I know what our moral obligations are, but what are our legal obligations? Have you heard back from anyone in Providence?"

"No, but I assume that with a murdered detective and a suspect at large, they have other things to deal with right now."

"You said when he called you last week he had information on Townsend."

He nodded.

"So McCabe and Swisher must be going around to all the places on their exhibit trying to find a connection to Townsend."

"That's my guess." He paused. "Perhaps we wait and let them do the dirty work for us?"

She looked over at her Chief of Detectives with a resigned smile. "My guess is you already played that scenario out before you called me."

"Yeah, I did. Maybe I'm crazy, but it didn't feel like I was doing my job if we went that route. And if it turns out the murder of the detective in Providence is connected . . . well."

"I hear you," she said, knowing he was right, even if there was a small tug on her practical instincts to allow things to play out.

She glanced at her watch and wondered if McCabe might still be in the office at a quarter past six. She looked up at Whitick. "I have to meet with Barnes's counsel and advise them. Do you agree?"

Despite his pained expression, he nodded. "What about Lee? What are you going to tell him?"

"The truth. And if he fires me . . ." She paused and gave a little chuckle. "Who knows, maybe I'll hire McCabe and Swisher to represent me in a whistleblower suit."

She looked through her contacts and decided to call McCabe's office rather than her cell phone, hoping she'd be gone for the day so it would buy her some time to figure out what to tell them. After the fourth ring it went to voice mail. "Erin, it's Barbara Taylor. Give me a call tomorrow. I'd like to set up a meeting with you and Mr. Swisher to discuss some new information I've been provided with. I should be available after ten thirty. Thanks."

"You want a beer or a glass of wine? Something to take the edge off," he offered.

She thought for a moment. "Why not? You have any white wine?"

"Yeah, I have a small wine cellar in my basement that sits under the front steps. Always keeps the wine at the perfect temperature."

"No, please don't open a bottle for me."

"Who said I was opening it for you?" he said, offering the closest thing to a smile he had shown since she arrived.

"Okay, as long as we're sharing. Mind if I use the bathroom?"

"Sure, be my guest."

They both got up, and while he slowly plodded across the kitchen, she headed toward the hallway and the guest bathroom.

His movements were instinctual, carved into his motor memory because he had done it hundreds of times before. But as soon as he opened the door to flick on the cellar light, she recognized the smell. "Na—!" she screamed, but the ensuing explosion devoured her scream as it did her body, and in that split second, Barbara Taylor and Tom Whitick ceased to exist. The ensuing fireball engulfed the house and their remains in equal measure, leaving only a gruesome reminder of the people they had once been.

As Erin was doing the dishes and cleaning up after dinner, she turned on the television to watch News 12. When the picture finally arrived, the scene of a house engulfed in flames greeted her.

"And as you just heard Ocean County Prosecutor Lee Gehrity say, not only are officials concerned for the safety of Chief of Detectives Thomas Whitick, who owns the home behind me, but fear is growing for First Assistant Prosecutor Barbara Taylor, whose

BY WAY OF SORROW

car was parked outside Chief Whitick's home and who has not been heard from since the explosion."

Erin immediately shut off the water and tried to process what she had just heard. Then she picked up her cell phone and called Duane's landline, hoping it wasn't bugged, and told him what was on the news.

"You there?" Duane asked after she went silent.

"No, I'm not sure where I am."

"E, you asked the other day about why they haven't come after us, and I said something like it was too much trouble. I don't feel that way anymore. Based on this, I think I'm going to take Cori and Austin somewhere safe. My suggestion is that you go stay with your folks or your brother. Just don't stay there. If they'd take out Whitick and Taylor, we're next."

"Yeah, sure," she said, her tone almost robotic. "I agree, get Cori and Austin out of Dodge, and when you get back, we'll figure out what's next."

She closed her phone and stared at the muted television, the familiar weather map now gracing the screen where only moments ago there had been images of Barbara and Whitick's funeral pyre.

She forced herself off of the couch, threw on her heavy winter coat, checked to make sure she had everything she needed in her purse, and headed out into the darkness toward the office.

There, she made copies of the motion for reconsideration, changed the CC on the cover letter from First Assistant Prosecutor Barbara Taylor to Assistant Prosecutor Roger Carmichael, pasted the certified mail cards on each, and headed back out. The advantage of having a PO Box was that the outside lobby of the post office would be open until nine p.m. No one was working, but she could drop the envelopes in the outgoing mail slot and know they'd be picked up at eight a.m.

It was a little before nine p.m. when Michael rang the bell. The door opened, and Will Townsend stepped to the side to allow Gardner to enter. Will said nothing as they made their way back to the kitchen, but the fury in his eyes said everything.

"I thought I told you no," Will said, pacing back and forth. "I told you to find another way. Now according to the news it wasn't only Whitick, but Taylor was in the house as well. I told you that I've known Tom Whitick for almost twenty years. What the fuck are you doing?"

Gardner's eyes were cold and he showed little reaction to Townsend's rant. "We had no choice," he finally said. "We had a bug in his house. The utility truck served two purposes, and one of them was to listen. He gave her everything and they were reaching out to meet with McCabe and Swisher. Will, if this unravels now, we're all in trouble. They had to be stopped."

Townsend hung his head. "No," he muttered, the anger spent. "It's spinning out of control. How many more? First it was just some whore. Then it was getting rid of Barnes. It looks to me like it's already unraveling."

"We only have to take care of the remaining two and it should be over."

"No! Absolutely not. Think about how that would look. The prosecutor and defense counsel wind up dead, and the defendant has a fractured skull. Why don't we just shine a spotlight on me and say, 'Hey, come investigate!'"

Michael studied Townsend's eyes and then looked at his watch. "Let me see what I can do," he said, taking out a burner phone. "I know I can call back the people on Swisher, but the one who is going to visit McCabe . . . Let's just say, he has a bit of a twisted interest in McCabe's anatomy. He's the one who broke into the apartment twice."

Michael typed quickly "ABORT" and then "CONFIRM" and hit send.

"Will, no matter what happens, none of this will come back to you. Everything is clean. There are no witnesses. Don't worry. You were there for me; I won't let anything happen to you. You know I'd take a bullet for you. And if something happens to McCabe, it will look like she . . . *he* was the victim of a demented rapist. Which, ironically, is exactly what he is."

He had followed her from her apartment to the office. He had almost decided to take her there. But his instructions were clear: Take no action before nine p.m.

When she headed back to her apartment after the post office, he knew it was his lucky day. *Perfect*. Hopefully, the street would be deserted enough that he could grab her as she opened the outside door, but if it wasn't, he'd just use the copy he'd made from the realtor's key.

She was a block from the door when his phone vibrated. *Shit*, he thought when he saw "ABORT." He momentarily thought about ignoring it. He could always say he had turned off his phone and didn't get the message in time. But Gardner could be a sick fuck, and there was no point in crossing him now. Eventually, either on the clock or for his own personal enjoyment, he'd have a chance to meet McCabe up close and personal.

"CONFIRMED," he typed, hit send, and turned down a side street.

CHAPTER 29

*E*RIN LAY THERE, LACKING THE WILL TO GET OUT OF BED. She had no appointments and wasn't due in court, and even if she had been, she wasn't sure it would have mattered. It was more than lack of sleep, it was everything—the newspaper articles, their phones being tapped, the threats, and now the murders, all happening with a regularity that seemed more in keeping with a crime drama on television than real life.

It wasn't like she and Barbara Taylor had been friends, but Erin felt like they had started to develop a mutual respect. Now she was dead. Erin tried to picture what it had been like for Barbara; she'd gotten up, gone to work, made plans for the next day just like Erin had. But literally in a flash, all of Barbara's hopes and plans were gone. Just gone. The thoughts just kept coming over and over, and all she could do was cry. It wasn't right. She wanted a do-over. She wanted everyone to be alive again. Why couldn't she wake herself from this nightmare?

Her cell phone startled her. She reached over and picked it up off the night table. "Hello," she said, her voice crackling and barely audible.

"E, where are you? Are you okay? I've tried the office three times and Cheryl said you weren't in and she didn't know where you were."

"I'm in bed, Swish. I . . . I . . ."

"Is everything okay?"

"No!" she screamed. "People are dying. Our client is in intensive care. For all I know, people are trying to kill us. No," she said as her voice trailed off to almost a whisper, "everything is definitely not okay."

"Where are you?"

"In my apartment."

There was a long pause. "I asked you to stay someplace else last night. Why are you still at your apartment?"

"Because I was too numb to go anywhere else."

"E, you're not safe there. I think someone broke into the office again last night. When I spoke to Cheryl, she said the motion papers we put together yesterday were missing. She can't find them."

"I mailed them."

"What?"

"I went to the office last night after watching the—I went and mailed them. I wanted to make sure if something happened to us, they were filed."

"Wait, you mailed them to the court and Barbara?"

"I mailed it to the court, but at that point I already knew Barbara was gone, so I mailed them to Carmichael and Gehrity." She grabbed a tissue and blew her nose. "Where are you? Please tell me you, Cori, and Austin are safe."

"We're fine. I'm going to leave in a little bit to head back to Jersey. Obviously, I don't want to say on the phone where we are, but Cori and Austin are going to stay here for a few days, just to make sure everything is okay."

"Okay. Good. Glad to hear you're safe."

"Listen, I should be back around five. Why don't we plan on having dinner together and figuring out next steps?"

"Sure."

"E, please be careful. Last night before we left, I called a friend of mine who's a Scotch Plains cop and asked him to keep an eye on my house. I spoke to him about an hour ago. Last night around nine, he stopped a car that was driving past my house for the second time. Since I live at the end of a cul-de-sac he thought it was a little strange. He told me that there were two guys in the car, and they said they were lost. He had no reason to get them out of the car and search them, so he let them go. He did run their license plate and it came back to a rental company in Woodbridge. Anyway, he just thought it was a little suspicious."

"I'll be careful; promise."

She finally dragged herself out of bed and eventually made her way to the office. She tried to busy herself with other files, but her mind just kept replaying the scene of Whitick's house ablaze. She had picked up the *Ledger* and *Herald News* on her way in, and both had stories on the explosion. The initial report was that there was a gas leak in the area. Prosecutor Gehrity mourned the loss of two "superstars" in his office and promised there would be a thorough investigation.

Duane rolled in around five, as promised, and they made their way over to the Cranford Hotel.

"I'm still numb," she said as she took a sip of her wine. "I'm having such a hard time processing that Barbara is dead. It's strange, toward the end I actually felt like we had a certain bond. That we both knew things were happening beyond our control, but we were doing the best we could for our respective clients. I know it's crazy and if we had tried the case, we probably would have hated each other, but at least for now, I felt she finally accepted me. Stupid, right?"

"No, E. I don't think it's stupid at all."

"When I finally got to the office this morning there was a voice mail from her."

"From Barbara?"

"Yeah, it came in at 6:16 last night. She said she had some new information and wanted to meet with us to discuss it."

Duane rubbed his chin. "Wow, we just missed her call. We had called her about fifteen minutes earlier. We had just left to go get a beer."

"I know. I realized that too. I'm assuming she was at Whitick's when she called, and so I guess it wouldn't have made any difference if we had been there to answer the phone. We would just have been on the phone when the explosion occurred."

"I'm guessing that Florio must have called Whitick like he told me he would. Maybe that's what they were talking about. Do you think she knew about Florio's call to Whitick a couple months ago?"

Erin gave it some thought. "Not sure. Barbara strikes me— sorry, struck me, as a fairly straight shooter. I think if she knew Whitick was hiding something, she would have done something." She swirled the wine in her glass, wishing somehow this was all just a bad dream. Neither of them said anything for a long time. All Erin could see was Whitick's house consumed by flames, and her mind kept going back to the last time they had been together, when Erin had warned Barbara about who she was dealing with. At the time it had never even crossed Erin's mind that Barbara would wind up dead.

"There was some good news today," Erin finally said. "I got a call from Tonya; Sharise opened her eyes. She still isn't responding to verbal commands yet, but Ogden was encouraged that she seems to be coming out of the coma."

"That is good news," Duane replied, too tired to even smile.

"Tonya also asked me if we'd represent Sharise in suing the county. Even if it *was* an accident, she thinks we should go after them."

"What'd you tell her?"

"That neither you nor I do any civil litigation, and we'll recommend someone to her. To which she replied, 'Nobody's taken care of my sister like the two of you, not even her own family. I want you handling the case. If you need to bring someone else in to help, that's fine, but I won't take no for an answer.'"

Duane gave a little snort. "Well, I guess we'll learn how to handle a civil case."

"I actually did a couple of car accident cases right after I left the PD's office. At that point, I took on anybody who was foolish enough to walk in the door."

"And Ben's partner, Elizabeth Sullivan, does a lot of civil stuff. I'm sure we could bring her on board."

She nodded. "Sounds good. A civil case is the least of our worries at this point. I'll find out what we have to do in terms of the notice and we'll go from there."

"By the way, Ben called me today about my investigation."

"And . . ."

"He said he had gotten a really strange call from Andy Barone from DOJ and Edward Champion, the First Assistant United States Attorney in the Newark office. Ben said they seemed more interested in what was going on in the Townsend case than in me. They asked if I'd be willing to meet with them after the holidays to discuss the case."

"Wait, discuss the investigation of you, or Sharise's case?"

"Sharise's case."

"That's bizarre," she said. "How would they know anything about Sharise's case?"

"Ben didn't know and they didn't say. Maybe the explosion? Beats me."

"What are you going to do?"

"After we talked it over, Ben went back to them and said as long as they don't ask me about the leak investigation, we'd be happy to meet."

"Wow. Do you really think they're interested in Townsend, or is this some kind of ploy?"

"Ben and Champion know each other, so we both assume it's on the level."

"Who knows, maybe he'll get what he deserves after all."

After they finished dinner Duane insisted on walking Erin back to her apartment. "Did you get a gun like I suggested?" he asked.

"No, you know I hate guns."

"I really wish you'd stay somewhere else," he said, trudging up her steps.

"It's safe," she replied.

"Bullshit," he fired back. "No one else lives here."

"I took some self-defense classes designed for women, and I added some additional security." She opened the door, turned on the light, and motioned him inside. "After the second break-in a week ago, I had the landlord install a single-sided deadbolt," she said, showing him the lock, which for her was at eye level. "The windows have alarms. This door is solid wood and by the time someone kicked in the door, I'd have called nine-one-one and the cops would be here. I'll be okay," she said with a sad smile. She then reached out, pulled him into a hug, and kissed him on the cheek. "But thanks for worrying about me."

His eyes went a little wide. "What was that for?" he asked, sounding a little sheepish.

"For worrying about me, and being my friend," she replied with a wink. "Where are you staying tonight?"

"Home. But don't forget, I have a gun and know how to use it. I'll be fine."

"You better be," she said emphatically. "I can't deal with any more bullshit in my life."

CHAPTER 30

WILL LAID THE MOTION PAPERS DOWN ON HIS DESK AND TOOK a deep breath, his eyes narrowing. This was not how he envisioned spending his morning.

"What do you think?" he asked Lee Gehrity, who was sitting on the other side of his desk.

"Roger Carmichael thinks we may be able to get Redman to deny their motion," Gehrity offered.

Will gave a sarcastic chuckle. "As much as I'm sure Bob Redman would like to help, Boston and Philly both have a complete DNA suspect profile on record. Redman doesn't even have to order Bill's profile to be entered into CODIS, just sent to those two places."

"That doesn't mean that Bill's DNA will be a conclusive match. After all, Rhode Island only had eight loci. Barbara says . . ." Gehrity paused. "Sorry, still hard to get used to the fact she's not here." He inhaled slowly and then continued. "Barbara used to tell me you needed thirteen loci for a conclusive match."

Will nodded ever so slightly. "You're right, this is far from conclusive evidence." He hesitated. "When is Redman going to consider this?"

"There's a conference scheduled a week from tomorrow, but I'm sure, in light of what's happened, we could get that put off until after the holidays."

"Assuming Redman sends Bill's DNA profile to Boston and Philly, how long before they come back with the results?"

"I'm told because this is so specific, it should only take a few days or so," Gehrity replied.

Will rubbed the side of his face with his hand. "Let me think about it, Lee. I'll make up my mind over the weekend and let you know what I want to do." Townsend stood up. "I do appreciate you bringing this over personally. I know this has been an incredibly difficult week for you. Like you, I have a difficult time coming to terms with the fact that Tom and Barbara are gone. A tremendous loss, both personally and professionally. How's Barbara's daughter doing?"

"I understand she's having a real hard time. First the divorce and now this—hard for any kid to deal with."

Will walked around his desk and, instead of taking Gehrity's offered hand, pulled him into a man hug and patted him on the back. "I'll see you tomorrow at Barbara's funeral and then Saturday at Tom's. It's going to be a tough few days for everyone. Hang in there," he offered as he escorted Gehrity to the office door.

After he had shown Gehrity out, Will turned and glared at Gardner. "What happened was unnecessary."

"We didn't know about Providence at the time, Will. However, it's still important that Taylor and Whitick are out of the picture. Remember, Whitick is the one who called McCabe, so we know he couldn't be trusted. He could have caused a lot of problems down the road. And judging from Taylor's reaction, she was about to turn on you too."

"Jesus, Michael, I knew these people."

Michael's eyes were cold as he stared at Will. "You still want to be governor, right?" He didn't wait for an answer. "Of course you do. And who knows, maybe from there you go national. You hired me seven years ago to be your fixer—so I fixed it. It had to be done. You know damn well if it turns out your son was a serial killer and that gets out, you wouldn't be able to get elected dog-catcher. You saved my career, Will. I've never forgotten that. It's my turn to save your career. You pay me good money to take care of the messy stuff, and I take my job very seriously."

Will walked past Gardner and slid into his desk chair. "So what now? How do we manage to keep this quiet?"

"My feeling is we try and delay things as long as possible."

"How's that help us?"

"Because there may be a way to legally buy their silence."

Will turned his chair so he was looking directly at Gardner. "I'm listening."

"First of all, let's confirm our worst fears. Let me see if we can get a copy of the DNA results from Philly homicide, where I have some connections. Then we take Bill's known sample to a forensics lab I know and let them tell us if they match. If they match, then we know. If they don't, maybe we do the same thing with the Boston results. In the meantime, ask Lee to request a ninety-day adjournment in light of the need to bring another sea-soned prosecutor in to get up to speed on the case."

"Okay."

"I'm assuming they are going to sue the county for negligence over Barnes's injuries. But they can't sue for six months, because they are legally required to give the county notice and time to in-vestigate or settle. So we find out if the DNA matches, and if it does, you get the county to settle. When they settle, they condi-tion it on Barnes and counsel keeping everything confidential—a nondisclosure agreement. The criminal case is dismissed, so nothing ever gets sent to Boston or Philly. As a result, there's never any confirmation Bill murdered anyone. They get some money, criminal case over, and no one ever knows about Bill."

Will smirked at Gardner. "You know there are more than a few moving pieces to that plan. For example, how are they going to settle a civil case when they probably won't even know how severe Barnes's injuries are?"

"I agree there's a lot of things that could go wrong, but it's better than letting a judge send out Bill's DNA in a couple of weeks. As to how you settle, just have the county throw a lot of money at them. Most of it will come from the county's insurance carrier anyway. Christ, it's not like he doesn't have a serious injury."

"Yeah, unfortunately, not serious enough," Townsend said mostly to himself.

"Barnes has been selling himself for years, you think he's going to turn down a million dollars?"

Will crossed his arms across his chest and leaned back in the chair. "It might work. Certainly, every freeholder who would have to approve a settlement is indebted to me." He paused. "Who the hell am I kidding? It's not like junior left me any fucking alternatives," he said, gesturing to the framed picture of his son on his bookcase.

"I don't want to be disturbed," Will barked through the phone at his secretary after Michael left. He walked over to the bookcase, grabbed the framed picture of his son off the shelf, and threw it across the room, the glass shattering when it hit the wall. *You fucking bastard. I gave you everything—the best schools, expensive cars, a trust fund—and this is how you repay me. I busted my ass for the last fifteen years so I could be where I am now and you're not going to fuck that up. No matter what it takes, I will be governor!*

He plopped down in a chair and stared at the shattered glass on the floor, wondering how he had gotten into this mess.

CHAPTER 31

*E*RIN AND DUANE WEREN'T SURPRISED WHEN THE PROSECU-
tor's office requested that the case be delayed, or when Redman
agreed to put everything on hold until March. Their frustration
with the delay was tempered somewhat by the fact that Sharise
was still not out of the woods. So with the case now on hold, and
any personal threats dissipated, their lives returned to some sem-
blance of normal just in time for Christmas.

Erin and her mother hadn't gotten together for a week, so they
agreed to meet for a quick brunch on the Saturday before Christmas. With temperatures hovering in the mid-fifties, she felt comfortable in just a long-sleeved blouse and her down vest as she
walked the three blocks to their favorite restaurant.

"You actually look like you've gotten some sleep," her mother
said with a wry grin as Erin slid into the booth opposite her.

"Is that a nice way of telling me I don't look like hell?"

"Whatever," her mother responded. "It's good to see you, and
especially good to see you not looking quite as harried and ex-

hausted as you have been the last couple of times we've gotten together."

"Thanks. With everything that's happened, the judge has put the case on hold until the beginning of March, so things have slowed down a little bit. I even got a chance to play some soccer in an indoor coed league."

"How'd that happen?"

"Actually, you'll get a kick out of this. I got a call from a friend of Lauren's. Lauren had to stop playing a few months ago because she's pregnant, and apparently Lauren recommended me as a replacement."

"That's kind of ironic," her mother said with a small laugh.

"Tell me about it," Erin said.

"You enjoy it?"

"Yeah, I did. I was a little rusty . . . okay, a lot rusty. It's been a few years since I actually played. But I got better as the game went along."

"The more things change . . ." her mother said with a grin. "On a more serious note, how's your client doing?"

"She's making progress," Erin replied, her eyes showing her excitement. "She's starting to follow commands, which, according to her doctors, is a great sign. She's still not communicating, but the doctors seem optimistic. So, fingers crossed. I'm heading down to the hospital to see her after we eat."

"It's terrible what happened to those two people from the prosecutor's office."

"Yeah," Erin said, exhaling as if she had been kicked in the gut. "I didn't know Whitick, but Taylor was a good woman. And the randomness of it has been hard to deal with."

She could feel her mother measuring her with her eyes. "You ever going to tell me everything that's gone on?"

"I'll let you read the first draft of the book. How about that?"

"Very funny. I know there's been a lot that you haven't told me because you don't want me to worry. Well, guess what? I'm your mother, I worry anyway."

"I know you do, Mom. I appreciate your concern. When this is all over, I'll tell you the whole sordid mess."

"I won't hold my breath," she said sarcastically.

Erin shrugged her shoulders.

"What are you doing Monday?" her mother asked.

Erin's eyes narrowed. "Why?"

"Because it's Christmas and I'd like to spend it with my children and grandchildren."

"I can't go through that again, Mom. Thanksgiving was bad enough. I am not ruining everyone's Christmas."

"I'm talking about Monday, not tomorrow. As much as I'd love you to be at dinner tomorrow night, I'm not going to make that mistake again. As usual, my side of the family is coming for Christmas Eve dinner, but Liz and Sean are having people over for Christmas Day. I think your dad is going to his sister Rose's, so why don't we go down to your brother's together?"

"Why aren't you going with Dad?"

"Because I am not spending another Christmas without seeing you."

"Sean and Liz are okay with this?"

Her mother gave her a look. "Do you really think I would invite you without checking with them first?"

Erin chuckled. "Yep, not a doubt in my mind you would."

"Well, I spoke to both of them, so there, Miss Smarty-pants. They'd love you to come, and the boys can't wait to see you."

"That sounds really nice," Erin replied with a smile that came from her heart. "I would love that. It also means I don't have to give you everyone's presents; I'll just leave them in the car and bring them on Monday." Erin paused and gave her mother a funny look. "Can I ask you a question? Actually, I need some advice."

"I'm listening."

"About a week or so ago I got a phone call from Mark."

"The man who has disappeared twice?" her mother asked in a tone that indicated she already knew the answer.

"Yes, Mom, the same one."

"Just checking."

"Anyway, we've talked on the phone and e-mailed a number of times since then, and he'd like to take me out to dinner tonight." She tilted her head to the side and the curl of her mouth conveyed her mixed feelings. "I guess I was just wondering what you thought."

"If you're going out tonight, isn't it a little late to ask me what I think?"

"No, if you convince me not to go, I'll call and cancel. After all, he owes me a couple cancellations."

Her mother's eyes seemed to twinkle just a little bit at that possibility. "You're right," she responded. "So why did you agree to go?"

"Curious, I guess. Curious as to why he keeps coming back; curious about my feelings; curious to see what happens."

"You prepared to get hurt again?"

"Yeah, I think so. I also think I'm going in with pretty low expectations. So . . ." She shrugged her shoulders.

"Well, he's obviously attracted to you, but my guess is he's trying to come to terms with what that attraction says about his own sexuality."

Erin cringed. "You sure know how to make me feel good about myself as a woman."

"I'm sorry. I wasn't blaming you. Just recognizing the fragility of the male ego." Her mother gave her a reassuring smile. "Go. See what happens. Who knows?"

"Thanks for those resounding words of encouragement," Erin said with a chuckle.

After she left her mom, she stopped at Duane and Corrine's to drop off a present for Austin and wish them all a Merry Christmas. Following the explosion, Duane had taken Corrine and Austin to stay with her folks for a week, but when nothing further happened, he brought them home for the holidays. At least for now, things seemed safe enough for them to be back.

On the way to the hospital, Erin stopped at the bakery and picked up a platter of Christmas cookies and a cheesecake to bring the nurses. Erin had discovered that, whether it was getting information about Sharise or staying a little past visiting hours, it was always helpful to be on the nurses' good side. By now, she had visited Sharise often enough that most of them recognized who she was.

As she approached the nurses' station, Sharise's nurse looked up and said, "I'm sorry, Ms. McCabe, but Mr. Barnes already has two visitors. If you'd like to wait in the visitors' lounge, I'll let his family know you're here."

"Thank you," Erin replied, wondering how Paul had made it in since he had a televised game on Christmas Eve against the Mavericks. "These are for all of you. Happy holidays," she said, putting the cookies and cheesecake up on the nurses' counter.

Several minutes later, Tonya walked into the lounge with another woman who appeared to be in her mid-forties. She was shorter than Tonya, but otherwise the physical resemblance was striking. "Erin," Tonya said. "I'd like you to meet my mother, Viola Barnes. Momma, this is one of Sammy's lawyers, Erin McCabe."

Erin extended her hand to cover her own surprise, but when Viola took it, she pulled Erin into a hug. "Thank you for everything you've done for my child. Tonya had been filling me in on the case and where things stand. I don't know where Sammy would be without you and your partner."

Erin was tempted to say *probably not in a hospital*, but knew her attempt at humor might seem unkind. "Thank you," Erin replied. "Duane and I are doing our best."

"Momma, do you mind waiting here while I take Erin to Sharise's room? I'd like to give Erin her Christmas present."

"You go ahead. I'll be here."

"What are you saying about a Christmas present?" Erin said as Tonya led her to Sharise's room, but she saw soon enough when

Tonya stepped aside to reveal Sharise sitting up in the elevated bed. "Hi," she said in a voice just above a whisper.

"Oh my God," Erin said, hurrying over. "Sharise, this is the best Christmas present I could have hoped for. It is so good to hear your voice."

"Good to be heard," Sharise replied weakly.

Erin turned to look at Tonya. "When did she come back to us?"

Tonya thought for a moment. "Sorry, I've lost track of time. Momma arrived Thursday afternoon, and just as we were getting ready to go back to the hotel, Sharise looked up at us and said, 'Momma, is that you?' "

Erin reached down and took Sharise's hand. "It's so great to have you back."

"Thanks," Sharise replied, squeezing Erin's hand.

"Do you think you could say hello to one other person?" Erin asked, retrieving her cell phone from her purse.

Sharise looked confused for a moment. "Duane, right?"

As soon as Duane answered, she handed the cell phone to Sharise.

"Hello, Duane," she said, her whisper sounding unintentionally sultry. Then, "What do you mean, who is this? It's Sharise." They watched as Sharise listened and a grin formed on her face. "Thank you, Duane, Merry Christmas to you too. I'm handing the phone back to Erin."

Erin took the phone and walked to the corner of the room, speaking with Duane. When she returned to Sharise's bedside, Sharise closed her eyes and said, "I'm really tired. I'm going to take a nap."

Tonya came over and lowered the head of Sharise's hospital bed and readjusted the covers. "Get some sleep."

"Can I ask a personal question?" Erin asked when they were back in the hallway.

"Sure," Tonya replied.

"I was surprised to see your mom here. Sharise had told me how disapproving she was of her being trans. What happened?"

Tonya nodded. "You're right, Mom has been tough. But I've been talking to her since Sharise's fall and last week she told me she wanted to come see Sam. I was thrilled and I made reservations for her to fly in. I mean, you know Sharise has been steadily improving, but as soon as Momma arrived and started talking to her, it was like something kicked in."

"I'm glad your mom came." Erin hesitated. "Your dad?"

Tonya shook her head. "No, that man is a tough one. Not sure he'll come around."

"I know how that can be. Oh, before I forget, we filed all the paperwork for Sharise to sue the county. They have six months to investigate, and assuming nothing happens, then she can file a lawsuit. We also filed all the papers for her name change."

"Thanks," Tonya said. "Who knows, maybe you guys can get her out of this mess and she can collect some money to start a new life. She deserves it."

They walked down to the waiting area, collected Viola, and went down to the cafeteria for a cup of coffee. After some small talk, Viola turned to Erin. "So Tonya tells me that you're like Sam and that you were born a man."

"Momma!" Tonya said, her tone a mix of embarrassment and reprimand.

"No, it's okay, Tonya," Erin said quickly. "To a certain extent that's true. I was born with a male anatomy, but I never felt like a man. As long as I can remember, I always felt like I should have been female. But I guess like Sam, I was afraid to tell people how I felt for fear they'd think I was crazy or wouldn't love me anymore."

"What made you change your mind?" she asked.

"I was falling apart. I just couldn't be the person everyone wanted me to be."

"Do you think Sam is like you and wants to be a woman?"

Erin smiled at Viola. "No, I know Sam is like me and is a woman. I know it's hard for you to understand. It's been hard for my family to understand. But we certainly didn't choose to be this way. It's just who we are and who we've always been."

"Does your family accept you now?"

"My mom and my brother and sister-in-law do—my dad, not so much."

"Thank you." Viola looked down into the Styrofoam coffee cup in her hands as if she was looking for answers. "I don't understand any of this, and I don't think I'll ever understand it. But I finally sat down and spoke with my pastor about Sam, and he said that God is not punishing Sam. God makes people with all different kinds of issues and still loves them. So even if I don't understand why he is the way he is, Sam is my child that God gave me." She looked up at Erin. "And I'd rather have a child who is alive than one who's dead."

It was just past six when Erin began her trek up the stairs to her apartment, leaving her just over an hour to get ready for her date with Mark. She had told her mom that she had low expectations for tonight, but that wasn't exactly true. The truth was that she was nervous and excited, hoping that this time things would go better. She was almost to the top of the stairs to her apartment when she was startled by a voice behind her.

"So nice to finally meet you, Mr. McCabe. I've stopped by to visit you a couple of times, but unfortunately you weren't home."

She turned quickly. Standing at the bottom of the stairs was a man who looked to be in his forties, wearing a short black jacket and jeans. He sported a baseball cap, the brim pulled down, so it was hard for her to get a good look at his face, but as he slowly raised his left arm, she saw that his gloved hand held a knife. The click of the blade snapping into place and the creak of the old wooden steps under his weight echoed through the stairwell as he slowly headed up the stairs toward her.

"Please continue to the top of the stairs, Mr. McCabe—or is it Ms. McCabe?" He paused, a malevolent smile smeared across his face. "Well, I guess we'll find out, won't we?" he said calmly.

She did a quick calculation and concluded she could never get her door unlocked before he reached her. *Don't retreat if you have a tactical advantage*, she remembered from self-defense class. *A knife isn't good, but at least he doesn't have a gun. You have the high ground, so stand your ground. He has to come to you.*

She stared at him, not moving.

He stopped his ascent up the stairs. "I told you to move to the top of the stairs, Mr. McCabe."

There were about eight stairs that separated them. If she charged him, he had enough time to react and use his knife to his advantage. *Wait him out.* "Thanks, I think I'm good where I am," she replied, trying to slow her breathing and collect her thoughts. *Stay calm. Stay focused. Use your training. Make him come to you.* Maybe if he came close enough, she could kick the knife out of his hand.

His smile disappeared. "That wasn't a request, Mr. McCabe, it was an order." In one motion he folded the blade of the knife back into the handle and reached into the waistband of his pants. When he raised his right arm, he held a 9mm handgun. "Let me say it one last time. Move to the top of the stairs, Mr. McCabe." His voice was cold. "I would much prefer to have fun with you while you're alive, but I have no qualms about killing you now."

She had seen guns before, but always in a holster or as evidence in a case. She had never had one pointed at her before. Looking at the barrel aimed at her, it appeared huge, and it momentarily took her breath away. She closed her eyes and drew in a deep breath, then slowly climbed the remaining three steps, trying as she did to slip her hand into her purse, feeling for the pepper spray she carried.

"Hand out of your purse," he commanded. "Now!"

She withdrew her hand from her purse and stopped when she reached the top step.

He stopped about four steps from the top, his gun pointed at her face. "See how easy it is when you do what you're told. Keep that in mind as we get to know each other." His eyes, now clearly visible as he looked up at her, conveyed all she needed to know about what he had in mind. "Now gently back up against the door."

Her mind was racing. This wasn't going to end well. He wore no mask, so he was identifiable, which meant he had no intention of her living beyond their encounter.

She inched backward toward the door, her eyes never leaving the barrel of the gun. She stopped when her back was against the door.

"Where are your keys?"

"In my purse," she said weakly.

"Slowly, crouch down and put your purse down on the floor. And if you try anything stupid, I *will* shoot you," he said, emphasizing the word *will*.

She slowly bent at the knees, lowering herself so she could do as instructed, all the while trying to come up with something, anything, to allow her to escape. She placed her purse on the floor in front of her, close to where she was standing. As she stood back up, she hoped that maybe, if he leaned forward to grab her purse, she might be able to kick him or the gun out of his hand.

His laugh was cold. "Do you really think I'm going to reach for the purse so you can kick me? Here's what I want you to do. . . ."

As he spoke, she weighed her options. It appeared there were only two: die out here with a bullet to the head, or allow him to get her into the apartment, where he would no doubt tie her up and torture her before he killed her. Neither was attractive, but there really was no choice. One way or the other she had drawn the death card. Despite the hope that maybe there was a way out, it looked like a quick bullet was the way to go.

He finished his instructions. For the briefest moment she wondered what death would be like. She inhaled slowly, staring him straight in the eyes, determined she would never let him get her inside her apartment. Now, she thought. *Do it now!*

CHAPTER 32

"*H*ELLO?"

"Peg?"

"Yes."

"It's Duane Swisher."

"Hi, Duane. How are you?"

"Peg, I'm calling about Erin. Something's happened."

"Is everything okay?" she asked, a sudden urgency in her tone.

"Umm, no. Actually, I'm not sure what's going on. I just got a call from a mutual friend, Mark Simpson. He and Erin were supposed to go out to dinner tonight, but when he got to her apartment to pick her up, the police were there and they told him Erin had been taken to Overlook Hospital."

"Oh my God, Duane. What happened?" she screamed.

"I don't know. I'm on my way to the hospital now." He hesitated, unsure if he should tell her more. "I'm not sure if it's accurate, but Mark thought that Erin may have been shot."

The scream from his phone echoed through his car. Then

there was silence before a different voice boomed, "Duane, it's Pat McCabe. What the hell's going on?"

"Honest, Pat, I wish I knew. All I know is that Erin has been taken to Overlook. I'm on my way to the hospital now."

"Has anyone tried his cell?" he asked.

"Yes," Duane replied. "I've tried several times and our friend has tried even more. No answer."

"Okay, Peg and I will meet you at the hospital."

The line went dead and Duane sped through the traffic, trying not to let his mind go where it was going. When he entered the emergency room waiting area, he saw Mark pacing back and forth near the triage desk.

"What's going on?"

"I don't know. They won't tell me anything and they won't let me in."

Duane grabbed him by the arm and approached the desk. "Hi, my name is Duane Swisher. I understand that my law partner, Erin McCabe, was brought in a while ago." As he was talking he removed his license from his wallet and took some papers from inside his coat pocket, handing them to the triage nurse. "This is Ms. McCabe's living will. I'm listed as one of her healthcare proxies." He turned and looked at Mark. "And this is her fiancé," he quickly ad-libbed.

The triage nurse took Duane's paperwork and looked at Mark suspiciously. "Hold on," she said, disappearing through a hospital door.

"Do you know anything else?" Duane asked, trying his best to remain calm.

"No, nobody will tell me anything," Mark responded.

"What did the cops tell you at the scene?"

"Nothing. Just that she was here."

"Who told you she had been shot?"

"Some woman." He shook his head. "Jesus, Swish, it's all a blur." He took a deep breath. "I was supposed to pick her up at seven thirty, but she wasn't answering her phone. When I got to her apartment there was a crowd of people and, I don't know, maybe four marked cop cars. I asked this lady who was standing there if she knew what had happened, and she said someone told her that a woman who lives in one of the apartments had been shot. At that point I began to panic and got a cop's attention. I said I was taking a friend out to dinner, and she lived in one of the apartments, could I get through to go get her? When I gave him the address, he gave me a strange look and asked me for my friend's name, then went over to talk to a lieutenant or something. They both came back, and he said, 'Look, there's been an incident here and Ms. McCabe's been taken to Overlook.' He said that's all he could tell me. I ran back to my car and called you."

"Fuck," Duane mumbled under his breath. "Fuck!"

The door to the emergency room opened and the triage nurse came out and handed Duane back his license and paperwork and said, "Follow me." They walked down the corridor to the nurses' station, where she stopped. "This is Dr. Mohdi. He can fill you in."

Mohdi looked at Duane and Mark. "You're here for Ms. McCabe?"

"Yes," they responded simultaneously.

Mohdi took off his glasses. "They took her up to surgery about fifteen, twenty minutes ago. I was the one who examined her when she came in. She has a gunshot wound that is considered non-life-threatening, although she lost a fair amount of blood, and a fractured, dislocated left elbow. We cleaned up the gunshot wound in the ER and she received about twenty stitches. She's lucky the bullet didn't hit any bones. I'm not sure how backed up the OR is, but the OR waiting room is on level four. I'd suggest you head over there and check in. That way they'll tell the surgeon you're there and he can speak to you when surgery is complete. She'll probably be kept overnight for observation, but, assuming no complications, she should be released tomorrow."

"She's going to be okay?" Duane asked.

"From what I saw, I don't see any reason why she won't be."

"Why is she in surgery?" Mark asked.

"To fix her elbow," he replied.

They both stood there, until finally Duane said, "Thank you, Doctor. We appreciate the information."

"You're welcome," he said, turning his attention back to one of the nurses, who handed him a chart to review.

Erin's parents were walking into the waiting area just as Duane and Mark walked back out of the ER. Duane immediately called to them. He began to fill them in on what Dr. Mohdi had told them, but Pat told him they already knew. Pat had called Sean as soon as he hung up from Duane, and Sean, using his connections, had gotten through to both the ER doctor and the surgeon.

Duane asked the woman at the information desk for directions, and all four of them made their way through the maze that led from the ER to the OR waiting room. Along the way, Duane introduced Mark to Erin's parents, and he couldn't help but notice both Pat's quizzical expression and Peg's slightly more critical gaze.

An hour later, a physician in surgical scrubs walked into the waiting area and asked if there was anyone there for Erin McCabe. The four of them stood up in unison and quickly introduced themselves.

Facing Erin's parents, he said, "Hi, I'm Dr. Miller. Your daughter had a fractured and dislocated elbow, which we have put back in place with a wire and two screws. I put it in an immobilizing brace, and with rehab, she should be fine. We also gave her some additional blood to help with the loss from the bullet wound, but there's no major damage. The bullet missed the hipbone and passed right through the fat pad. It's high enough that even if it leaves a scar, it should be covered by her bikini."

He looked at his watch and missed Pat McCabe cringe at the mention of "her bikini."

"Assuming she wants to go home tonight, she should be ready to go in an hour or so, but if she'd like to spend the night, it shouldn't be a problem. We usually have room this time of year. I gave her prescriptions for pain and an antibiotic to make sure she doesn't develop an infection, and I spoke with her brother before the surgery, so hopefully he can take a look at everything over the holiday. But if for any reason she'd like to come back for me to take a look at it, my contact information will be on her discharge sheet. As soon as she's fully awake, the nurse will come out and bring you back. Any questions?"

"Lots," her father answered, "but not for you."

About forty-five minutes later, Erin was still a little groggy when a nurse escorted her visitors in to see her. Erin squinted at the four of them gathered around her bed, looking from one to the next. Then, focusing on her mother, she said in a hoarse whisper, "'Oh, Auntie Em, it's you.'" She looked from her dad to Duane and then Mark. "'And you were there, and you, and you . . . But you couldn't have been, could you?'"

Silence hung in the room for several seconds before her mother said, "Listen, Dorothy, if you want to get home, you'll open those eyes of yours, otherwise you'll be stuck here in Oz tonight."

Erin opened her eyes wider and she gave her mother the stupidest grin. "'Oh, Auntie Em, there's no place like home.'"

Thirty minutes later, she was awake and dressed. Sitting on the edge of the bed, she looked at the four of them. "Look, I know you all want to know what happened, but first things first—I need a place to stay tonight because right now my place is a crime scene."

Her mother's look was priceless. "I just assumed you were staying with us."

Erin raised her eyebrows and allowed her mother to follow her gaze as she looked at her father.

"Of course," he said somewhat sheepishly.

"You sure?" Erin asked directly.

"Oh, for Christ's sake. I know I'm not with the program here, but someone took a shot at my . . . child, and I'm not a total asshole. Yes, I'm sure."

Erin allowed herself a small grin, mostly at her father's inability to say the word *daughter*.

"Okay. So why don't we head back to your house and I'll fill you all in on what happened." She looked over at Duane and Mark. "If either of you need to go, I can fill you in tomorrow."

They looked at each other and shook their heads no.

She gingerly stood up from the bed. She was a little woozy at first, reaching out to her mom to steady herself. But after several seconds she felt steadier. "I'm going to go with Mark. Why don't you go ahead? We'll meet you there."

Her father nodded with a sidelong look in Mark's direction. Her mother gave her a hug. "Are you okay?"

"Yeah, I think I am," she responded. "I'm still here, even though about five hours ago I thought my time was up. So right now, no complaints. It's okay, Mom," she found herself reassuring her teary mother. "I'm okay."

After her parents left, the nurse wheeled her to the exit in a wheelchair while Mark went to get his car. When he pulled up, he and the nurse helped her into the car, trying not to bump her elbow or the wound on her right hip.

"Sorry for all the excitement tonight," she said.

"No problem," he replied. "Just glad you're okay."

"Yeah, me too." She turned so she was facing him, wincing a little from the pain in her hip. "Maybe we're just destined never to have that first date."

He quickly looked in her direction. "I'll admit that I've had any number of brick walls when it comes to you; most of them I built. But I've come to realize how badly I want to get to know you. And the realization that tonight I apparently came very close to losing that opportunity has made me more determined than ever to have that first date." He paused. "And hopefully more after that."

For the first time since she heard the noise behind her on the stairs, she started crying like a baby. Mark immediately found a place to pull over and parked the car. "I hope your reaction is to everything that happened to you tonight, and not to the prospect of going on a date with me?"

She looked up at him, and her sobs became interspersed with several chuckles. "What, you think I asked you to drive me to my parents so I could tell you I never wanted to see you again?"

He gave her the same warm smile he did when they met for the first time in Duane's backyard. "I hope not, but after the way I've treated you, I wouldn't blame you if you did."

She went to look for her purse to get a tissue, when she remembered she didn't have it with her. "You wouldn't have a tissue, would you?"

He reached into his pocket and handed her a handkerchief. "It's clean, I promise. My mom raised me right. Always take a clean handkerchief."

She took it and wiped her eyes and then blew her nose. "Thanks."

"You okay?" he asked.

"No," she replied, "but I think I will be." She put the handkerchief on her lap and took his hand back in hers, giving it a gentle squeeze. "Thank you," she said. "We better get going or my parents will be calling the cops."

CHAPTER 33

W HEN SHE AND MARK ARRIVED, HER PARENTS AND DUANE were already sitting around the kitchen table having a cup of coffee. Erin sat down gingerly and her mother made her a cup of tea.

She glanced around the table. "I know you all want to know what happened, but please, I suspect I may get a little shaky in parts, so just let me go without interruption."

"Where are your keys?"

"In my purse," she said weakly.

"Slowly, crouch down and put your purse down on the floor. And if you try anything stupid, I will shoot you."

She couldn't help but notice that the gun was pointed directly at her head. He moved across the steps so he was positioned on the left side of the stairwell.

"Do you really think I'm going to reach for the purse so you can kick me? Here's what I want you to do. Now, gently, with your left foot, nudge your purse forward so it's near the edge of the landing."

Her purse was a medium-size black leather Dolce & Gabbana satchel, about the size of a football. Born out of desperation, a stupid idea came to her as she looked at it there on the floor. It had little chance for success, but it was the only chance she had. She figured that if it didn't work, at least it would be over quickly.

She inhaled slowly, trying to calm herself, hoping her rusty skills would translate from ball to satchel. She gently reached out as he had directed and touched her purse with her left foot. As she did, she continued to look directly at him. "Use your eyes to fool a defender" was advice that had been drilled into her.

He had taken a half step farther toward her and was now positioned with his right leg on the second step and his left leg on the third step as he prepared to reach out and snatch the purse from the landing. As he began to lean forward, his eyes were focused squarely on her face, his target if he pulled the trigger. She gently pointed her toes down so that the instep of her left foot was squarely behind the purse. Now, *she thought.* Do it now. *Quickly she flicked her foot, just like she used to do with a soccer ball, propelling the purse at his face. As she did, she instantly spun to her right. He fired just as the purse struck him in the face, but the purse distracted him just enough that the bullet missed her head by inches. She charged at him, hoping to knock him down the steps, but he'd recovered enough to grab on to the handrail, his gun now pointed at the ceiling.*

He grappled with her, trying to bring the gun down to get off another shot. But as he was bringing the gun down, he lost his grip on her and she clutched her left fist with her right hand, and using that to add force, she swung her left elbow at his head as hard as she could. She was aiming for his temple, hoping to crush his skull, but she missed and her elbow smashed into his jaw. There was a distinctive pop as his head snapped to the right, causing him to scream in pain. As fast as she could, she charged past him down the steps, grabbing the newel post to swing herself around as she hit the landing. Just as she did, a shot rang out and she heard him cursing. She sprinted past Dr. Gold's office and down the next flight of stairs to the street. She burst through the door and turned left onto North Avenue, knowing it was three blocks to the police station.

She burst through the door of police headquarters screaming. Two of-

ficers at the desk immediately grabbed her. "Lady, calm down," one of them said. "What's going on?"

"There's a man with a gun." She gasped for breath. "He broke into my building. He shot at me."

"Dave," the other officer said, "she's bleeding. She may be hit."

"This is Jensen at the front desk. I need an EMT ASAP."

They guided Erin to a chair and sat her down. "What's your address?"

"27A North Avenue," she replied, trying to catch her breath.

"Can you give me a description of the person who shot you?"

After she did, the officer reported over his radio. "I have shots fired at 27A North Avenue. All units respond. Suspect is a white male, approximately mid-forties, about five-eight. Wearing a baseball cap, a black jacket, and jeans."

"Oh," she added, "he may have a broken jaw."

The officer looked at her quizzically. "Suspect may also have an injury to his jaw," he repeated into his radio.

Her heart was pounding, the adrenaline pumping through her. Then the pain set in. Her left elbow was throbbing, and her right hip was suddenly on fire.

"We're going to need an ambulance," she heard the EMT say to the officer who had been talking to her. "She's bleeding—definitely been shot. She appears to have lost a fair amount of blood, but it doesn't look like it hit anything vital."

She held out her left arm. "I think I did something to my left elbow too," she said, wincing as moving her arm had become very painful.

"Any idea how you injured your arm?" the EMT asked.

"Yeah, probably when I slammed it into his jaw."

As the EMT examined her arm, everything came rushing back—the look in his eye, the barrel of the gun pointed at her face, the bullet whizzing by her head. She suddenly started trembling uncontrollably. They brought in a stretcher and placed her on it. But even after they strapped her in place, she couldn't stop shaking.

"You're going to be okay," she heard somebody say as they wheeled her out to the ambulance.

* * *

Erin looked around the table and they were all staring at her. Finally, Duane asked, "Was it the guy who broke in twice?"

She closed her eyes, the memories fresh. "Yeah, it was him. He said he was glad to finally meet me."

"Wait," her father said. "Your apartment's been broken into twice?"

She nodded.

"Why didn't I know about this?"

She didn't want to argue now. "Long story, Dad. But not for tonight. I'm exhausted, everything is really starting to ache, and I have to get to police headquarters tomorrow to hopefully get my purse and look at mug shots."

"I'll take you," Duane offered.

"Swish, it's Christmas Eve. I'm sure you have enough to do."

"What time?" he replied.

"Nine?"

"Perfect." He came up next to her, bent over, and gave her a hug. "Can you ID him?"

"Don't know. I might be able to. But I think we both know he won't be in any photo arrays."

He nodded. "Yeah, you're right." He straightened up, now towering over her. "Glad you're still with us," he offered with a small smile. "See you in the morning."

She stood up slowly and her mother came over to her side. "I'll call you tomorrow," she said to Mark. "Thanks for our chat earlier. Maybe we're done with all the brick walls."

He stood up, walked over, and gave her a kiss on the cheek. "I hope so," he said.

Her mother led her slowly out of the room and guided her up the stairs to her old bedroom. A room she hadn't seen in the three years since she transitioned, a room that still looked like it did when she last lived here right before law school—a guy's room. On the bookcase were the books she read growing up, her soccer trophies, and a framed picture of the New York Giants celebrating Super Bowl XXV. She crawled under the covers and quickly fell asleep.

Erin awoke to her mother shaking her.

"Erin. Erin, honey, wake up."

She looked through the haze of sleep, trying to understand where she was. "What?" she mumbled.

"You were screaming," her mother said soothingly.

Her eyes were barely open. "I saw Barbara," she said, suddenly realizing she was shaking, her heart racing.

Her mother looked at her blankly.

"The prosecutor," Erin offered. "She was burned. Her face . . . there was nothing left. It was . . . it was horrible."

"It was a dream," her mother told her.

"No, I saw her. She was warning me."

Her mother lay down next to her. "It's okay," she said. She draped her arm over Erin. "You're going to be okay."

CHAPTER 34

"*H*OW YOU FEELING?" DUANE ASKED AS THEY WALKED TO the car.

"Sore," she responded.

"That's it? Sore?"

She nodded.

He handed her the newspaper. "Page four if you care to read about it," he said.

"I kind of know what happened. What's the paper's spin?"

"How the police think it's someone obsessed and angry over you being transgender."

"That's what I love about law enforcement: Never let the facts get in the way of your theory of the case," she said with a sigh.

"I spoke to Paul Tillis last night about what happened," he said, opening the car door for her before walking around to the driver's seat.

"Why?"

"I wanted him to contact the private security company guarding Sharise's hospital room and make sure their people were alerted and ready for any potential trouble."

She didn't say anything for several minutes. "I think this guy acted alone," she finally said.

"What makes you say that?" Duane asked.

"Just a gut feeling. This guy looked like a sicko, but he must have been a professional given he had broken in twice before. But last night, there was a look in his eye. He was there to have fun killing me."

He glanced over at her.

"Yeah, I know. I'm incredibly lucky," she said with a sigh. "When I think of all the random things—the weather was warm, so I didn't have on a heavy coat and was able to hit him hard with my elbow. I was wearing running shoes instead of heels. And he took two shots at me and somehow I'm still here." She paused. "Yeah, really lucky."

"You seem really far away. You sure you're okay?"

She turned to face him. "I dreamt about Taylor last night."

Duane shifted uncomfortably in his seat. "Anything in particular?"

She turned and stared out the window. "It was pretty horrific," she said, cringing with the images of her dream still vivid in her head. "She was burned all over."

"You still see your shrink?" he asked.

"Yeah, I'll make an appointment," she added, resignation in her voice. "I guess as time goes on, the memories will fade, but just being here is . . . I don't know, overwhelming. I don't know what being dead is like, but when I flicked my purse into his face, I expected to find out."

"I'm glad you didn't."

When they got to police headquarters, Detective Hagen was waiting for them. After Erin signed some property forms to get her purse back, he told her that she was free to go back to her apartment. They spent some time reviewing her statement to make sure she hadn't left anything out. She looked at some photo array books but didn't see anyone who looked like the guy. Before they left, Hagen told her that they had some good leads. They had found blood on the stairs so they could run some DNA tests and they had found both bullets, so they'd be able to do forensics on them. Hagen was confident they'd find the guy who had done it. She and Duane were less sure, but kept their thoughts to themselves.

Afterward, she called Mark and arranged to meet him at Nomahegan Park. But first they had one more stop to make.

"You sure you're ready to go in there?" Duane asked, as she opened the outside door.

"As long as I have you with me, big guy, 'though I walk through the valley of the shadow of death, I will fear no evil,'" she said. "Besides, I need some clothes."

At the end of the hallway, where the landing turned, she could see where the police had dug out the second bullet, the one that went through her hip, from the wall. She took a deep breath and started up the stairs, wincing in pain from the gunshot wound. Just before the top of the stairs, she stopped and looked down at the stair treads. She grabbed the banister, the images of the night before suddenly replaying in vivid detail. She bit down hard on her lower lip, trying to quell the emotions.

Duane, who was standing behind her, reached out to steady her.

"This is where we struggled," she offered, more to herself than to Duane. She turned and looked up at the top of the steps, taking in the view that her assailant had. She slowly climbed the last three stairs. The bullet hole in the door was right at eye level.

She took out her keys and unlocked the door, but before she could open it, Duane said, "Let me."

He opened the door and went in, looking around to make sure there were no signs that anyone had been inside other than the police. Then, she quickly gathered some clothes and cosmetics, and packed them into her suitcase. They met Mark in the parking lot of the park, where Duane transferred Erin's suitcase and cosmetics bag to the trunk of Mark's car.

"Merry Christmas," she said, giving Duane a one-armed hug. "Please give my love to Cori."

"You sure you're okay with me taking off this week?" he asked.

"Absolutely. I'll hold down the fort. Things will be fine. You enjoy your family. I'm sure Austin will be having a blast with whatever Santa brought him. Have a good time and relax."

"You too," he replied. "By the way, you're joining us New Year's Eve, aren't you?"

"I'll try."

He gave her a knowing look. "Lauren and her husband aren't going to be there. They're visiting his family somewhere in Michigan."

She smiled at him. "Thanks for letting me know."

He returned her smile. "You're welcome. And, assuming you come, please feel free to bring a friend."

She chuckled. "Thanks."

The weather was more like the day before Easter than the day before Christmas. Temperatures were in the mid-fifties and the bright sunshine made it feel even warmer. She and Mark walked to one of the benches overlooking the lake in the park and sat down.

"Look," he said, "I know it's none of my business, but from catching snippets of what you and Duane were talking about, it sounds like the two of you have been through a lot. If you want to unload, I'm happy to just listen."

She really hadn't planned on it, but once she started, it poured out of her. She left out everything about Sharise's legal position, but when she finished, he was staring at her with a look of disbelief.

"Wow," he said. "That's unbelievable. It's hard to believe no one is investigating this."

"Not hard when the person they'd have to investigate is one of the most powerful politicians in the state."

They sat in silence for several minutes, her mind stuck on Barbara Taylor and the house engulfed in flames.

"What are you doing for Christmas?" he asked.

"Not sure what I'm doing tonight," she replied. "My mom always has her family for Christmas Eve dinner, but I'm not sure I want to answer a thousand questions, or worse, deal with the quizzical looks. Tomorrow my mom and I are going to my brother's to spend Christmas with them. What about you?"

"I'm going to my sister's tonight for dinner, and tomorrow I'll be at my mom's with the whole family." He paused. "Would you like to come with me tonight?"

She was surprised by his offer. "Um, I don't know. Seems a little awkward to meet part of your family without even having had a date."

"Well, if it makes it any easier, this is the part of my family that I suspect will welcome you with open arms."

"Yeah, but you just can't show up with an uninvited guest. That would be rather rude."

"I already asked my sister if it was all right."

She found herself getting lost in his eyes, mystified by her feelings. The one thing she could no longer deny was that she found him attractive. She knew she had been sexually attracted to Lauren. She hadn't made that up. And she had always believed that had Lauren been willing to live with her as a woman, she would have continued to be sexually attracted to her. So when did it shift? And why? Even Lisa, her therapist, had nothing concrete to offer: "It happens sometimes. It doesn't mean your past feelings weren't real and it doesn't mean your current feelings aren't real either. There's no reason to fight it. Enjoy it." Enjoy it? Life was confusing enough right now.

"Earth to Erin," Mark said with a small laugh.

"Sorry. I guess that would be nice."

"Okay. It's a date."

She cringed. "You sure you want to use that word? We haven't had a whole lot of success with it."

"I think we're past that," he offered, as he leaned over and kissed her.

When she opened her eyes, he graced her with the warmest smile. She leaned into him and he wrapped his arms around her and for the first time in a long time, she felt a moment of peace.

Will pointed to the newspaper on the table. "What the hell's going on?"

"Merry Christmas to you too." When Will raised his eyebrows, Gardner explained, "I tried to get you this morning, but it went right to voice mail."

"It's Sunday, as well as being Christmas Eve. Sheila and I were at church. Even I'm entitled to an hour of peace and quiet."

"No argument," Gardner replied. "I was just trying to get to you because I wanted you to hear it from me instead of reading it in the newspaper, as you apparently did."

"Okay," Will said. "Please fill in the details."

"I had mentioned to you that the guy who broke into Mc-Cabe's apartment twice was a bit of a sick fuck."

"You did."

"Well, apparently last night he decided to have his own little adventure."

"He was freelancing?"

"Exactly."

"I'm confused; the article says McCabe escaped with minor injuries."

"That's accurate. McCabe's very much alive. From what I'm told, she has a non-life-threatening gunshot wound and some kind of arm injury. However, the guy we used is dead."

"That's not in the article. How the hell did he die?"

Michael's stare showed no emotion. "I received a message last night from an intermediary, advising me that our man was in a bit of a panic. Apparently, he took a pretty good shot to the jaw and had left blood over the stairwell at McCabe's apartment. He knew what that meant—DNA. He also knew he had violated a cardinal rule by going off on his own, and he suggested to the intermediary that he needed to leave the country quickly. My feeling was that his plan left something to be desired." He stroked his upper lip between his fingers. "I learned earlier this morning that he was found dead of what appears to be a self-inflicted gunshot to the head."

Will took in the measure of his former XO. "I presume you're confident that the investigation will confirm it was a suicide?"

"Extremely. I've also been told that the weapon he used was the same weapon used in the incident with McCabe."

Will nodded almost imperceptibly. "Okay, thank you. I don't need any more loose ends at this point."

Michael ran his right hand through the tuft of hair on the right side of his head. "Understood."

CHAPTER 35

*T*HE HOLIDAYS WERE A BLUR. MOLLY AND ROBIN HAD MADE Erin feel at home, and if Mark was uncomfortable, he never showed it. Then her father shocked her when he went with her and her mother to Sean and Liz's on Christmas Day. He didn't say much during the trip or while they were there, but she considered it a major victory that they had driven in the same car and had dinner at the same table without incident. She also got to spend time with her nephews, which filled her with a joy she hadn't felt in a long time. The day after Christmas she visited her brother's office. He took X-rays and examined her arm, and was very happy with the work the surgeon had done. He told her that she should be able to begin physical therapy in about three weeks.

The police contacted her on Friday of Christmas week to let her know that they believed they had located the person who assaulted her. As soon as she looked at the first photo, she knew it was him. After she identified him, they told her that he was dead of a self-inflicted gunshot wound. They had obtained a positive

DNA match from the blood found on the steps to her apartment, and ballistics matched the gun he used to commit suicide to the gun that had been fired at her. They also discovered articles clipped out of various newspapers about her from the beginning of the case scattered throughout his apartment. Based on this, the fact that he had no criminal record, and that he had served multiple tours in Afghanistan and Iraq, the police concluded that he was mentally unstable and biased against transgender people. She suspected there was a far different story, but knew it was pointless to argue.

She and Mark had gone to the Swishers' for New Year's Eve and had wound up spending the night at Mark's place. When he dropped her off at her parents', she and her mom sat at the kitchen table and had brunch while her father slept in.

"You really need to get some friends."

"Thanks, Mom."

"No, seriously. Don't you have any close friends that you can talk to about this?"

Erin looked down, embarrassed by her mom's directness. "Not exactly. I didn't have a lot of girlfriends before, and most of my guy friends didn't stick with me through the transition."

Peg McBride looked at her daughter. "Yeah, this is definitely not something to talk to a guy about. I guess I just don't understand it."

"I don't understand it either. I mean, I was never attracted to guys before."

"Well, it appears like you are now."

Erin looked down at her French toast and giggled. *Thank you, Captain Obvious.*

"Are you sure you weren't just gay and we could have avoided this whole trans thing?"

"Mom, I swear I didn't secretly have the hots for guys before this."

"So what is it? It's probably hormones," she continued without waiting for Erin to answer. "I remember when I went through menopause, sweet Jesus, my hormones drove me insane. I was up, I was down, I was hot, I was cold. One minute I wanted to rip your father's clothes off, and the next, I just wanted to rip him apart."

"I don't think it's my hormones, Mom. I think it's just everything."

"That makes no sense. I don't even know what that means."

"I agree. Honest, I don't know what it is."

"I have to admit he's very handsome. So, did you have sex?"

"Mom! For God's sake, how can you ask me that?"

"What, I can't ask my daughter if she had sex?"

"No!"

"No, I can't ask, or no, you didn't?"

"Yes. No. You can't ask and no, we didn't."

"Why not?"

"Why what?"

"Why can't I ask?"

"Because you're my mother."

"What's that got to do with anything? Mothers and daughters talk about these things."

"How do you know mothers and daughters talk about this stuff? You've never had a daughter before."

"I had a mother," she responded defiantly.

"So you're telling me that you and Nanny talked about having sex?"

"Oh God, no," she laughed. "I'm not sure I ever even heard my mother say the word *sex*."

"That's my point."

"What's your point?"

"That mothers and daughters don't talk about these things."

"That's not true. I have friends whose daughters talk to them about their sex lives."

"Really?"

"Sometimes. Usually when things aren't going right."

"Well, that's different from fathers and sons. Fathers never talk to their sons about sex."

"Men never talk about sex period, even when it's the only thing on their mind. No offense, but men are weird."

"No offense taken. I'm no longer on the team, remember?"

"Right." She paused, scrutinized Erin. "So why didn't you have sex?"

"Jesus, Mom."

"Just curious."

"It was our second date. Besides, this is all new to me."

"You're not getting any younger, you know."

"Mom, I don't have to worry about my biological clock. It's not ticking."

Peg seemed momentarily confused and then a grin started to spread across her face. "I knew that," she chuckled. "Interesting."

"What is?"

"The fact that you're a virgin . . . again."

"There is one other thing," Erin said softly. "I will confess that I'm nervous about it."

"The 'it' being intercourse, I presume."

Erin nodded.

"Can I ask why?" her mother asked.

"I don't know, what if after all of this I don't enjoy it?"

Her mother laughed. "Well, then I guess we'll know you're really a woman."

"Mom. Come on, I'm trying to be serious," she said, almost pleading.

"You're right, I'm sorry," her mother offered, her tone apologetic. "Erin, honey, no one has to tell you that sex is different for men and women—after all, you've been on both sides of the bed. And I sure as hell can't tell you what it's like for a man, but, from my perspective, it certainly *seems* a lot simpler. Assuming it gets hard, you're off to the races. And for most women it's not that simple. That said, most of the time, if the man you're with is loving and wants you to enjoy it too, it can be wonderful. The best advice I can give you is don't think about it, just enjoy it and let whatever is going to happen, happen."

Erin nodded. "Thanks."

"You're welcome," her mother replied with a gentle smile.

They sat in silence for several minutes until Erin asked, "How's Dad? I think he's said fifteen words to me in the week I've been here."

"Don't worry, on a good week he says twenty-five to me."

"Stop! I love Dad, and it bothers me that he is still struggling with this."

"Hon, I wish I understood it. I think on some level your dad just thinks it's all made up and you're choosing to live this way." Peg held up her hand to stop Erin from responding. "I know you're not, and he and I have talked about it numerous times. I can tell you that the fact that you were almost killed devastated him. The night you told us what had happened, after you went to bed, he sat here and cried. He realized he almost lost one of his children. And to be honest, I know the whole thing with Mark is really freaking him out. All I can tell you is just be yourself and leave the door open. He may not understand it, but he still loves you. One day he'll come around."

CHAPTER 36

*E*RIN WOKE UP TO HIM PULLING THE COVERS BACK FROM HER chest, a gun pointed in her face. "Make a sound and you're dead," he said, his tone remarkably calm.

She stared at him in disbelief.

"You actually believed I was dead," he mocked. "Well, aren't you a naïve bitch? No, I came back to finish what I started," he said, throwing his head back with a laugh. The sound of his laugh grew louder and echoed off the walls. He was so loud, surely he'd wake her parents. But as the room came into sharper focus, she realized she was back in her apartment. When? How?

He suddenly stopped laughing. "Bye," he said, pulling the trigger.

Her body convulsed and he was gone. She sat up with a start, her breathing coming in staccato bursts. Her nightgown, soaked in sweat, was clinging to her body.

Slowly she got out of bed and made her way to the bathroom. She sat on the toilet, her stomach churning, trying to reassure her-

self that it was a dream. With her good arm, she peeled off her
wet nightgown and made her way back to the bedroom.

Lying in bed, she turned fitfully from side to side. Her brain,
now awake, began involuntarily reviewing where they were with
Sharise's case. Things were not going as they had hoped. Right
after the holidays, Duane had received the call from George
Phillips, the Ocean County counsel, who wanted to set up a
meeting to see if Sharise's civil case could be settled. Despite
Duane's reluctance, he couldn't convince Phillips that the timing
wasn't right. "Let's just sit and talk," Phillips insisted. "You've
got nothing to lose."

After meeting with Tonya and Sharise, they decided that since
Sharise's fall had occurred only a couple of months earlier, they
would keep their settlement demands high. Even with Ogden
giving Sharise a good prognosis, it was still far from certain that
she'd make a complete recovery.

The meeting had been a disaster. To their surprise, Gehrity
and Carmichael had come, in addition to Phillips and Charles
Hayden, a representative of the county's insurance carrier.
Phillips explained that he had invited Gehrity and Carmichael in
hopes that a global resolution could be reached, but when all
Gehrity offered was a plea to aggravated manslaughter with a
ten-year cap on any sentence, and refused to consent to having
Townsend's DNA sent to Massachusetts or Pennsylvania, he and
Erin had gotten into a shouting match, and the plea negotiations
quickly came to an end.

It was more of the same when they turned to the civil case.
While conceding that Sharise had suffered a serious injury, Hayden
offered $300,000 to settle the case. Duane advised them that they
were looking for five million, and after some back and forth, the negotiations ended with them at three million and rejecting the
county's final offer of $750,000.

It had been a month since their meeting with Phillips and
Gehrity, and they'd heard nothing further about a plea or settle-

ment. Now they had the conference in front of Redman, and both she and Duane were beginning to get nervous. She had been sure the DNA would match, but the prosecutor's office's refusal to budge on the plea had shaken her confidence. What if they had missed the opportunity to get Sharise both a good plea and a nice settlement was her last thought before she fell back to sleep.

"Do you think we overplayed our hand?" Duane asked as they drove to the conference with Redman.

"Don't know," Erin replied. "I just find it strange that we've heard nothing. I almost feel like they're trying to delay things, but I don't know why."

"Well, we'll soon find out."

Erin closed her eyes, contemplating all that had happened since the last time she had been in front of Redman; Barbara had still been alive, Sharise was healthy . . . things had been so different.

Her life had changed too. Her arm had healed and physically she was back to normal, but she'd realized she could never live in her third-floor walkup again. There was just too much emotional baggage. After two weeks of living with her parents, she knew staying there wasn't a viable long-term option either. Her dad's silence had morphed from being awkward to upsetting. She knew it would be only a matter of time before one of them said what was on their mind, and that wouldn't be good for anyone. It hadn't taken her long to find an apartment literally a stone's throw from the office. It wasn't luxury living, but the Riverside Apartments at least offered her the security of neighbors.

She and Mark were still seeing each other on a regular basis. And while she was still mystified by her attraction to him, there was no longer any questioning that she was a heterosexual woman.

"The delay may work to our benefit," Duane said, snapping her out of her thoughts. "Ben and I are meeting with Champion and Barone from DOJ next Wednesday."

"About Townsend?"

"Yeah, Ben made sure that the only thing on the agenda was Sharise's case."

"I still find that totally bizarre. How can her case even be on their radar?"

"No idea. But I guess I'll find that out too."

Redman was standing at the door to his chambers when his clerk led both counsel teams in. As Gehrity walked in, he turned to the judge and said, "Judge, I believe you know Assistant Prosecutor Chris Henderson; he'll be taking over the lead role in this matter."

"Yes, of course," Redman replied. After they were all seated, Redman said, "So where do we stand with this matter? Counsel, how is your client doing?"

"She's currently in a rehab facility still recovering from her TBI."

"I'm glad to hear she's recovering. In terms of moving forward, is she competent to assist in her own defense?"

"Judge, if we were going to trial next week, I'd have serious concerns. However, we still have a number of preliminary matters; the DNA motion, the motion to change venue, both of which I think we can proceed with."

"What about plea negotiations? Is she competent to understand and enter a plea if an acceptable offer was made?"

"Judge, we haven't had to cross that bridge because no acceptable offer has been made."

Redman gave Erin a quizzical look. "Mr. Prosecutor," he said, turning in Gehrity's direction, "where are you in terms of your plea offer?"

"Judge, I've been speaking with the vic—I'm sorry, with Mr. Townsend's family, and I conveyed to counsel that the family was anxious to conclude the case, so we offered to allow Mr. Barnes to plead guilty to aggravated manslaughter, with a flat ten, no parole disqualifier."

"That's a very generous offer, Mr. Prosecutor." Redman's eyes shifted back to Erin. "Counsel, I presume you've recommended that to your client."

Erin saw where this was going and decided to jump in with

both feet. "Actually, Judge, as I said, my client has rejected the offer and I concur with her decision. We believe that when the court hears our renewed motion on the DNA evidence you'll grant the motion, and we further believe that the DNA will show conclusively that Mr. Townsend was involved in the murder of two transgender prostitutes, one in Boston and one in Philadelphia. So we are extremely confident that our client will be found not guilty of murder or manslaughter." She looked at Gehrity. "To resolve the matter, my client is willing to plead guilty to third-degree theft as long as the sentence is time served."

"Well, Judge, we're making some progress," Gehrity interjected with a sarcastic chuckle. "The last time I spoke to Ms. McCabe, she wanted an outright dismissal." He shifted his body so he was facing Erin. "Counsel should be aware that if we have to go through the DNA motion, the offer will be withdrawn and our original thirty years will be the only deal offered."

"Gentlemen," Redman said, directing his attention to Gehrity, Carmichael, and Henderson, "why you don't step out for a moment and allow me to speak to defense counsel?"

After they had stepped out, Redman stared at Erin and Duane. "Are you crazy? You're seriously rejecting the plea offered by the State?"

"Yes, Judge," Erin replied.

"Ms. McCabe, I caution you, if your client is found guilty of murder or manslaughter, I will give him the maximum. He's aware of that?"

"She is, Judge," Erin replied.

Redman raised his eyes to the ceiling. "And you heard the prosecutor, if the motions go forward, the offer is withdrawn?"

"I heard what he said, Judge, which, given my client's condition, doesn't seem fair. You're asking her to make a final decision on a plea offer when I'm not satisfied she's competent to make that decision. If that is truly going to be the State's position, we will need to delay the motions until her doctors clear her to make those kinds of life-altering decisions."

Redman shook his head, his disgust apparent. "I have no intention of delaying this case indefinitely. All right, get the prosecutor back in here."

When they retook their seats, Redman asked, "Mr. Henderson, are you up to speed on this case and ready to go?"

"I should be soon, Judge. If Your Honor could give me another two to three weeks before scheduling anything, it would be appreciated."

"Fine," Redman said. "Ms. McCabe, how about from your perspective?"

"Judge, as I indicated, there is the pending motion to send Mr. Townsend's DNA to the Pennsylvania and Massachusetts State labs for analysis to see if it matches DNA collected at the scenes of murders in Philadelphia and Boston. We also have our motion to change venue. Finally, as I just indicated to Your Honor, given that our client has suffered a very severe traumatic brain injury, I'm requesting that all motions be carried until she is cleared by her doctors to make those kinds of decisions."

"Ms. McCabe, I have no intention of allowing this case to languish indefinitely. Mr. Henderson, file your response to the DNA motion by March 27. If you have any reply, Ms. McCabe, please get it to me by April 2 and I'll hear it on April 6. We'll schedule the change of venue motion after the DNA motion is decided."

As they rose to leave, Redman removed his glasses. "Counsel, I urge you to have another conversation with your client over the current plea offer. I think he'll be making a big mistake if he doesn't take it."

They left the courthouse and stopped at the rehab facility to discuss what had happened with Sharise. Days earlier they had urged Tonya to visit so she could be part of any discussions.

Entering the room, Erin stopped dead, thinking she had made a mistake. There, sitting in a chair in the far corner, was a very attractive African-American woman wearing a long powder-blue skirt and navy top, her hair freshly braided, and her makeup muted but done to perfection. Erin quickly looked from the woman to Tonya, who was sitting on the edge of the bed, sporting a broad smile.

"Oh my God!" Erin exclaimed. "Sharise, you're gorgeous." She nearly ran across the room to hug her client.

After they described the conference with the judge, Sharise leaned forward in her chair. "You telling me to take the deal?"

"No," Erin replied. "I'm still confident that we'll win the motion and the DNA will match. But I need to make sure you know that if we lose the motion, or if the DNA isn't a match, the offer will be withdrawn, and if you're found guilty, he'll throw the book at you. With the current offer of ten years, no parole disqualifier, it means with the time you've already served, you'd probably do three years before you were paroled. Three years in prison is a hell of a lot less than thirty years without parole. You'll be out when you're twenty-two. And, the chances are you wouldn't be the only transgender person in state prison, so it's probably safer than the county jail."

Sharise looked off into space for a long time. "I don't want to spend no rest of my life in jail. Do you think they'll still offer me seven hundred and fifty thousand to settle the civil case?"

"Probably," Duane responded.

"It isn't fair that the judge is forcing us to make the decision now," Tonya said. "I know my sister is doing great, but she's still recovering."

Erin nodded. "We agree. And if the judge doesn't give us an adjournment of the motion, we'll file a motion so we have a record to appeal him if we need to, but right now he appears to be sticking to his position."

"I need to talk to Tonya," Sharise said. "Maybe it's time to end all this and move on. All I got to do is survive a few years in prison and I be okay. Let me think about it."

"Of course," Erin replied. "Just so you know, if you decide to take the deal, you have to give what's called a factual basis for the crime. In other words, you'll have to tell the judge under oath that you killed Townsend and it wasn't in self-defense."

Sharise's eyes looked incredibly sad. "Sometimes you do what you gotta do to survive. I wanna survive, Erin. I wanna have a life."

Sharise and Tonya sat quietly after they left.

"I can't spend the rest of my life in jail," Sharise said, breaking the silence.

"Can you do three years in a men's prison?" Tonya asked.

"I've been trapped in a man's prison my entire life," Sharise replied without emotion. "Three years be a walk in the park." She looked down at the floor. "She's disappointed."

"Who is?" Tonya asked.

"My lawyer."

"She just wants what's best for you," Tonya said.

"I know. Up until you came, she the only one who stood by me." Her voice rose as she spoke. "They even tried to kill her. But she know, she know." Her tone was now defiant.

"She knows what?" Tonya asked.

"She know that white boy tried to kill me and if I go to jail, it's because his daddy be rich and powerful."

"What really happened that night, Sharise?"

Sharise looked at her sister. She had never told anyone the truth. She had even lied to Erin and Duane. But somehow, with help from Lenore, they had figured out most of it.

"He pick me up about a week before. We went a few blocks and parked. He pay me fifty dollars and I gave him a blow job. When we done, he look at me and ask if I was a trannie. Before I could answer, he say to me, 'Don't worry, I like trannies.' So I told him. He said, next time he come back, we'd get a room and have some fun. He axe me, how much to fuck me. I say two hundred. A week later, he come back and we go to the motel. He give me fifty and says he give me the rest when we done. He says for me to take off my clothes except my panties and lie on the bed. He takes off all his clothes and he gets on top of me and tells me to start touching him. I do, but he ain't getting hard. He seems like he getting upset, and I tell him don't worry, honey, we make it work. Suddenly he pulls the front of my panties down so he can see my dick, and then he leans forward and starts rubbing up by my neck. Now I can feel him getting hard and he starting to rub against me. I tell him I got a condom in my purse, which is on the bed next to me. All of a sudden he puts his hands around my neck and starts choking me. I try to push his arms away, but he way too strong. He be all excited and moaning, and I realize he's getting off on choking me. I'm trying to get him off me and I'm throwing my arms all around when my hand hits my purse. I'm just about to black out when my hand finds my knife in my purse. I pull it out, hit the button so the blade comes out, and he so excited he never sees it coming when I stick the knife in him."

Sharise wiped the tears from her face. "I never want to kill anyone. But I don't want to spend the rest of my life in jail either. What should I do? I don't want my lawyer to think I be a murderer."

"Sharise, honey, Erin's not the one facing jail, you are. No matter what happens when your case is over, she'll go home and sleep in her bed. You can't worry about her. You have to take care of yourself."

"Be just my luck, I settle the case for lots of money and then have to spend the rest of my life in jail for murdering someone who tried to kill me." She sighed as she looked at her sister. "Where my guardian angel be at when I need her?"

"I may not be your guardian angel, but I am your legal guardian, Sharise. I'll help you decide."

"Why are you so upset?" Duane asked.

"Don't know."

"Sure you do, you're disappointed she might take the deal."

"Swish, I know Townsend's a murderer."

"No, you don't know, E, and that's the whole point. We strongly suspect, but we can't be certain."

"I'm pretty damn sure."

"Sure enough to risk spending the rest of your life in jail if you're wrong? Because that's what you're asking her to risk."

"I know," she mumbled under her breath. "This sucks! They're squeezing us. I just can't believe Gehrity and Redman are forcing her to make a decision before the DNA analysis," she said. "How is that justice? I thought the system was called the justice system. It's not even close."

He gave her a sad smile. "I remember my first day of law school, the professor walked in and said, 'I'm going to teach you how to be lawyers. If you want to learn about justice, the theological seminary is on the other side of campus.'" He paused. "It's not a level playing field, E. Money and power still matter."

"You really need to work on your pep talks," she said. "I'm not feeling inspired."

"Well, maybe there's your reason why they've been dragging things out. The plea and the money become harder to walk away from over time."

"I guess. . . . But what if I have an idea to make them fish or cut bait?"

"I'm listening," he replied.

"Okay, look, before you say anything, I admit it's a little farfetched; no, it's really farfetched."

"If there's one thing I've learned from you, nothing is farfetched," Duane offered with a smirk. "I'm all ears."

"Lauren and the baby are doing well, right?"

"Lauren and the baby? What are you talking about?"

"Just answer my question. They're doing well?"

"Yeah, Cori and I were over two weeks ago. Everyone's doing great."

"And you and her husband, Steve, get along?"

"Yeah. Why?"

"Perfect. I need you to set up a time when we can meet with Steve. We need a favor from him."

CHAPTER 37

*E*DWARD CHAMPION HAD BEEN FIRST ASSISTANT UNITED States Attorney under Jim Giles for almost five years, but there were still times that he had a tough time figuring out his boss. He liked Giles—although Giles's physical appearance was as ordinary as applesauce, there was a certain charm and charisma to the man that drew people's attention to him when he walked into the room. And even though he was only forty-four, no one could deny that, for a guy who had never run for political office, he was skilled in the arts of politics, and that, for someone who had never been a prosecutor, he had developed a keen sense of which cases to pursue and which to pass on.

But when it came to cases with political overtones, Champion knew that his boss was unpredictable. There had been times when Giles had incurred the wrath of his own party by pursuing cases against Republican politicians, but Champion often wondered if those cases were motivated by a different type of politics, the personal kind. Now there were the rumors that Giles had been quietly talking about a run for governor and Champion wondered how, or if, that would enter into Giles's calculus with regard to going after Townsend.

When Giles entered the conference room, both Champion and Alan Fischman, head of the Civil Rights Division, stood up. "Sit down," Giles said with a wave of his hand. He flipped the papers he was carrying onto the table so that they slid across the tabletop.

"I read DOJ's report, and, Ed, I read your report on your meeting with Swisher," he offered. "Let me ask the two of you this: If DOJ had the tap on Swisher, and they believe Townsend was behind all these murders, why aren't they going after him?" He paused, and laughed mockingly. "Oh yeah, that's right, because Townsend's Forty-Three's fair-haired boy in New Jersey. What was I thinking? Come on, guys, there's no there, there. Do either of you think we have probable cause to get an indictment, no less convince a jury he's guilty beyond a reasonable doubt?"

"I think there's enough to have the FBI open an investigation," Champion replied.

"Ed, you and I rarely disagree, but for Christ's sake, all you have here is a tape of some disgraced FBI agent, now a defense lawyer, and a lot of speculation on his part about Townsend's involvement. Even DOJ sniffing around hasn't found any evidence that these things are connected directly to Townsend. Besides, half of this shit didn't even take place in Jersey. Our office is supposed to look into the murder of a hooker in Vegas, a dead cop in Rhode Island, and a gas explosion at the shore? Why should our office coordinate a multistate investigation into a conspiracy to violate the civil rights of a cross-dressing alleged murderer? Where's DOJ? What am I missing?"

Champion looked at Fischman, who simply shook his head. "I'm not sure you are missing anything, Jim. I guess the only other thing I'd add," Champion said, "is that I spoke with Phil Gabriel, who's running Jersey Sting, to see if they've gotten anything on Townsend. Phil told me that they have a lot of people talking about Townsend, but they haven't been able to get anything solid and nothing that connects to any of this stuff."

"Look, guys," Giles began, "you know I don't shy away from going after politicians, so I appreciate you bringing this to me. But I have the reputation of this office to think about, and I'm not having the office's reputation tarnished by going after one of the top politicians in the state unless we have a decent shot at convicting him." He pointed to the report still lying in front of Champion. "I was struck by the number of coincidences that have happened, and I know that none of us at this table is a big believer in coincidences, but we need more to go on than a visceral reaction or a gut feeling. We're prosecutors and we have an obligation not to go after someone just to ruin their reputation; we run the risk of ruining this office's reputation for impartiality in the process."

Champion and Fischman nodded in agreement.

"So why did Chris Bentley need to speak to you so urgently?" Will asked as he poured himself a scotch.

"Ostensibly, to let you know that DOJ has forwarded information to Giles, and that Giles is seriously considering opening an investigation of you in connection with the Barnes case for violating his civil rights," Gardner answered.

"And the real reason?" Will asked, shaking his glass to cool the scotch on the ice.

"It wasn't put this directly, but clearly Bentley is guiding Giles and his political ambitions. He flat out said that Giles was considering a run for governor, and knew that you were too. Said it would be a shame if the investigation interfered with your plans. The unsaid subtext being that, perhaps if you decided *not* to run for governor, things might just go away."

"Bullshit!" Will barked. "You know that's total bullshit. If he thought he had enough to go after me, he'd try to bury me in a heartbeat. Cocky motherfucker thinks he can eliminate me that easily. If he truly thought he could indict me, there's no way he'd tip his hand like this. Jim Giles may be many things, but he isn't stupid."

"I agree with you. I think it's a ploy. But I give Bentley credit, he's crafty and careful. He said something else that figures into the mix. He said you weren't the only major politician who might have their tit in the wringer."

Will's face scrunched, trying to figure out who Bentley was implicating. "Carlisle?" he said, his eyes suddenly widening.

"That's how I took it. What he said was that the governor might have an appointment to make in the near future. My thinking is since the governor gets to replace a sitting U.S. senator until a special election, Carlisle resigning certainly seems to check off the boxes."

Will took a long sip from his drink. "Interesting. There've been rumors Carlisle got caught up in that crazy sting, but honestly, I thought he was too smart for that."

"Like I said, no names were mentioned. But that's my guess."

Will poured two more fingers of scotch into his glass, walked over to the black leather couch, and made himself comfortable. "So what's Giles want, the appointment to take Carlisle's spot, or to be governor?"

"Perhaps both," Gardner responded.

"What do you mean, both?" Will asked skeptically.

Gardner's face betrayed almost a look of admiration as he started laying out the potential machinations. "Let's suppose Carlisle steps down in the next few months. The governor appoints a replacement and then by law must call a special election to fill out the remainder of the term. Since Carlisle was just reelected, his term doesn't expire until 2012. So hypothetically, Giles could get the appointment, run as an incumbent in November to serve out the remainder of the term and, if he wins, still run for governor in 2009, knowing that if he loses, he goes back to the senate."

Will leaned back into the couch and pursed his lips. "That's pretty Machiavellian," he said with a hint of respect. "Why couldn't I do that?"

Gardner smirked. "I know you. Why would you ever want to

give up what you've built here by going to Washington? You'd become irrelevant in months."

A smile slowly started to form on Will's lips. "You're right. I have no desire to go to that cesspool unless it's to move to Pennsylvania Avenue." He paused, stroking his chin. "What's Gehrity doing with the case?"

"Offered Barnes a plea to manslaughter. McCabe is trying to force the DNA motion to be heard and she's looking for a plea to theft, time served."

"Fuck her. She's a bitch. I wish your guy had killed her just on general principle. What about the settlement of the civil case?"

"Seven hundred and fifty on the table, they're looking for three million."

"Jesus fucking Christ, should have killed the whole lot of them." He looked up at Gardner. "Don't look at me like that. If I had let you do what you wanted to do, I would have been hauled before so many grand juries my head would be spinning." He raised his eyes to the ceiling. "I'm venting, okay?"

Gardner nodded.

"Listen, I can't afford to lose this game of chicken. But if we time things right, we can bury what we have to do."

"What do you have in mind?" Gardner asked.

Will gave him a crooked smile. "Here's what I want you to discuss with Mr. Bentley."

"So, how'd it go with the boss today?"

"Not so good," Ed Champion replied. "He suggested that if it was such a good case, you boys at DOJ would be all over it. So he wants no part of it."

"I can't say I'm surprised," Andy Barone said. "'When you strike at a king, you must kill him.'"

Champion laughed. "Ralph Waldo Emerson. Trust me. I think he's well aware of that."

"I'm impressed you know your poets. But do yourself a favor and remember that Townsend's a very smart and ruthless guy, who also happens to have friends in high places."

"Yeah, but I thought maybe he'd let us have the FBI take a look."

Barone laughed. "Ed, we can't even keep the secrets secret. Townsend would get wind of it, and then Giles would pay the price. Look, you know if I thought there was enough there, I'd go after the SOB. There just isn't enough, especially given his connections."

"I get it. Just a little disappointed because I do think Townsend had a hand in this and I'd like to see him exposed."

"Be careful, Don Quixote, careers can be ruined tilting at windmills."

Champion laughed. "And here I thought my job was to defend truth, justice, and the American way."

"It is, but you also have to learn when to pick your fights."

"Speaking of picking fights, what are you going to do with Swisher and the leak investigation?" Champion asked.

"We're closing the investigation. We can't pin it on him. We got nothing. Honestly, I never really thought it was him. There's always been another person we were interested in, but the boys upstairs told us not to go there. A little too sensitive going after a sitting judge."

"Sonya?" he said, his surprise evident.

"Never heard that from me, my friend. But let's just say she was dating a reporter from the *Times* when she was at your office. There's always been some suspicion of pillow talk, but . . . well, you know how it works when daddy is a big donor."

"Andy, you guys ran Swisher out of the Bureau and you never really thought it was him. Why?"

"Sacrificial lamb, I don't know. The decision was made above my pay grade."

"Don't you care?"

"Sure, I care. It sucks."

"Why him?"

"He had access to the leaked information, and . . ."

"And?"

"Look, you think it was a coincidence they went after the Ivy League–educated Black guy?" He paused. "But what do I know?"

CHAPTER 38

DUANE AND ERIN STOOD ON EITHER SIDE OF SHARISE.

"Ms. McCabe, you've gone over all the plea forms with your client?" Redman asked, peering over the top of his reading glasses.

"I have, Your Honor."

The courtroom was almost empty, not surprising for a Friday afternoon, but very surprising given what was about to take place. The only spectators were Tonya, Paul, and Sharise's mom on one side of the courtroom, and the same malevolent-looking individual who had attended the original motion hearings—Michael Gardner, if Erin remembered correctly—on the other side.

"And you're satisfied that your client is entering this plea knowingly and voluntarily?"

"I am."

"Very well. I will swear your client in for purposes of placing a factual basis on the record."

Redman looked down at the court order Erin had given him

prior to the start of the proceedings, which legally changed "Samuel Emmanuel Barnes" to "Sharise Elona Barnes." He looked up to take in the defendant, who, in a black dress and heels, looked every bit the woman her name said she was.

He took a deep breath. "Do you, Sharise Barnes, swear or affirm that the testimony you are about to give will be the truth, the whole truth, and nothing but the truth?"

"Yes, Judge."

Erin turned and faced Sharise. "Ms. Barnes, on April 17, 2006, just a little over a year ago, you were working as a prostitute in Atlantic City. Is that correct?"

"Yes."

"At that time, did you become acquainted with an individual by the name of William E. Townsend, Jr.?"

"Yes," Sharise responded softly, a nervous catch in her voice.

Erin had no doubt that Lauren had prevailed upon her husband to meet with them. Sure, Steve knew Duane, but meeting with Erin—his wife's ex-husband—that must have been a tougher sell. Not to mention that a precondition of the meeting was that Steve had to agree that the meeting was totally off the record.

After some initial chitchat between Duane and Steve, they got down to business. Erin laid it on the line right from the start; they were there looking for a favor, and they were using him. He almost left Duane's kitchen right then, but when Erin said that it was literally a matter of life or death, he bit his lip and told them to go ahead. They explained everything they knew and suspected, and then told him they needed one thing from him, a phone call to Will Townsend saying that as the metro assignments editor, he would like to send a reporter out to discuss the deaths of a number of individuals connected with his son's murder case. They explained why timing was critical in terms of Sharise's plea, and promised him that if Sharise were forced to plead guilty to manslaughter, they would go on the record and give the *Times* an exclusive on everything that had happened in the case. But they also warned him that if they got what they wanted, there'd surely be a nondisclosure agreement, and there'd be no story, at least not from them. He asked them what would happen if Townsend agreed to meet with a reporter, and they promised they would give him enough information to make for a fascinating interview. They also knew, but didn't tell him, that if Townsend did agree to meet, it meant that Townsend knew the DNA did not match his son's.

Erin looked down, her sigh almost audible. The script was part of the plea agreement, and as much as she wanted to deviate, she knew she couldn't. "While you were in the room with Mr. Townsend he was impaled on a knife and died, is that correct?"

"Yes," Sharise replied, wanting to scream, *He put his hands around my neck and was trying to kill me,* but she too had agreed that her plea elocution would leave out the fact he tried to kill her.

"Can you tell the court what happened after Mr. Townsend was dead?" Erin asked.

"I got scared. I don't know where I was 'cause he had taken me to some strange motel. So I took thirty dollars from his wallet, his bank card, and the keys to his car. I drove back to AC, got some clothes, then went to Philadelphia and took a train to New York City."

"Did you use his bank card?"

"Yes, I took three hundred dollars from an ATM in Atlantic City before going to Philly."

Steve had gotten through and actually spoke to Townsend, who, as Steve told them, had been very courteous in declining to speak to a reporter, citing that his son's death had taken such an emotional toll on his family. Three days later, Duane received a call from Phillips wanting to reopen negotiations on the civil case. After numerous calls back and forth, they finally agreed on a settlement of $2.1 million.

The next day, Erin received a call from Carmichael, who indicated that his office might be willing to offer a plea to robbery instead of manslaughter. Erin pointed out that robbery was a second-degree offense, meaning that Sharise might actually wind up doing more jail time with a plea to robbery than the flat ten they had offered on manslaughter. Two days later, Carmichael agreed on a plea to theft, with five years' probation, no additional jail time.

They gathered in the hallway outside the courtroom after Redman had sentenced Sharise in accordance with the plea bargain. Viola and Tonya cried tears of joy and hugged Erin and Duane in turn, thanking them for everything they had done. Then it was Sharise's turn.

"You," she said to Duane, "is my Black knight in shining armor. I'm glad you no longer in no FBI because, without you, I still be sitting in jail." She wrapped her arms around his neck and gave him a kiss on the cheek. "I know you be a married man," she whispered, "and I hope your wife knows she is one lucky woman." When she stepped back, she had a huge smile.

"Thank you," Duane said. "Not sure she always feels so lucky."

Sharise turned to Erin. "You, girl, are my fierce bitch. The first time I saw you, I thought they gonna eat you alive. But, honey, now I know you be sent by my guardian angel, 'cause you done save my life." She wrapped her arms around Erin and pulled her into a bear hug. "I don't plan on ever getting into no trouble ever again, but, girl, if I ever do, I want you with me."

"You better not get yourself into any more trouble," Erin said, the tears making their way slowly down her cheeks. "But don't worry, whatever comes your way, as long as I'm around, you'll never walk alone." Erin took both of Sharise's hands in hers. "I want you to know there were times when I wasn't sure I had the strength to go on. But whenever I felt that way, I thought of you and how courageous you are, and that always gave me the strength to carry on. So as you like to say, you are my fierce bitch. Thank you." They embraced again and for the first time in her life, Sharise cried tears of joy.

Duane and Erin drove back to the office in silence, both of them physically and mentally exhausted.

"I'm so happy for Sharise," she said, breaking the silence. "But part of me feels like we failed. Should we have done things differently?"

"E, if I had told you back in September that this case would end with Sharise Elona Barnes pleading guilty to third-degree theft and walking out of the courthouse a millionaire, what would you have said?"

"Give me a hit off of whatever it is you're smoking because it must be good shit," she said with a forced laugh.

"Exactly."

Just after they crossed the Driscoll Bridge, Duane reached for his cell phone, which was vibrating in his jacket pocket, and handed it to Erin. She looked at the display. "It's Ben," she said.

"Answer it and put it on speaker."

"Hey, Ben. It's Erin. I've been reduced to being Swish's answering service. I'm putting you on speaker."

"Hi," Ben replied.

"What's up?" Duane asked.

"Put on WNYC and then call me back."

"Okay," she said, giving Duane a quizzical look. She turned the radio on and found WNYC.

"*In a series of shocking and fast-breaking developments today, the New Jersey political world was rocked when James "Jim" Giles, the U.S. Attorney for the State of New Jersey, unexpectedly announced that he was resigning his position, effective immediately. Until the president names his replacement, his First Assistant, Edward Champion, will become the acting United States Attorney. That news was followed by a stunning announcement that Senator John Carlisle, the senior United States Senator from New Jersey, had resigned, effective immediately. There had been some rumors that Senator Carlisle had been captured talking on wiretaps in a federal investigation, but the only reason given by the senator and his staff today was personal reasons that required the senator to devote more time to his family.*

"Then as you just heard moments ago, Governor Rogers announced that he was appointing Jim Giles to temporarily fill Senator Carlisle's seat until a special election could be held in November. Giles, in turn, followed the governor to the podium to thank the governor for the appointment, and also thanked State Senator William Townsend for recommending him to the governor for consideration.

"It's been a whirlwind of a day, and we'll be back at the top of the five o'clock hour for more detailed analysis of what has taken place and its impact on New Jersey and national politics."

"Holy shit," Erin said, turning the radio off. "What do you make of all of that?"

Duane glanced over at her with a knowing smirk. "It all makes sense now."

"Well, I'm glad it does to one of us. Explain?"

"You noticed there were no reporters in the courtroom."

"Yeah."

"Well, that's because they were all probably running around covering pieces of these stories. On top of that, what do you want more than anything on a day when you want a story about you to get buried?"

She shrugged. "An even bigger story?"

"Exactly," he said. "Tomorrow the papers will be full of stories about Giles and Carlisle, and speculation on why Carlisle stepped down. If there's anything on Sharise's plea and settlement, it will be buried on page fifteen. Townsend gets no adverse publicity, and the only people who can put it all together, the two of us and Sharise, are barred by her settlement agreement from talking about it."

She put her hands on top of her head and rested her arms on either side of her head. "Ugh," she mumbled.

She tried to convince herself that they had done what they could. Duane had told everything to the feds. They had given the information to the *New York Times*, albeit off the record. They had thrown the seeds out there. It wasn't their job to bring the guilty to justice. Yet she couldn't shake the feeling that they could have done more.

Her mind wandered. She still thought about Barbara a lot. There were days when she played the last voice mail message from Barbara over and over, listening to Barbara's voice and knowing that Barbara did not know that she had only minutes to live. The official investigation said that a gas leak caused by the sudden cold temperatures had allowed gas to accumulate in Whitick's basement. The speculation was that one of them had opened the cellar door, flicked on the light switch, and the resulting spark had ignited the gas. Erin believed everything except that the leak was accidental.

What had happened in those last seconds, Erin wondered. Did Barbara know what was about to happen? *At least*, Erin thought, *she had been given a chance to dodge death*. Barbara wasn't that lucky. And that was life; it could be so arbitrary. At some point your time was up, and it was over.

CHAPTER 39

November 7, 2007

"**N**o!" ERIN SCREAMED, THROWING A PILLOW AT THE TELE-vision. It was shortly after midnight when News 12 called the re-sults of the U.S. Senate special election. Jim Giles had won a close election, beating his Democratic challenger, Marie Honick, by less than two thousand votes. As the coverage shifted to Giles Headquarters in Freehold, Erin watched as the proud victor pa-raded onto the stage, followed by his wife and two teenage sons. As he stood in front of the microphone, exalting in the cheers of "Gi-les, Gi-les, Gi-les!" William E. Townsend, Sr., stood behind him. Despite Erin's hopes that one day Townsend's house of cards would collapse, not only had he survived, but his political tentacles now reached into the United States Senate.

After the settlement and plea, several reporters had sought her out to find out what had happened. All of them wanted to know how they managed to get the plea deal they had gotten for Sharise, but she was prohibited by the settlement. She had tried to give a couple of the reporters some subtle hints, but she couldn't jeopardize Sharise's new life by breaching the nondisclosure provision.

As soon as Giles began his victory speech, she turned off the television in disgust and made her way to bed. The dreams came less often now, but with Townsend's face still lingering in her consciousness as she drifted off, she knew tonight might be one of the nights that Barbara visited her.

"You okay? You look a little wiped out," her mother said as Erin settled in opposite her.

"Yeah, I was up late last night."

"How was Indianapolis?"

"It was interesting," Erin replied. "I'm not about to move there, but Conseco Fieldhouse was nice, and watching the game from one of the suites was a trip. You know me, I'm not a basketball fan, but it's like watching from a restaurant. There was food and a bar. Of course, Mark and Swish were like two kids in the candy store, and Paul was really good to them. Right after the game ended, two security people came in with VIP passes and they got to go down to the locker room to meet Paul and the other players. It was like they had died and gone to heaven. Cori and I are lucky we got them on the plane Sunday night to come home."

"Sounds like you had a good time."

"It was fun," she said.

"And how's Sharise?"

Erin's face lit up. "She's doing so well, it's unbelievable. You'd never know she had a TBI. Paul set her up with his financial adviser, so all her money is safely invested. She's renting a really nice two-bedroom townhouse in Carmel, which is just outside Indianapolis. Her place is about a mile from where Paul and Tonya live." She paused, her smile growing. "This is the best part. After she moved back in April, she got her GED and she's now taking some classes at a community college. She told me that she's thinking of going to college full-time next year. So when I asked her what she wanted to do, she laughed and said, 'Be a badass lawyer.'"

"Well, she has a great role model."

Erin bit her lower lip, trying not to get emotional. "You know there was a point at one of the hearings, after I had gotten my head handed to me by the judge, and when I sat down next to Sharise she said to me, 'Thank you. You the first person in my life who stood up and defended me for who I am.'" Erin reached across the table and squeezed her mom's hand. "I know how she felt. You're that person for me. Thank you."

"You're welcome," her mom replied, squeezing Erin's hand. "I'm incredibly proud of you and the woman you are."

"Thanks," Erin said, the color rising in her cheeks.

The waitress came by and poured each of them more coffee.

"Did you watch the election results last night?" her mother asked.

"Unfortunately."

"So the guy on the stage immediately to the right of Giles when he gave his acceptance speech, was that Townsend?"

Erin nodded.

"For a guy who wasn't running, he sure looked very happy."

"Oh, he's running, he just wasn't on the ballot this time. From what I hear he may well be the next governor of the state."

"Can't you get anyone to investigate him?"

In a moment of weakness, right before they finalized the settlement, before she was bound by a confidentiality provision, Erin had told her mom everything—about Lenore, Florio, Barbara, Whitick, and her wannabe killer who had ended up dead, supposedly from a self-inflicted gunshot wound. Her mom had been horrified. She had also been dumbfounded that Townsend had gotten away with everything.

"Mom, we've been through this. Swish and his attorney sat

down with lawyers from the Justice Department and the U.S. Attorney's office and told them everything. Then last night you saw the guy who was the head of the U.S. Attorney's office at the time Swish met with them, standing next to Townsend, and both of them were grinning ear to ear."

"I guess at my age I should be more cynical, but I foolishly thought it wasn't possible to get away with the stuff he's done. I mean, how many other people are dead because of him, and he's up onstage celebrating?" She took a deep breath. "Hard to believe."

Yes, Erin thought, *hard to believe and even harder to stomach.*

"Things with Mark still good?" her mother asked.

"Yeah," she said with a smile. "It should be an interesting holiday season with his family." She snickered. "But I did get him into the Pacers' locker room, so that covers a lot of sins."

"Speaking of the holidays," her mother began, "both of you are coming for Thanksgiving, right?"

Erin sighed. "I don't know, Mom. This year Dad will have not only me to contend with, but my boyfriend as well. Not sure he's ready for that."

"He'll adjust," her mother added defiantly.

"That's what you said last year and we all know how that worked out."

"Dinner at six, cocktails at five."

Later they stood out on the sidewalk saying their goodbyes. "If I don't see you before, I'll see you on Thanksgiving," her mother said.

"You don't give up, do you?" Erin replied with a grin.

"Never," her mother responded. "And if you're not doing anything the Wednesday evening before Thanksgiving, come over and I'll show you how to make my famous pumpkin pie and my rice pudding."

"Why do I need to know how to do that?"

Her mother looked at her, shaking her head. "Erin, my dear, I told you once that there are two ways to a man's heart. It seems like you've figured out the first one. Now it's time to learn the second."

"Mom, you realize how stereotypical that is, don't you?"

"Oh my God, you're a feminist too," she said with a chuckle. "Good for you. So how about because it's a mother-daughter tradition—my grandmother showed my mother, my mother showed me, now it's my turn to show you."

She leaned in and gave Erin a peck on the cheek. "See you in two weeks."

Two weeks later

Erin paused before turning the doorknob. "Are you sure I look all right?" she asked.

"You look fine."

Erin turned her head to the side. "Has anyone ever told you that telling a woman she looks fine isn't really a compliment?"

Mark shook his head. "Sorry," he said with a smile. "I think you look perfect. But then again, I thought you looked perfect in the first five things you picked out to wear. Why are you so nervous? It's your family, and they've all met me," he said, giving her a reassuring tug around her waist. "Relax."

She knew he was right; they had all met him. She and Mark had been to Sean and Liz's for dinner, and the boys had gotten to know Mark because he often joined her on Sundays to go to their games. No, it was only one member of her family she was worried about. She took a deep breath and pushed the door open.

Like the year before, Patrick and Brennan were sitting on the couch in the living room playing with some device. This year, however, there were no excited screams. They hit pause, came over and gave her a hug, said hello to Mark, and quickly went back to their game.

She and Mark made their way into the kitchen, where her mother, Sean, and Liz were chatting as her mother scrambled around the kitchen. They all exchanged greetings and her brother even gave her a hug, but she couldn't help but notice that her dad was absent. "Where's Dad?" she finally asked.

There was an awkward silence before her mother said, "He's in the den watching football."

Might as well get this over with now. She took Mark by the hand and led him to the den. She opened the door and there was her dad, eyes glued to the game. "Hi, Dad." He looked up. "You remember Mark," she continued.

Her father's eyes shifted from her to Mark. "How could I forget?"

"Nice to see you again," Mark replied.

"Yeah," her father said.

"Who's winning?" Mark asked.

"Detroit," her father said, turning his attention back to the game.

To Erin an eternity seemed to pass with nothing being said. *Shit, here we go again.* "Let's go see if my mom needs help," Erin said, pulling Mark toward the door.

"Wait," her father said, causing her to stop. "Mark, can I speak alone with . . . her."

"Of course," Mark replied.

"Please sit," her father said, muting the volume and motioning to the easy chair. She looked at him and noticed he looked pale, older than his sixty-six years.

"Look, it's no secret I'm not happy about your change. But I don't want a repeat of what happened last year," he said, slowly rubbing his chin. "This," he said, gesturing to her with his hands, "has been really hard for me, because I was so proud of you as my son. But . . . I tried to raise you and your brother in a way that encouraged you to pursue your dreams." He looked at her and shook his head. "Of course, this isn't exactly what I had in mind."

"Sorry—"

"No," he interrupted. "Please. Let me finish." He hesitated and then leaned forward. "As your mother is quick to tell me, I'm an old fart and I need to get with the program." He looked at her with a sad grin. "I will confess to being an old fart. I don't understand any of this, I never wanted you to do it, and I wish to God you hadn't. But you are my child and I need to get past this because, believe it or not, I do want you to be happy." His voice quivered. "I . . ." He paused and swallowed. "Why don't you go help your mom. She's thrilled you're here."

"Sure," she said as she rose from the chair. When she reached the door, she paused and looked at him. "Thanks. I hope you know how much that means to me." She wanted to say more but was afraid she'd lose it.

Later, they all took their seats around the table and Brennan said grace. The room grew noisy as platters with turkey, mashed potatoes, gravy, and cranberry sauce were passed from one to the other. As Erin passed the potatoes to Mark, she looked across the table at her mom, who hadn't stopped smiling since they sat down. Erin was momentarily transfixed watching her mom joke with Patrick, then teasing Sean, sharing herself with everyone at the table in her own unique way.

"Pass the salt, please . . ." She looked up to see her father staring at her. "Erin," he added.

She smiled at her father. "Sure, Dad," she said, extending her arm. "Here you go." The conversations resumed and for the first time in years she knew she was going to have a Thanksgiving dinner that couldn't be beat.

Acknowledgments

First and foremost, I'd like to thank you, the readers. Whether you walked into your local bookstore, ordered it online, downloaded it, took it out of the library, listened to it in your car, borrowed it from a friend, or found it left in the recycle bin—thank you. Thank you for investing your valuable time in reading (or listening to) a story I created. I hope you've enjoyed it.

I owe so much to my agent, Carrie Pestrito, who believed in me long before I did. I know this book wouldn't exist without her. Likewise, to my wonderful editor at Kensington Books, John Scognamiglio, who had the courage to publish a book with two transgender main characters, written by an unknown trans author. John, thank you from the bottom of my heart.

Similarly, I want to thank all the folks at Kensington Books who have helped make this a better novel. I'm sure there are a few editors who are still scratching their heads wondering how I made it this far in life without knowing when to use a comma. And to Crystal McCoy, who has guided me through the publication process, encouraged me, and helped to market my book, thank you.

My favorite character in the book may be Erin's mom, Peg McCabe. She is loosely based on my own mom. My mom is my hero. Whatever reservations she had about her child being transgender, she put them aside and has continued to love me as only a mother could love her child. Her wonderful sense of humor and refusal to "act her age" have inspired me. Thank you, Mom!

There is simply no way that I could ever adequately acknowledge Jan, who, despite the changes our relationship has undergone, has remained my best friend. She has always encouraged me to pursue my dreams, even when those dreams weren't in her best interest. I am forever grateful that she is part of my life.

A special thank-you to our children Tim, Colin, and Kate, for putting up with me and continuing to love me, despite the changes. A second thank-you to Colin (sorry, Tim and Kate—Colin read the early drafts), for reading the early drafts and encouraging me to go on. The publication of his novel, *The Ferryman Institute*, inspired me to keep plugging away. To my daughter-in-law, Carly, and my granddaughters, Alice and Caroline, you are all a special part of my life. And to my future daughter-in-law, Stephine, and her daughter, Madison, so happy you are part of our growing family.

To my siblings, Doreen, Virginia (aka Ginna), and Tom, my in-laws, outlaws, uncles, aunts, nieces, nephews, and cousins—thank you. I am one of the lucky trans folks whose entire family somehow managed to make the transition with me. All of you are the best family anyone could ask for.

I owe a major debt to Andrea Robinson, an independent editor, whom Carrie recommended. Andrea took a manuscript that looked like it was written as a student project in an ESL class, and helped shape it into the novel it became. Andrea, I cannot thank you enough for your sage advice, your patience, and for helping me in more ways than you can ever imagine.

To the people who read this along the way and offered advice, thoughts, and encouragement—Lori Becker, Lynn Centonze, Don DeCesare, Lisa O'Connor, Celeste Fiore, Linda Tartaglia, and Gary Paul Wright—thank you.

To those who read my first effort at writing a novel, which never saw the light of day (thankfully), but who nevertheless encouraged me to stay at it—my son, Colin, Luanne Peterpaul, Andrea Robinson, Lori Becker, Lisa O'Connor, Janet Bayer, Nancy DelPizzo, Joanne Ramundo, Emily Jo Donatello, Jane Pedicini, and Barbara Balboni—thank you.

To my GluckWalrath family (my day job) who have all been incredibly supportive of my extracurricular activities—Michael, Chris, Jim, Dave, Meghan, Vicky, Fay, Caitlin, Colby, Char, Diane, Kendal, Marsha, Carolyn, Steve, and a very special thanks to Patti, who has to put up with me every day, which can be hard—I know because I have to put up with me every day too.

To all trans, non-binary, and gender non-conforming people—this is for you. You are my inspiration. Thank you!

Robyn Gigl's unique protagonist, transgender attorney Erin McCabe, returns in a fascinating and timely legal thriller that delves into the dark world of human trafficking by the rich and powerful . . .

At first, the death of millionaire businessman Charles Parsons seems like a straightforward suicide. There's no sign of forced entry or struggle in his lavish New Jersey mansion—just a single gunshot wound from his own weapon. But days later, a different story emerges. Computer techs pick up a voice recording that incriminates Parsons's adoptive daughter, Ann, who duly confesses and pleads guilty.

Erin McCabe has little interest in reviewing such a slam-dunk case—even after she has a mysterious meeting with one of the investigating detectives, who reveals that Ann, like Erin, is a trans woman. Yet despite their misgivings, Erin and her law partner, Duane Swisher, ultimately can't ignore the pieces that don't fit.

As their investigation deepens, Erin and Swish convince Ann to withdraw her guilty plea. But Ann clearly knows more than she's willing to share, even if it means a life sentence. Who is she protecting, and why?

Fighting against time and a prosecutor hell-bent on notching another conviction, the two work tirelessly—Erin inside the courtroom, Swish in the field—to clear Ann's name. But despite Parsons's former associates' determination to keep his—and their own—illegal activities buried, a horrifying truth emerges—a web of human exploitation, unchecked greed, and murder. Soon, a quest to see justice served becomes a desperate struggle to survive . . .

Please turn the page for an exciting sneak peek of
Robyn Gigl's next
Erin McCabe legal thriller
SURVIVOR'S GUILT
coming soon wherever print and e-books are sold!

CHAPTER 1

April 4, 2008

"*H*EY, STRANGER," DUANE SWISHER SAID, STANDING IN the doorway of her office. "How you doing?"

Erin McCabe looked up, brushed her long, copper-colored hair back from her face, and smiled. She and Duane had been partners in the law firm of McCabe & Swisher for the last five years, specializing in representing defendants in criminal cases.

"Oh, living the dream—one nightmare at a time," she responded, gesturing to the piles of papers stacked haphazardly on her desk among the empty Dunkin' Donuts cups.

"So has Judge Fowler incorporated casual Friday into his trial calendar?" he asked jokingly.

She smiled at his reference to the fact that she was wearing jeans and a Dixie Chicks T-shirt. "No. No trial today. Judge Fowler schedules his sentencing hearings for every other Friday, so I get to come to the office in jeans and see your smiling face." She reached down and picked up a brief in opposition to a motion to dismiss an indictment that she had filed in one of their cases. "And try to catch up on all the shit that's been accumulating while I'm on trial."

After pulling back one of the chairs in front of her desk, Duane plopped down. He stretched his legs out in front of the chair as he uncurled his six-foot-two-inch frame. Unlike Erin's casual Friday attire, Swish wore a charcoal-gray suit with a light pink shirt, neither of which did anything to disguise that at thirty-seven he was still in great shape and only a few pounds heavier from when he was All Ivy at Brown. Swish, as everyone called him, both because of his last name and his prowess from three-point range on the basketball court, was not only her law partner, he was probably her best friend too. They made an interesting pair. Even though Erin was only six months younger, Swish, with his chiseled physique, dark brown skin, and well-trimmed goatee, made a commanding appearance. Whereas Erin, with her girl-next-door looks, dusting of freckles that ran across the bridge of her nose, and slim athletic figure was often mistaken for being younger and less experienced, a perception that she wasn't afraid to use to her advantage in the courtroom.

"How's the trial going?"

"Remind me again why we agreed to take this case?" she asked.

He chuckled. "We got a big retainer."

"Right." She shook her head and inhaled. "Swish, these guys are definitely the gang that couldn't shoot straight. They set up an offshore gambling operation in Costa Rica, installed sophisticated encryption software to protect the website . . . and then talked about what they were doing on the phone like they were making dinner plans."

"So what's the defense?"

"The three guys at the top are arguing that they thought it was legal," she said, gesturing with her hands that she had little faith in the merits of their argument. "Our guy, Justin Mackey, claims that all he did was design and sell encryption software, and that he had no idea what anyone was using it for."

Swish shrugged. "Sounds like a plausible defense."

"He seems to think so, but I'm a little less sanguine. Unfortunately, even though he claims he didn't know what anyone was using the software for, he did a lot of talking on the phone and the wiretaps picked up some pretty damning conversations between him and one of the top guys. Plus, he liked to bet—a lot. Gonna be tough to sell that he didn't know what they were using his software for. And for someone who was supposedly into all this encryption shit to keep everything secret, he certainly didn't seem too concerned about talking about things openly on the phone."

"Any chance of a plea?" Swish asked.

"The State offered some decent deals early on, but no takers," she said. "My sense is these guys are protecting someone else."

"Even our guy?"

"Yeah. He clearly knows more than what he's letting on to me. That said, I'm not sure he even knows who he's protecting." She shook her head, allowing her frustration to show. She liked Justin. He was young, twenty-eight, lived with his mom and seemed like a decent guy. As they prepared for trial and she had gotten to know him, her take was that he had just gotten in over his head, probably because not only did he bet a lot, but from what she had heard listening to the wiretap recordings, he also lost—a lot.

"How much longer do you have to go?" he asked.

"I expect the State is going to wrap up early next week. So we're in the home stretch."

"Any defense case?"

She cringed. "Not from me. I can't put him on the stand, they'd kill him on cross with the wiretaps."

"Sorry," he said. "Anything I can help you with?"

"No. I don't think so. If there's any silver lining it's that we're in front of Judge Fowler. Assuming Mackey gets convicted, I'm pretty sure Fowler won't revoke his bail prior to sentencing and, since it's Justin's first offense, I'm hoping he doesn't get more than eighteen months."

"Here if you need anything," he offered.

"Thanks. Anything new here?"

"I had the motion to suppress in the Creswell case in front of Judge Anita Reynolds down in Ocean County."

Erin smiled. Judge Reynolds had briefly presided over the case involving their client Sharise Barnes. Sharise's case had made Erin famous, or, more accurately, infamous, at least in much of New Jersey. Then again, defending a transgender woman of color accused of murdering the son of a now guberna-torial candidate had a tendency to generate publicity, especially when Erin's own status as a transgender woman figured promi-nently in the coverage. "I liked Reynolds. I wish she had con-tinued to handle Sharise's case," Erin said. "How'd the motion go?" she asked.

"She reserved, but I think she's going to grant it. I mean she should. They came into the guy's house without a warrant, after he refused to let them in, and then claimed they saw drug para-phernalia in plain view—in his bedroom on the second floor."

She laughed. "Yeah, you're right. I like your chances on that one."

He stared at her for several seconds. "I was with Mark at our game on Wednesday night and he asked how you were doing."

Erin flinched at the mention of Mark's name. She and Mark Simpson had dated for over a year, but she had recently ended their relationship and the wounds left behind were still open and painful. He had been the first man she had ever fallen in love with. And somehow, after a few false starts, he had gotten beyond the fact that she was a trans woman, and he had loved her for who she was—something that after she transitioned she assumed she'd never experience with a man or a woman. She knew Swish still saw Mark every week because they played on the same team in a men's basketball league. Trying to avoid where she knew this conversation was headed, she gave Swish her best "please don't go there" look, but she could tell from his expression that either her look didn't convey the intended message or even if he got it he was going to ignore it.

"Tell Mark I said hello," she finally said.

"Come on, E," he fired back. "I know it's none of my business, but Mark's a big boy—he can make his own decisions. If the roles were reversed, you'd be mad as hell that he was making decisions for you."

She closed her eyes and slowly drew in a deep breath. Even now, a month later, the look on Mark's face when she told him she was ending things was still vivid. It was not unlike how she felt years earlier when her wife had told her they needed to separate—a mixture of pain and disbelief. She opened her eyes. "Swish, you're right," she said. "It's none of your business."

Swish cocked his head to one side, his eyes widened, taking her in, then rose from his chair, his eyes never leaving hers. "Got it," he said brusquely before making his way out of her office.

Shit. She got up from behind her desk and walked over to one of the windows. Her office was on the outskirts of the business district in Cranford, perched in one of the second-floor turrets of a former Victorian home that had been converted into an office building twenty years ago. She loved Swish like a brother—not surprising given how much they'd been through together. Before they became partners, Swish had been an FBI agent, and probably still would be if he hadn't been forced to resign when he was set up to be the fall guy for a leak of classified materials involving the illegal surveillance of Muslim Americans after 9/11. When he left the Bureau he seemed to have a lot of options open to him, but to Erin's surprise when she had asked him to partner with her, he agreed and the firm of McCabe & Swisher was born. Of course, at the time, Erin was still living as Ian McCabe. It was only a year after they became partners that

Erin had come out as a transgender woman, and the resulting fallout had almost crushed her. Some losses had been harder than others, none more so than her former wife, Lauren; her dad, Patrick; and her brother, Sean. Her mom; Swish; and his wife, Corrine, were the only ones who never wavered in their support. Without them, she wouldn't have made it.

Still, as close as they were, it was too painful for her to talk to Swish about Mark right now. She needed to stay focused on the trial and find some way to separate her client from the other defendants, some way to convince the jury that Justin wasn't responsible for the huge offshore operations the prosecution had meticulously laid out over the last three weeks. Then, and only then, could she focus on her life again.

She grabbed her coffee off her desk and headed down the hallway to Swish's office. His office occupied one of the former bedrooms to the original home and, unlike the clutter and chaos of her office, his was always neat and orderly with everything in its place. There was never so much as a stray paper clip lying out on his glass desk.

"You got a minute?" she asked, standing in the doorway.

He looked up and nodded.

She took a few tentative steps into his office and stopped. "Swish, I'm sorry. I truly am," she said, biting her lower lip. "I know you're trying to be a good friend to Mark—and to me—but I'm just not in a good place right now. You know how I get when I'm on trial. I can't focus on anything else, and honestly, Swish, talking about Mark right now just hurts too much."

She could tell by his expression he wanted to say more, but it was a sign of how deep their friendship ran that he didn't. "You're right. Focus on what you need to do. We'll talk when the trial's over."

"Thanks," she replied, trying to paste a smile on her face. "I appreciate it."

CHAPTER 2

Aaron Tinsley studied his client's computer. He missed his days as a hacker, something he had started doing when he was fifteen. While the prospect of five years in prison for hacking into the NRA's e-mails had been a convincing enticement to get on the straight and narrow, it was still hard for him to wrap his head around the fact that at twenty-two he was now a white hat doing IT security. While his boss was a decent guy, a former hacker himself, and it did have the advantage of a regular paycheck, it meant his days were mostly filled with boring stuff.

Still, every once in a while, he came across something that provided him with the same thrill as hacking. Today was one of those days.

Up until about six p.m. last night, Aaron hadn't even known where Westfield, New Jersey, was. But his boss had called him with what he said was a "special assignment" for a guy by the name of Charles Parsons who was having computer problems. *Must be real special*, Aaron had thought, if they were willing to pay him double time to go out on a Sunday. Surveying his surroundings, Aaron had no idea how much Parsons's house was worth, but it was easily the biggest house he had ever been in. The home office he was working in probably had more square footage than Aaron's entire one-bedroom apartment in Queens.

As he searched deeper through the mostly unseen files on his client's laptop, he had to admit that he was enjoying the hunt. He examined the computer's registry, trying to find the hidden program he had begun to suspect was buried in the software code. Whoever had done this was a real pro. He was almost envious.

"I need to get on my computer. Are you almost done?" Charles Parsons asked, startling Aaron.

Aaron had been so engrossed in his search he was surprised to see Parsons standing in the middle of the room. Parsons, who was well tanned even though it was early April, appeared to be around six feet, with broad shoulders. Aaron couldn't even hazard a guess at his age, but his wrinkle-free face, contrasted with a shock of wavy gray hair, left the impression that Parsons was well acquainted with a plastic surgeon. Catching Parsons's annoyed stare, Aaron realized that he was still grinning in admiration for the cleverness of the hacker.

"What are you smiling at?" Parsons snapped.

Aaron willed his face into seriousness. "Sorry. Um, can we go talk in another room?" he said.

"What the fuck are you babbling about?" Parsons shot back.

Aaron powered down the laptop, closed it, and took Parsons by the arm, escorting him out of the office. "Mr. Parsons, please, let's go into your kitchen."

"What the hell is going on?" Parsons said, yanking his arm from Aaron's grasp as they left the room. "I asked you to check to see if I have a virus, and you're acting like my computer has the bubonic plague."

Aaron sat on one of the stools in front of the marble island in Parsons's massive, well-appointed kitchen. "That's actually not a bad analogy," he offered, nodding his head. "Yeah, you have a virus, which it looks like you picked up from some porn website. That's easy enough to fix. Unfortunately, you have a much bigger problem. How long have you been running the encryption software?"

"Why? What's that got to do with anything?" Parsons asked, his eyes narrowing as he gazed suspiciously at Aaron.

"I'm not sure yet, but I think that may have a rootkit embedded in it. Which means your laptop, and probably any other computers you use that are running the same software on them, are infected with the same rootkit."

"What the fuck is a rootkit?"

Aaron shook his head from side to side. "In layman's terms, it's a program that allows whoever installed it to monitor everything you do on your computer."

"Wait, are you saying someone can see what websites I visited?" Parsons said, cocking his head to the side and rubbing his forefinger across his lips, his tone suddenly less defiant.

"Yes, but . . ." Aaron hesitated. "Well, it's much worse than that. It means that whoever is watching can record every keystroke you make. So that if you go to a website where you have a password, they can steal your password and lock you out. I think they've also taken over the microphone and camera to watch and listen to you. That's why I wanted to speak to you in here."

Parsons's stare conveyed disbelief. "Watch me? From my computer? You can't be fucking serious?"

"Yeah," Aaron nodded. "Unfortunately, I am."

"What's that got to do with my encryption software?"

"As best I can tell, the rootkit is embedded in it. So if you have the same software on your desktop, or any other computers, you probably have it on those as well."

Parsons's blank stare conveyed his failure to grasp the full impact of what Aaron was telling him.

"Look," Aaron said, speaking slowly now, "if this is what I

think it is, it means that as long as you've had this software on your computer, whoever's responsible for it has seen everything you've done. Every e-mail, every transaction, every download—everything."

"But everything's encrypted. That's the whole purpose of the software. So only people with . . ." He stopped midsentence, panic spreading across his face with the realization that the encryption software was compromised. "Whoever this is, they can see everything?"

"Yeah, most likely," Aaron repeated.

"No. No, that can't be possible," Parsons said, his face suddenly ashen.

"When did you have it installed?" Aaron asked, enjoying the sudden shift in power as he watched Parsons's desperation grow. *Who knows*, he thought. *Maybe if I play this right and fix the problem, Parsons might pay me something extra under the table.*

"Um, I don't know—about a year and a half ago, I guess," he replied.

"And where did you get it?" Aaron said. "I mean, it's not something you bought at Staples."

"Some friends recommended it." When he saw Aaron's skeptical look, he got defensive. "I trust these guys. We do some business together and the business they're in requires secrecy, like mine. They said this software was the best."

"Any changes to it since then?"

"I got a new laptop about a year ago."

"Anything else?" Aaron asked.

"Yeah, about six months or so ago the guy who designed and installed the software came back and installed an update saying they needed to patch some potential security issue."

"Bingo," Aaron said, the final piece of the puzzle finally dropping into place. "It looks like whoever designed it built in a little something extra when they installed the update, because as good as it is as encryption software, it's even a better rootkit."

"I need this fixed now," Parsons said, growing angry. "I need access to my data. If someone has been watching me for six months, I need to secure things before someone steals my information."

Aaron didn't feel like incurring Parsons's wrath by telling him it was probably too late. The hacker had access for six months. Plus, they either already knew Aaron had been reviewing the computer's registry and that he had likely uncovered the rootkit, or they'd know soon enough. Not to mention that the only way to retrieve the encrypted data was to use the infected software. As Aaron weighed the options, he couldn't help but admire how thoroughly this mystery designer had fucked his client.

"You understand," Aaron started cautiously, "there are basically two pieces to the encryption software: One encrypts any e-mails you send and receive, the second encrypts any data that you're storing so no one can read it unless they have the same software."

Parsons nodded.

"Here's the problem," Aaron said slowly. "I'm assuming you encrypted and downloaded a lot of data you don't want anyone else to see." Aaron didn't wait for Parsons's response—his face told him the answer. "Assuming that's true, you can't access the information without unencrypting it, which requires you to use the program. So what we need to do is get you off the Internet so whoever is running this thing will lose access to your computer. Then we need to unencrypt all your data and get a brand-new laptop."

Parsons's head was bouncing like a bobblehead toy. "This can't be happening! Motherfucker!" he spat out, then started grabbing things and throwing them against the blue tiled walls. He started with the fruit in a ceramic bowl on the island, then the bowl, then anything he could get his hands on—a glass, a coffee mug. He finally stopped, his breath coming in short staccato bursts as he wrapped his hands behind his head, holding it as if trying to keep it from exploding. He looked at Aaron with the look of a cornered wild animal. "I need that data. I have to make sure . . ." He stopped. "There's a lot of important financial information that I've downloaded. I can't let that fall into the wrong hands."

Aaron scratched his head. "Where's the data now?"

"I have it on four external hard drives."

Aaron took a deep breath. "As I said, the easiest thing to do is get you offline, connect your hard drives, open and unencrypt the data on them, move it unencrypted to a new computer or hard drive, and then resave it using new encryption software."

"Can I do that on my own?"

"How good are you on a computer?"

He shook his head in disgust. "Can you show me how to do it? There's a lot of sensitive data, so once you show me, hopefully I can handle it from there."

"Sure. But in the meantime, whoever installed the rootkit has access to your data. So time is of the essence."

Parsons mumbled under his breath. "There may be another solution," he said. "I have an idea. I'll call you later. But in the meantime, go get me a new laptop and do whatever you have to do to get some new encryption software, so you're ready to show me how to do it as soon I need you."

Aaron let himself out through the front door and headed out to his car, happy to be getting out of the house. Any thoughts of making Parsons happy and getting a few extra bucks under the table had evaporated as he'd watched Parsons explode. This was not a guy he wanted to deal with any more than he had to. Get the job done and get out of town. He wasn't sure what Parsons was thinking when he said he might have another solution, but, by the look on Parsons's face, Aaron was sure he didn't want to know.

Parsons walked into his bedroom and pulled out the four hard drives, stared at them, now aware that someone else might know everything that was on them. Who the fuck would do this to him? He didn't trust his partners, but he couldn't imagine any of them would risk incurring his wrath by hacking him. He tried to remember the name of the guy who had installed the software and who had recommended him. He needed answers and he needed them now. He picked up the phone and dialed her number. Of all of them, she was the one who had always been loyal to him.

"Cass, it's me. I . . . we have a major problem. I just had an IT guy in here and he tells me our encryption software has some fucking rootworm or something in it."

"What the hell is that?" she asked.

Parsons hesitated, weighing what he wanted to tell her to avoid giving her too much information. "It allows someone to see what I'm doing on my computer," he replied.

"Charles, are you serious? This could be devastating."

"Listen to me. I don't need you to tell me how fucking bad this could be; I just need you to find the guy who installed this. Do you remember the little shit's name—McKay or something?"

"Mackey," she said.

"Yes, that's it. Justin Mackey. Tell Max and Carl to find him and bring him to the warehouse in Elizabeth. We need to have a little chat with him."

CHAPTER 3

I DON'T NEED THIS ON A MONDAY MORNING, ERIN THOUGHT, standing at the entrance and scanning the nearly empty diner. This being New Jersey, the diner capital of the world, there hadn't been a problem finding an open one even at the ungodly hour of four thirty in the morning. After spotting Justin in the far corner, she slowly made her way over and slid into the booth opposite him.

Mackey had called in a panic forty-five minutes earlier, telling her that he had to talk to her. Although Mackey might not have been the brightest bulb in the luminary, he had never been an alarmist, so she managed to drag herself out of bed, splash some water on her face, throw on some clothes, and make her way to the Lido Diner.

She ordered coffee, too tired to be angry. He looked like hell, his eyes bloodshot and puffy, an indication that he had gotten less sleep than her. His stained T-shirt and jeans looked like he had grabbed them off his bedroom floor.

"I'm sorry," he said before she could ask him anything. "I

would never have bothered you at this hour if it wasn't important," he said, running his hands through his uncombed hair. "I needed to see you to let you know that I have to disappear for a while."

"Disappear for a while? Justin, what are you talking about?"

"I'm not coming to court today, or probably for the rest of the trial. I have to get out of town."

Erin wasn't sure if it was the coffee kicking in or her client telling her that he was jumping bail, but she was suddenly awake. "Justin, you understand you're on bail. If you don't show up not only will the judge revoke your bail, but you'll be committing a separate crime: bail jumping. I know the trial isn't going the way you hoped, but even if you're convicted, I don't think Judge Fowler will give you more than two or three years tops. And because it's your first offense, you'll probably serve less than a year before you get parole. But if you run, you're really going to piss off the prosecutor and the judge, and assuming at some point you get caught, there's no telling what sentence you'll get."

"You don't understand, Erin. It's got nothing to do with this case," he said, nervously looking around the diner. "Despite what I'm charged with, I didn't design this software. Some guy named Luke, who I've never even met, designed all of it. He hired me and I just did what I was told."

Erin motioned for him to lower his voice. Between his emotions and the empty diner, it sounded like he was using a megaphone.

"It's Luke who did this, not me. It's not my fault."

"Stop! Justin, you've got to slow down. You're not making any sense. Who's Luke? What does any of this have to do with your case or with you disappearing?"

"I'm sorry. I'm just a little rattled."

As he took a sip of his coffee, Erin noticed that his hand was shaking.

"About a year and a half ago, I was a programmer at a start-up in the city. I was also betting and losing big-time. I owed my bookie a ton of money, like twenty-five grand, when he suddenly offered me a way out. They wanted to move their operations off-shore and were looking for software to encrypt everything. It couldn't be anything off the shelf; it had to be unique. He told me if I could design or find encryption software that worked and install it, he'd write off my debt. So that's how I found Luke. He was looking for someone to handle installation of his own encryption software. He gave me the names and contact info for about a dozen of his customers in New York and New Jersey, and then paid me two hundred dollars a pop to go to their houses and install it. Truth is, I didn't care what he paid me—I just wanted access to the software so I could get out of debt to my bookie."

Justin paused, shaking his head. "About a year ago when I got indicted, Luke found out that I had used his software with-out his permission. He sent me a text and he was pissed. He told me if I ever used his software without permission again, he'd sue me. I told him I had screwed up and that I'd never do it again. Then about six months ago he contacted me and said I could make things right with him if I went out to the same peo-ple and installed an update he had developed. So I did. He even paid me to do it."

Maybe it was the early morning hour, but Erin was having trouble following this. "Okay," she said, "but what Luke is do-ing sounds perfectly legal. Why do you have to disappear?"

He looked up from his coffee at Erin and bit his lip. "Around midnight, I got a text from Luke. It said that one of the people I had installed the software for had discovered a hidden feature and Luke was worried I'd get blamed for it. He said they were going to come looking for me and suggested that since some of the people involved could be dangerous I should lay low for a while until he could take care of it for me. His message said that it might take a few months, but he'd straighten it out and I'd be okay."

"Do you know what he's talking about—a 'hidden feature' in the software?"

Justin cupped his hands on the sides of his neck and looked like he was on the verge of tears. "I'm not sure. But my guess is there was a virus or something in the update he had me install. Generally updates take a couple of minutes to install, but it took as long to download and install the update as it did to do the original software."

"Justin, this is crazy. Let's just call Luke and find out exactly what's going on."

"I can't. I have no way to contact him."

"You just told me you got a text message from him."

"It was from an unknown number; he always blocks his number and uses burner phones. But he puts enough info in the text so I know it's legitimate."

"How's he pay you?"

"PayPal."

"You have any idea where he is?"

"Not a clue. If I had to guess, I'd say somewhere on the West Coast because he's a software designer and his texts are always at weird times."

He slid his phone across the table to her with Luke's text open. She scrolled through it, trying to make sense of everything. *It's too early in the morning for this*, she thought.

"Okay," she said, "you said you only installed the software and updates on about twelve computers. Let's go to the prosecutor with this and, assuming there was some kind of virus in the software update, let the prosecutor's office figure out what is going on between Luke and these people. If you skip out now, it'll just be worse for you when the police find you. And, if these people are truly dangerous, you'll be protected."

He inhaled, appearing to weigh his options.

"No," he said with a sigh. "Some of these people have big bucks and they're pretty fucking scary—sorry, excuse my French." He paused, seemingly embarrassed at having used the F-word in front of her. "I don't want to mess with them. I'm going to do what Luke suggests and lay low for a while and hope he can get me out of this mess."

"Justin, please think about this. If you run, you're only going to expose yourself to more jail time. And if these people are really dangerous, you're better off trying to work out a deal and getting protection. Just because Luke got you into this mess doesn't mean he's going to be able to get you out of it. Let me work this out for you."

He gave her a sad smile. "Thanks. I really appreciate everything you've done for me in the case. The truth is, I wanted to take the original plea deal, but the guys at the top wouldn't let me. So I was stuck. I know I didn't give you much to work with to defend me. Sorry." And with that he threw twenty dollars on the table to cover the two cups of coffee and walked out of the diner without looking back.

As she sat there staring into her coffee cup, a waitress came by holding a fresh pot. "Need a refill?"

Erin looked up and nodded.

"Don't worry about him, honey. You can do better," the waitress offered with a wink.

Erin, too tired to explain, simply said, "Thanks." She looked at her watch—five a.m.—too early to call Duane. Assuming Justin didn't show up in court, what was she going to say when the judge asked where her client was? She couldn't lie to the judge, but at least some of what Justin had told her was protected by attorney-client privilege. Then there was the fact that Justin genuinely believed his life was in danger. But what could she do? It wasn't like she could walk into a police station and give them anything to follow up on. *"What kind of car was he driving?" "I don't know." "Where was he going?" "I don't know." "Who was he afraid of?" "I don't know." "What did he do wrong?" "I can't tell you, he's my client."* Yeah, that would go well.

Erin finished her coffee, threw her jacket back on, and headed out into the brisk April morning. The sun wouldn't rise for another hour, but the purples and pinks of the morning twilight already dominated the sky. As beautiful as it was, it would have been even more spectacular had she been able to see it while jogging next to the Atlantic Ocean. She and Duane had just come off a very successful year, and she had used her share to purchase a two-bedroom condo overlooking the ocean in Bradley Beach. She had moved into it in January and soon came to love how deserted things were in the middle of winter. She was looking forward to the trial being over so she could head back to Bradley.

For now, however, because she had to be in Newark every morning for the trial, it was back to her apartment in Cranford.

She was only a mile from her apartment when she noticed the dark sedan. Unless her mind was playing tricks on her, she had seen the same car as she left the diner. Her apartment was on Riverside Drive, a one-way street that ran along the Rahway River. At this time of morning, it should be easy to figure out if she was being followed. The hard thing would be to figure out what to do if she was.

Reaching into her purse to retrieve her BlackBerry, she weighed her options. With the Cranford Police Headquarters three blocks from her apartment, she could always call 911 and then head straight there.

She checked her rearview mirror. The sedan was two and a half blocks back. She made the left onto Riverside, then, to continue on Riverside, she had to make a quick right. As she did, she accelerated, hoping that because of the quick turns and bends in Riverside whoever was following her would momentarily lose sight of her car. That allowed her to make a right turn onto Central Avenue. As she did, she checked her mirror again and saw the sedan continue down Riverside, past Central.

She was relieved she had lost them, but had little doubt now that she was being followed.

She made a right back onto Springfield and then another quick right back onto Riverside, completing her square circle.

Now she had to decide where to go. If whoever was following her knew where she lived, they might be waiting near her apartment. Fortunately, she knew a back way to get to the parking lot of her building without ever having to go down Riverside.

She made her way down the side streets, all the time focused on looking for a dark sedan. She momentarily thought about heading to the police department, but, like the quandary she faced with Justin, what would she tell them? She had no make or model of the car, no license plate, nothing to go on. Instead she pulled her car into the parking area behind her building and had her keys and phone ready as she hopped out of the car. After a quick 360, making sure no one was waiting, she bolted for the back door.

As she headed to the stairs to get to her third-floor apartment, the memory of an encounter on a different set of apartment stairs came flooding back. That time the attacker had come prepared to kill her, and she'd barely survived—this time, not knowing why she was being followed, she wasn't taking any chances.

She made her way slowly up the stairs, listening for any noise that would indicate someone was lurking in the stairwell. When she got to the second floor, she opened the door enough so she could peer down the hallway. When she was satisfied it was deserted, she walked down the hallway to the other set of stairs in the building. As she had done before, she cautiously made her way to the third floor and cracked the door to look down the hallway—nothing.

She quickly made her way down the hall to her door, unlocked it, and pushed it open, her phone in hand in the event she had to dial 911. She walked into her living room, looking to see if anything appeared amiss. When she was finally satisfied no one had been in her apartment, she made her way to her bedroom window, which looked out on Riverside Drive.

There was no sedan in sight.

She double-checked the locks on her door, and then slumped into her couch, the adrenaline slowly draining from her system. After her heart rate returned to normal, she looked at her phone still tightly clutched in her hand and dialed Duane's cell. He picked up on the third ring.

"Hey, everything okay?" he answered.

"Not exactly," she replied.

An hour later, Duane was in Erin's kitchen, pouring himself a cup of coffee. He had parked at the office and walked the two blocks to her place on the hunt for a dark-colored sedan. He almost never carried his gun—as a Black man, he ran the risk of being shot before he could even explain to a cop that as a former FBI agent he had a right to carry a weapon—but he had taken it this morning.

"Listen," he said. "The fact that you were tailed is bothering me."

"As soon as I lost them, they disappeared. Who knows, maybe it was just my imagination."

"Neither one of us believes that," he replied.

He heard her moving around her bedroom, getting dressed for court, and he took her silence as a hint to change the subject.

"You know the prosecutor is definitely going to press you if Justin doesn't show up. Bail jumping is a crime. So if the judge asks, you can't say you haven't heard from him. And if you claim you can't say anything because the information you have is privileged, the judge may argue that the privilege doesn't protect him from committing the crime of bail jumping."

"But the truth is, he's already gone, and I don't know where he is," Erin called from the bedroom. "Besides, if he doesn't show up, he's already committed the crime, so it's past criminal conduct and protected by the privilege."

"Just be prepared for the worst," he offered.

She walked into the kitchen, wearing a navy blue business suit over a white silk blouse. "Will do," she replied.

"You mind if I give Ben a call and see what he thinks?" he asked. Ben Silver was one of the top criminal lawyers in the state and had represented Duane when he was under investigation by the Department of Justice.

"Not at all. My gut says I can't say anything, but I'd love to hear Ben's take." She rubbed her eyes, then put a hand on his arm. "I appreciate you always being there for me."

"It's what friends are for," he said, hoping his grin was reassuring.

"I know, but I've been a bit of a shit recently."

"You've been fine," he said.

It was a lie, but he could tell from her expression that she appreciated it just the same.